BUCHI EMECHETA was born in Lagos, Nigeria. Her father, a railway worker, died when she was very young. At the age of 10 she won a scholarship to the Methodist Girls' High School, but by the time she was 17 she had left school, married and had a child. She accompanied her husband to London, where he was a student. Aged 22, she finally left him, and took an Honours Degree in Sociology while supporting her five children and writing in the early morning.

Her first book, *In the Ditch*, details her experience as a poor, single parent in London. It was followed by *Second-Class Citizen*, *The Bride Price*, *The Slave Girl* (which was awarded the Jock Campbell Award), the internationally renowned *The Joys of Motherhood*, *Destination Biafra*, *Naira Power*, *Double Yoke*, *Gwendolen*, *The Rape of Shavi* and *Kehinde*, as well as a number of children's books and a play, *A Kind of Marriage*, produced on BBC television. Her autobiography, *Head Above Water*, appeared in 1986 with much acclaim.

In 2005, Emecheta was presented with an honorary OBE (Order of the British Empire) in recognition of her services to literature.

ELLEKE BOEHMER is currently Professor of World Literature in English at Oxford University. She has written three well-received novels, *Screens Against the Sky* (1990), which was shortlisted for the David Higham Prize, *An Immaculate Figure* (1993) and *Bloodlines* (2000), as well as the well-known *Colonial and Postcolonial Literature: Migrant Metaphors* (Oxford University Press, 1995; 2005). She has published the monographs *Empire, the National, and the Postcolonial, 1890–1920* (Oxford University Press, 2002) and *Stories of Women: Gender and Narrative in the Postcolonial Nation* (Manchester University Press, 2005), and several editions including Robert Baden-Powell's *Scouting for Boys* (2004). In 2008, she will publish *Nelson Mandela* and a novel *Nile Baby*.

BUCHI EMECHETA was born in Lagos, Nigeria. Her father, a railway worker, died when she was very young. At the age of 16 she won a scholarship to the Methodist Girls' High School but by the time she was 17 she had left school, married and had a child. She accompanied her husband to London, where he was a student. Aged 22 she finally left him, and took an Honours Degree in Sociology while supporting her five children and writing in the early morning.

Her first book, In the Ditch, described her experiences as a single parent in London. It was followed by Second Class Citizen, the Joys of Motherhood, The Slave Girl which was awarded the Jock Campbell Award, and the internationally renowned The Rape of Shavi, Head Above Water, Gwendolen, Double Yoke, Kehinde etc. The Joys of Motherhood, as well as a number of children's books, and a play A Kind of Marriage produced on BBC television. Her autobiography, Head Above Water, appeared in 1986 with much acclaim.

In 2005, Emecheta was presented with an Honorary OBE (Order of the British Empire) in recognition of her services to literature.

ELLEKE BOEHMER is currently Professor of World Literature in English at Oxford University. She has written three novels; her second Screens against the Sky (1990), which was shortlisted for the David Higham Prize; An Immaculate Figure (1993); and Bloodlines (2000); as well as the well-known Colonial and Postcolonial Literature: Migrant Metaphors (Oxford University Press, 1995; 2005). She has published the monographs Empire, the National, and the Postcolonial 1890–1920 (Oxford University Press, 2002) and Stories of Women: Gender and Narrative in the Nationalism (Manchester University Press, 2005), and several editions, including Robert Baden-Powell, Scouting for Boys (2004). In 2008, she will publish Nelson Mandela and a novel Nile Baby.

BUCHI EMECHETA

THE JOYS OF MOTHERHOOD

INTRODUCTION BY ELLEKE BOEHMER

Heinemann

Heinemann is an imprint of Pearson Education Limited, a company
incorporated in England and Wales, having its registered office at Edinburgh
Gate, Harlow, Essex, CM20 2JE. Registered company number: 872828

www.africanwriters.com

Heinemann is a registered trademark of Pearson Education Limited

Text © Buchi Emecheta 1979
Introduction © Elleke Boehmer 2008

First published by Alison and Busby 1979
First published in the African Writers Series 1979
This edition published by Pearson Education Limited 2008

12 11 10 09 08
10 9 8 7 6 5 4 3 2 1

British Library Cataloguing in Publication Data.
A catalogue record for this book is available from the British Library.

ISBN   978 0 435913 54 0

Typeset by Sara Rafferty
Cover design by Tony Richardson
Cover artwork from an original by Synthia Saint Jam
Printed by Multivista Global Limited

Acknowledgements
Every effort has been made to contact copyright holders of material
reproduced in this book. Any omissions will be rectified in subsequent
printings if notice is given to the publishers.

INTRODUCTION

With its doggedly downbeat portrait of Nnu Ego, the worn-out West African Every-woman and ironic icon of maternal self-sacrifice, Buchi Emecheta's *The Joys of Motherhood* (1979) has long stood as an acclaimed classic of modern African fiction. At every turn in her beleaguered life, Nnu Ego discovers that the promised joys of wifehood and motherhood – both the material rewards and the emotional fulfilments – in fact bring little more than disappointment and bitterness. Despite the upswing in the political fortunes of her country Nigeria in the period when the novel is set – the Second World War and subsequent years – the weight of her gender history militates against the prosperity and self-reliance she works so hard to achieve. The expectations attached to the roles of mother and wife in her culture – and indeed in cultures worldwide – encourage her preparedness for prizes that never come her way. All that she has invested in her children, especially her sons, they disregard in the very act of their claiming the successes towards which she has propelled them.

The Joys of Motherhood was the fourth novel to appear from Buchi Emecheta (1944–), a Nigerian-born novelist resident in London from 1962 onwards. Early on in her career, Emecheta's work established a name for its women-centred perspectives and determined focus on the leading female characters' spirited struggle for survival, often against the pressures of patriarchal and colonial tradition. Novels such as *The Bride Price* (1976) and *Destination Biafra* (1982) feature dynamic, driven and hard-working heroines whose actions often bring them into conflict with shiftless, irresponsible male counterparts whom they succeed either in outwitting or evading, if gradually. For her apparent tendency to stereotype gender relations, and men in particular, Emecheta has at times drawn sharp criticism – and this despite her fierce disavowal of feminism as it was expressed in the western, largely middle-class formations that predominated in the 1960s and 1970s. 'If I am now a feminist', she once insisted, 'I am an African feminist', or, on another occasion, 'a feminist with a small *f*.[1]

Yet *The Joys of Motherhood* has, from its first publication, tended to rise above the charges of stereotyping and reverse gender prejudice that have at times been unjustly levelled at other of Emecheta's works. A careful, often qualified exposé of the abuses that ordinary African women face, the novel stands out both in Emecheta's oeuvre and in its literary and cultural context, for its meticulous social observation accompanied by an attention to character formation that is painstaking and realist yet carries strong symbolic overtones. For example, the narrative pairs the long-suffering Nnu Ego with her feisty co-wife Adaku, a contrastive match that finds its counterpart in the earlier fateful juxtaposition of her mother Ona, chief Nwokocha Agbadi's spirited beloved, and the slave woman whose vindictive chi or personal spirit entered Nnu Ego at birth. Throughout, Emecheta builds an intricate structure of intersecting ironies based on such opposing pairs. Ona dies hoping that her daughter will, firstly, 'have a life of her own', and, secondly, be allowed to 'be a woman' (26). But as Nnu Ego, mother of two sets of girl twins, in time discovers, the two conditions are always to remain mutually exclusive.

In its broader historical context, *The Joys of Motherhood* is noteworthy too for its unsparing delineation of the changing shape of West African gender relations across the twentieth century, a time when colonialism seriously undermined the relative interdependence of men and women that had once marked social organisation. So in her second husband, the Lagos 'house-boy' Nnaife, Nnu Ego encounters a product of traditional patriarchy

1 Quoted in Gina Wisker, *Post-Colonial and African American Women's Writing* (Basingstoke: Palgrave Macmillan, 2000), 148.

whose sense of entitlement the male biases of colonial rule have reinforced, yet who is at the same time feminised and demeaned by the work opportunities available to him in the colonial city. In Nnu Ego's eyes, Nnaife with his job of laundering the white madam's clothes (48–49) has become a 'woman-made man' who carries a soft belly (42) like that of a pregnant woman. Moreover, unlike her father Agbadi with his several wives in his prosperous village situation, from the time Nnaife takes as second wife his dead brother's spouse Adaku, he is unable to provide for Nnu Ego in the ways appropriate to a senior wife, by granting her a separate dwelling. As Nnu Ego and her friend Cordelia discuss early on, they inhabit a hierarchical social structure marked by different levels of oppression, in which they – as African women – find themselves at the very base: 'If [their men's] masters treat them badly, they take it out on us' (54). As senior wife, Nnu Ego must suffer all the sacrifice that attends upon her position, yet may enjoy none of its traditional bounty.

Working out this double burden of her womanhood and her colonised position, Nnu Ego's destiny as a mother in *The Joys of Motherhood* unfolds through the medium of an episodic plot structure: a form that immediately evokes the humdrum, 'one-thing-after-another' nature of her existence. After the flashback that brackets the opening four chapters, sparked by her distress at the loss of her first child, the narrative tracks the day-to-day accumulation of disappointments, losses and humiliations that together constitute her life. Such a life, we as readers find, stymies any possibility of happiness and, unsurprisingly, ends one day when she sinks down 'by the roadside', 'with no child to hold her hand and no friend to talk to her' (254). A would-be good mother, Nnu Ego has consistently met with misfortune. No matter the extent of her sacrifice, throughout the novel she has reaped very poor rewards. Yet, relentless as the novel's anti-climactic impulses may seem, generations of its readers have found its storyline compelling for its boldness and honesty, its refusal to compromise and make accommodations with happy endings, or with the persistent, near-universal assumption that childbearing represents the goal and culmination point of a woman's existence.

Almost uniquely for her time, Emecheta in *The Joys of Motherhood* takes to task an embedded tradition in post-independence African writing of raising mother figures on symbolic pedestals, a tradition that has produced what novelist Zadie Smith calls a 'new fetishisation of the black female'.[2] Against the exacerbated gender hierarchies that the colonial system produced, anti-colonial nationalist movements by contrast promoted inverted gender attitudes and structures, in particular a vehement masculinity, in order to help dismantle the oppressions of the past. This process – one that critic Sangeeta Ray terms the *en-gendering* of the independent nation – simultaneously involved the assertion of new forms of male dominance (as epitomised in Nnaife's growing condescension towards his wives), *and* a compensatory elevation of women, especially mothers, in the metaphorical realms of social life.[3] Mother figures were pictured in nationalist songs ·and stories, for instance, as gigantically strong and heroically praiseworthy, enduring and surviving oppression from all sides. In reality, however, such powerful mother symbols did not empower women. Instead, as men sought to regain control over the women who had found limited outlets for their desire for freedom and self-expression under colonialism, masculine authority in the independence period became the more deeply entrenched. 'The lap of the Mother Nation' turned out not to be 'as soft and

2   Zadie Smith, 'What does Soulful Mean?' *The Guardian Review* (1 September 2007): 4–6.

3   See Sangeeta Ray, *En-Gendering India: Woman and Nation in Colonial and Postcolonial Narratives* (Durham NC, Duke University Press, 2000)

capacious for women as it [was] for men'.[4]

Emecheta in *The Joys of Motherhood* of course makes short work of the delusory inflation of the African woman ideal. Yet she does so not only in contradistinction to masculinist trends within post-independence African writing. The fetishisation of the black woman, especially the mother-figure, is a process in which numbers of African, African-American and diasporic women writers have, for good reason, participated. Their work, too, has been powerfully informed by the consolations it offers. Speaking from cultural backgrounds that are conventionally often strongly matri-focal, such writers have been especially concerned to overturn the perception, shared by Nnu Ego, that the black woman is at the very bottom of the social pile. Instead, writers like the African-American Alice Walker, for example, have idealised African women as custodians of tradition and guarantors of their daughters' futures, though in ways that can seem over-compensatory, a type of special pleading. Emecheta evidently avoids symbol-building of this kind in her work.

Yet, despite her refusal of aspects of mother-idealisation, Emecheta is at the same time prominently interested in placing her work within a lineage of African women's writing – a lineage which sustains her, and which she in turn elaborates upon. On one level *The Joys of Motherhood* can be read as a cynical, Lagos-centred response to its pre-eminent forerunner text *Efuru* which had appeared from the pioneer Nigerian woman novelist Flora Nwapa some thirteen years before. *Efuru*, an eponymous village tale narrated largely through dialogue and proverb, concerns a childless woman who becomes the worshipper of a female water deity, a goddess likewise independent and without children. The novel

4   See Elleke Boehmer, *Stories of Women: Gender and Narrative in the Postcolonial Nation* (Manchester: Manchester UP, 2005), 88–105 for further analysis of this phenomenon.

ends with an acknowledgement that both Efuru and the 'woman of the lake' have achieved an almost inexplicable fulfilment outside of wifehood and motherhood. Its last lines read: 'She gave women beauty and wealth but she had no child. She had never experienced the joy of motherhood. Why then did women worship her?'[5] With her story of the downtrodden Nnu Ego, Emecheta sets out to answer Nwapa's question about motherhood's doubtful joys.

As is clear from its beginning, indeed from its title which carries connotations not only of Emecheta's foremother but also of the clichéed ideal of maternal happiness, *The Joys of Motherhood* uses dramatic irony to memorable effect in order to make its point about that condition's scant delights. In a narrative that straddles the Nigerian mid-century leading up to independence (1960), Nnu Ego's name, pronounced 'new ego' and meaning 'priceless', bears the anglophone associations, too, of renewed cultural self-confidence and new selfhood (23). However, the realities of life for colonial Nigerian women, we as readers see, steadily break down Nnu Ego's inner resourcefulness and self-possession. She is the lovechild who in her first marriage herself finds she can bear no children. In her second marriage to Nnaife, her initial delight at overcoming her apparent barrenness is cancelled by the death of her first child, and the economic independence she experiences when her husband is away at sea, diminishes as soon as he returns home to become 'lord and master' (125).

Yet sisterhood, too, offers little comfort, as when Nnaife and in effect Nnu Ego too inherit, and must support, his dead brother's wife and children. Nnu Ego finds herself in a bitterly competitive relationship with her new co-wife Adaku, the mother of daughters only, who defies the censure attached to successful trading and prostitution by thriving on the material benefits of both. Nnu Ego,

5 Flora Nwapa, *Efuru* (London: Heinemann, 1966), 221.

by contrast, purportedly a blessed mother of sons, whom she works to give a western education, is abandoned by them, her virtue as self-effacing mother going unrecompensed. Her death is singularly lonely, every one of her seven live children having left her. In death however she obtains a certain justice, refusing to answer her community's prayers for children; yet for this, once again, she is resented.

With its dedication to 'all mothers', *The Joys of Motherhood* exposes the overall emotional and spiritual barrenness an African woman like Nnu Ego can experience no matter how richly she is endowed with children. Working to empower the lives of others, she forfeits her own self-reliance. Her many strengths and capacity for endurance go into the reproduction of a social world in which her own role remains marginal. Towards the end of the novel she offers up a heartfelt cry that requires no further glossing: 'God, when will you create a woman who will be fulfilled in herself, a full human being, not anybody's appendage? ... What have I gained from all this? Yes, I have many children but what do I have to feed them on? *On my life.* ... Until we change all this, it is still a man's world, which women will always help to build.' (211, emphasis added).

Though it is almost thirty years since *The Joys of Motherhood* was first published, we continue to live in societies where the rights as opposed to the duties of mothers and other child-rearers remain under-recognised and poorly theorised, including within feminism and other women's rights movements. In such a world Nnu Ego's clear-sighted and moving story with its unswerving plea for change will for many years to come retain its assured status as a twentieth-century African classic.

Elleke Boehmer
Oxford, 2008

To all mothers

1 THE MOTHER

Nnu Ego backed out of the room, her eyes unfocused and glazed, looking into vacancy. Her feet were light and she walked as if in a daze, not conscious of using those feet. She collided with the door, moved away from it and across the veranda, on to the green grass that formed part of the servants' quarters. The grass was moist with dew under her bare feet. Her whole body felt the hazy mist in the air, and part of her felt herself brushing against the white master's washing on the line. This made her whirl round with a jerk, like a puppet reaching the end of its string. She now faced the road, having decided to use her eyes, her front instead of her back. She ran, her feet lighter still, as if her eyes now that she was using them gave her extra lightness. She ran, past the master's bungalow, past the side garden, and shot into the untarred gravel road; her senses were momentarily stunned by the colour of the road which seemed to be that of blood and water. She hurried on beyond this short road that led to the big tarred one, ran like someone pursued, looking behind her only once to make sure she was not being followed. She ran as if she would never stop.

The year was 1934 and the place was Lagos, then a British colony. The Yaba housing estate, a little distance from the island, had been built by the British for the British, though many Africans like Nnu Ego's husband worked there as servants and houseboys; a few foreign blacks who were junior clerks lived in some of the modest estate houses. Even then Lagos was growing fast and would soon be the capital of a newly formed country called Nigeria.

Nnu Ego darted past the Zabo market stalls covered with red corrugated-iron sheets which, just like the wet grass and the gravel on the ground, were glistening with the morning dew. She in her state did not seem to be seeing all this, yet her subconscious was taking it in. Little sharp stones in the footpath pricked her soles as

1

she reached Baddley Avenue; she felt and at the same time did not feel the pain. This was also true of the pain in her young and unsupported breasts, now filling fast with milk since the birth of her baby boy four weeks before.

Her baby ... her baby! Nnu Ego's arms involuntarily went to hold her aching breasts, more for assurance of her motherhood than to ease their weight. She felt the milk trickling out, wetting her buba blouse; and the other choking pain got heavier, nearing her throat, as if determined to squeeze the very life out of her there and then. But, unlike the milk, this pain could not come out, though it urged her on, and she was running, running away from it. Yet it was there inside her. There was only one way to rid herself of it. For how would she be able to face the world after what had happened? No, it was better not to try. It was best to end it all this way, the only good way.

Her strength was unflagging. One or two early risers saw her, tried to stop her and ask where she was going. For they saw a young woman of twenty-five, with long hair not too tidily plaited and with no head-tie to cover it, wearing a loose house buba and a faded lappa to match tied tightly around her thin waist, and they guessed that all was far from well. Apart from the fact that her outfit was too shabby to be worn outside her home and her hair too untidy to be left uncovered, there was an unearthly kind of wildness in her eyes that betrayed a troubled spirit. But so agile and so swift were her movements that she dodged the many who tried to help her.

By the time she reached Oyingbo market, the sun was peeping out from behind the morning clouds. She was nearing a busy part of the town and there were already people about. The early market sellers were making their way to the stalls in single file, their various bundles tied and balanced unwaveringly on their heads. She collided with an angry Hausa beggar who, vacating one of the open stalls where he had spent the night, was heading for

2

the tarred road to start his day's begging. He was blind and walked with his stick held menacingly straight in front of him; his other hand clutched shakily at his begging calabash. Nnu Ego in her haste almost knocked the poor man down, running straight into him as if she too was without the use of her eyes. There followed a loud curse, and an unintelligible outpouring from the mouth of the beggar in his native Hausa language, which few people in Lagos understood. His calabash went flying from his shaky hand, and he swung his stick in the air to emphasise his loud curse.

'*Dan duru ba*!' he shouted. He imagined that, early as it was, he was being attacked by money snatchers who were wont to rob the beggars, especially blind ones, of their daily alms. Nnu Ego just managed to escape the fury of the beggar's stick as she picked up the calabash for him. She did this wordlessly though she was breathing hard. There was nothing she could have said to this man who was enjoying his anger, recounting what he thought was about to happen to him in Hausa. He went on cursing and swinging his stick in the air as Nnu Ego left him.

She began to feel fatigued, and from time to time whimpered like a frightened child; yet she walked fast, resentful that she should feel any physical hurt at all. As she walked, pain and anger fought inside her; sometimes anger came to the fore, but the emotional pain always won. And that was what she wanted to end, very, very quickly. She would soon be there, she told herself. It would all soon be over, right there under the deep water that ran below Carter Bridge. Then she would be able to seek out and meet her *chi*, her personal god, and she would ask her why she had punished her so. She knew her *chi* was a woman, not just because to her way of thinking only a woman would be so thorough in punishing another. Apart from that, had she not been told many times at home in Ibuza that her *chi* was a slave woman who had been forced to die with her mistress when the latter was being buried? So the slave woman was making sure that Nnu Ego's own

3

life was nothing but a catalogue of disasters. Well, now she was going to her, to the unforgiving slave princess from a foreign land, to talk it all over with her, not on this earth but in the land of the dead, there deep beneath the waters of the sea.

It is said that those about to die, be it by drowning or by a gradual terminal illness, use their last few moments of consciousness going through their life kaleidoscopically, and Nnu Ego was no exception. Hers had started twenty-five years previously in a little Ibo town called Ibuza.

Nwokocha Agbadi was a very wealthy local chief. He was a great wrestler, and was glib and gifted in oratory. His speeches were highly spiced with sharp anecdotes and thoughtful proverbs. He was taller than most and, since he was born in an age when physical prowess determined one's role in life, people naturally accepted him as a leader. Like most handsome men who are aware of their charismatic image, he had many women in his time. Whenever they raided a neighbouring village, Agbadi was sure to come back with the best-looking women. He had a soft spot for those from big houses, daughters of chiefs and rich men. He knew from experience that such women had an extra confidence and sauciness even in captivity. And that type of arrogance, which even captivity could not diminish, seemed to excite some wicked trait in him. In his young days, a woman who gave in to a man without first fighting for her honour was never respected. To regard a woman who is quiet and timid as desirable was something that came after his time, with Christianity and other changes. Most of the women Nwokocha Agbadi chose as his wives and even slaves were those who could match his arrogance, his biting sarcasm, his painful jokes, and also, when the mood called, his human tenderness.

He married a few women in the traditional sense, but as he watched each of them sink into domesticity and motherhood he was soon bored and would go further afield for some other exciting, tall and proud female. This predilection of his extended to his mistresses as well.

Agbadi was from Ogboli, a village of people who, legend said, had lived in that part of what is now Ibuza before the Eastern Ibo people from Isu came and settled there with them. The Ogboli people allowed the founder of Ibuza to stay, and bestowed titles on him and his descendants. They also inherited most of the widows of the newcomers. This was the arrangement for a long time, until the people of Ibuza grew in number and strength, and those of Ogboli somehow diminished. It is still not known why this was so, though some claim that many of them emigrated to neighbouring towns like Asaba. But that is by the way. The Ibuza people, who came from the eastern part of Nigeria, fought and won many civil battles against their hosts. They won their freedom of movement to the extent that they started crowning themselves and refused to send their wives to the Ogboli people again.

During the time of Nwokocha Agbadi the town had become known as Ibuza, and Ogboli was then one of the villages that made up the town. The glory was still there, and the Ogboli people still regarded themselves as the sons of the soil, even though the soil had long been taken away from under their feet. Two of Agbadi's wives came from Ibuza, two from his own village of Ogboli, three were slaves he had captured during his wanderings; and he also had two mistresses.

One of these mistresses was a very beautiful young woman who managed to combine stubbornness with arrogance. So stubborn was she that she refused to live with Agbadi. Men being what they are, he preferred spending his free time with her, with this woman who enjoyed humiliating him by refusing to be his wife. Many a night she would send him away, saying she did not feel like having anything to do with him, even though Agbadi was not supposed to be the kind of man women should say such things to. But she refused to be dazzled by his wealth, his name or his handsomeness. People said that Nwokocha Agbadi spent all his life on this earth courting his Ona.

Ona was Agbadi's name for her, not the name originally given to her. Her father was a chief, too, and Agbadi had seen her as a child following her father about. People used to find it strange that a chief like Obi Umunna would go about unashamedly pulling

6

a tiny toddler with him. But her father told people that his little girl was his ornament. Agbadi then said, jokingly, 'Why don't you wear her round your neck, like an *ona*, a "priceless jewel"?' People had laughed. But the name stuck. It never occurred to him that he would be one of the men to ask for her when she grew up. Her father, despite having several wives, had few children, and in fact no living son at all, but Ona grew to fill her father's expectation. He had maintained that she must never marry; his daughter was never going to stoop to any man. She was free to have men, however, and if she bore a son, he would take her father's name, thereby rectifying the omission nature had made.

She was of medium height, and had skin like that of half-ripe palm nuts, smooth, light coffee in colour. Her hair, closely cropped, fitted her skull like a hat atop a head that seemed to be thrust out of her shoulders by a strong, long powerful neck. When she walked, her expensive waist-beads, made of the best coral, murmured, and for men raised in that culture, who knew the sound of each bead, this added to her allurement. She had been used all her life to walking in bush paths, so she knew the tricks of avoiding thorns, using the balls of her feet rather than putting her full weight on her soles. This gave her movement the air of a mysterious and yet exciting cat. She had a trick of pointing her chin forward, as if she saw with it instead of her eyes, which were black-rimmed and seemed sunken into her head. Like most of her people, she had little patience for walking, and as she ran, in the same way as young girls would run to the stream or run out of their homesteads to find out what was going on, she would cup her hands to support her breasts, which swung with bare health. She seldom wore any tops, neither did she tie her lappa over her breasts like the old women. But she had many waist lappas, and expensive changes of coral beads for her neck and waist. Greenish-black tattoos stood out richly against her brown skin. Though she was always scantily dressed, she frequently made people aware of being a conservative, haughty presence, cold as steel and remote as any woman royally born. When she sat, and curled her long legs together in feminine modesty, one knew that she had style, this only daughter of Obi Umunna.

Nwokocha Agbadi would not have minded sending all his wives away just to live with this one woman. But that was not to be. People said she had had him bewitched, that she had a kind of power over him; what person in his right mind would leave his big spacious household and women who were willing to worship and serve him in all things to go after a rude, egocentric woman who had been spoilt by her father? This story gained credence particularly when Agbadi's young wives showed signs of sexual neglect. He would be reminded to do his duty by them, then when they became pregnant he would not be seen in their huts until the time came for him to mate them again. But whenever he returned from his many wanderings he would go and stay with his Ona.

It was during one rainy season that Nwokocha Agbadi went to hunt some elephants which he and his age-group knew would be crossing the bush marshes called Ude. He came too near one of the heavy creatures on this occasion, and that single slip almost led to a terrible disaster. He was thrown with a mighty tusk into a nearby wild sugar-cane bush and he landed in the bubbly black mud. The animal was so enraged that, uncharacteristically for a big elephant, it chased after him blindly, bellowing like a great locomotive, so that the very ground seemed about to give way at its heavy approach. Agbadi reacted quickly. He was pinned to the sugar-cane bush unable to move his body, none the less with a practised hand he aimed his spear and threw it under the belly of the angry animal. It roared, but still made a determined assault on Agbadi, almost tearing his arm from his shoulder, attacking him with a fury increased by the painful spear under it. The elephant roared and fell, but not before it had wounded Agbadi so badly that he himself suspected he was nearing his end. The other hunters, hearing the commotion, rushed to the scene and quickly finished off the elephant, which was still very alive and kicking furiously. They saw Nwokocha Agbadi bleeding to death. His shoulder bone was thrust out of his skin, and the elephant's tusks had indented his side. The men gathered and with bamboo splints tied the twisted shoulder, though they could do little about the bleeding side; judging from the pool of blood that was fast forming around him, they doubted that he would last long. Agbadi soon passed out and it seemed to all that he had died. The oldest man of the group took his *otuogwu* cloth which he had left in a dry hilly place by the stream, rolled Agbadi in it as if he were a dead person, then the anxious hunters carried him in a bigger bamboo crate which they had quickly constructed, and made their way gradually and sadly home.

The procession of dignified men emerging from the belly of the bush into the town was a moving spectacle. It was obvious to those farmers on their way to their lands that something was very wrong, but if they suspected the truth, they could not yet show grief: Nwokocha Agbadi was not only a chief but an important one, therefore the disclosure of his death would have to comply with certain cultural laws – there must be gun shots, and two or three goats must be slaughtered before the announcement. Anyone who started grieving before the official proclamation would be made to pay fines equivalent to three goats. So people watched the hunters' approach in awe, wondering who it was that had been so mummified. Women and children ran from their homesteads to witness the sight, and observant people noticed that the only chief missing among the returning hunters was Nwokocha Agbadi. His carriers were followed by four hefty male slaves dragging the dead elephant, groaning and sweating with the weight of the beast. People knew then that Agbadi had either been badly wounded or killed while hunting the elephant! Word circulated in whispers.

When Ona heard of it, the more vulnerable personality underneath her daily steely mask came out. She dashed out from where she was sitting by her father and soon caught up with the carriers.

'Tell me, please say something, is my lover dead?' she asked anxiously as she galloped after them on the balls of her feet, her waist-beads rumbling to the rhythm of her movements.

She held on first to this man, asking the same question, then to that one, begging him to say something. She pestered Agbadi's closest and oldest friend Obi Idayi, so much so that he lost his temper. He had ignored her for some time, and never had any love for this wild uncontrolled woman. He did not know what Agbadi found in her. Now he stopped in his heavy stride and snapped.

'In life you tortured him, teased him with your body. Now that he is dead, you cry for his manhood.'

Ona was stunned. She held her hands over her head and spoke like someone hypnotised: 'It can't be. It just can't be.'

Some older women standing by hushed her, saying, 'He may be your lover, girl, but don't forget that he is Nwokocha Agbadi. Watch your tongue.'

With fear and apprehension lightening her brain, Ona followed the carriers to Ogboli.

Agbadi was placed in the centre of his courtyard. The medicine man was able to detect a very faint life in him, although his breathing was toilsome and indicated that he was a dying man. They had to massage his heart into activity again. All his wives were shooed away, but Ona fought and clawed to be allowed to stay and would let no one touch Agbadi except herself. His people did not much like her, yet they respected her as the only woman who could make Agbadi really happy, so the medicine man let her attend to him. So frightened was she in the aftermath of the accident that, together with the men sitting around Agbadi, she forgot that food was meant to be eaten and that night was meant for sleep.

Goats were slaughtered every day to appease Agbadi's *chi*;

10

others were left alive by river banks and at Ude to appease the other gods. The thought of going home never occurred to Ona, not even on the fourth day. Nor did her possessive father call for her, for he understood her plight; hers were civilised people and they trusted her. For the first time, she realised how attached she was to this man Nwokocha Agbadi, though he was cruel in his imperiousness. His tongue was biting like the edge of a circumcision blade. He ruled his family and children as if he were a god. Yet he gave her his love without reservation, and she enjoyed it; she suspected, however, that her fate would be the same as that of his other women should she consent to become one of his wives. No, maybe the best way to keep his love was not to let that happen. But if he were to die now ... God, she would will herself death too! All the same, she would rather have her tongue pulled out of her head than let that beast of a man know how much she cared. That, she decided, would be his lot for being so domineering and having such a foul temper. She watched over him closely and told herself that she would go if he should start showing signs of being on the mend.

On the fifth day he opened his eyes without any help from the medicine man. Ona was so surprised that she simply stared back at him. Her first impulsive act was to scream her joy; then she remembered her self control. Agbadi looked at her for a split second, his eyes unfocused. For that small time, he looked so dependent that Ona felt like gathering him in her arms and singing to him, as one would do to a baby. He started to chew the side of his mouth, a habit of his which she knew from experience was normally the prelude to a hurtful remark. He looked at her sitting there cross-legged beside him, one of her knees almost touching his head which was supported by a wooden head-rest. He said nothing but his sharp mind had taken in the whole situation. Still biting the corner of his lower lip, he allowed his eyes to wander over her from head to toe. Then he simply rolled away and closed his eyes again. She did not doubt that the light in the open courtyard where he was lying was too strong for his eyes, since he had not opened them for five long days, but she had not missed his look of derision. What a way to thank her for all her help!

She did not tell anyone that Agbadi had regained consciousness; she watched hopefully, yet with fear, for further signs of recovery. That evening while she was trying to ease the bamboo splints that had been fixed to straighten his shoulder, two men had to hold his strong long legs to prevent him from kicking. He groaned in pain, and she was told to mop up the fresh blood oozing from the wound. She heard herself saying, 'You have borne the pain like a man. The bones are set now; you only have the wound, and this will heal in a day or two.'

Agbadi's eyes flew open, and this time they were clear and evil. His white teeth flashed in a sardonic smile. He chuckled wickedly, then said roughly, 'What would you have done without your lover, Ona?'

'If you don't stop talking that way, I shall throw this calabash of medicine at you and walk out of here back to my father's compound. You're much better now, judging from the sharpness of your tongue.'

Her eyes burned with hot tears, but she controlled and never shed them, sensing that nothing would please her lover more than to see her face awash with tears of frustration. She got up from Agbadi's goatskin rug and began to make her way out of the compound.

'You can't go now. You have to finish what you started,' Agbadi observed.

She whirled round. 'Who is going to stop me? Who dares to stop me? You?' she wailed, very near hysteria. 'Bah! You think you have the right to play God, just because you are Agbadi? You have your wives – they can look after you. You have your slaves – let them mop up your stinking blood!'

'My wives are too much in love with me to stand by and see

me in pain. I need a heartless woman like you ... a woman whose heart is made of stone to stay and watch men remove my splints and not drown me with tears. I will die if you go.'

'You will die if I go?' Ona sneered, jutting her pointed chin into the air and throwing back her head in feigned amusement. 'A statement like that coming from the great Agbadi! So you are just an ordinary person after all – no, not an ordinary man but a spoilt child who cries when his mother leaves him. Nwokocha Agbadi, hurry up and die, because I'm going back to my father's compound. My heart is not made of stone but I would rather die than let it soften for the likes of you.'

'I did not say I am dying because you are so indispensable ...' This was followed by his low, mocking laughter. He was joined by his close friend Idayi, and they seemed to be enjoying her discomfiture.

Then Idayi coughed gently. 'Look, Agbadi,' he warned, 'if you don't stop chuckling you'll start to bleed again. As for you, our Ona, you have lain there by him these five days, when he had lost his power of speech. Now that he can talk, you want him to kneel down and say 'thank you', eh?'

'Yes, why not? Haven't I done enough for that? I left my father's compound to come here – '

'I didn't ask you to come, remember,' Agbadi put in, determined to be the proud hunter till death.

'Oh, you have nerve!'

'All right, all right,' Idayi intervened again, seeing that Ona was becoming more and more angry. If her self-control was allowed to snap she might well throw the calabash as she threatened. 'In a day or two he will get better, Ona. Then you can go back to your people. We are grateful to you and to your father, I assure you. If Agbadi were to lower himself to thank you, I am sure you would stop caring for him. You need a man, Ona, not a snail. We all know you. For a while I thought we were losing our giant forever. Well,

13

don't worry, he is still too weak to bother any woman for many days, but what he needs is the comfort of your nearness, though he won't admit it. The sun is going down now; he needs to be brought his blood meal, if you want him to heal properly,' Idayi said with his usual studied calmness.

Ona went to do as she was told, thinking to herself how unfair it was that Agbadi should accuse her of having a heart of stone. How else could she behave since she could not marry him? Because her father had no son, she had been dedicated to the gods to produce children in his name, not that of any husband. Oh, how torn she was between two men: she had to be loyal to her father, as well as to her lover Agbadi.

There were many friends and wellwishers in Agbadi's compound when she brought the meal from the medicine man's hut, knelt down and silently began to feed Agbadi.

Then the familiar salutation 'He who keeps peace' could be heard from people outside, and Ona knew that her father Obi Umunna had come to pay Agbadi a visit. Agbadi looked at her in silent appeal and the message was clear: he did not want her to leave yet.

'How can you be so strong and yet so soft, Agbadi?' she asked him in a low voice so that the well-wishers would not hear.

In answer, he simply smiled non-committally.

Obi Umunna approached and said airily: 'So how is the lucky man? You are very lucky, my friend. Bring your best drink and kolanuts and let us pray for long life and thank your *chi* for rescuing you.'

'You are right,' Idayi agreed. 'I was just telling your daughter that for a while we thought we would lose him. But, my friend, I hope you are not here to take her home. She is not ready yet.'

'And how is my Ona?' Obi Umunna asked after watching her for a few moments.

14

'He who keeps peace,' she replied, 'I am being well looked after, Father.'

'Good; but remember that you are not married to Agbadi. I don't want his money. You must come home as soon as he is better.'

'Why do you not turn her into a man?' Agbadi said bitingly. 'Clinging to your daughter as if – '

'I am not here to argue with you, Agbadi; you are sick. And we have gone through this argument so many times before. My daughter will marry no one.'

Ona purposely spooned some of the meal near Agbadi's nose, as a way of telling him not to insult her father in her presence.

Agbadi coughed and remarked: 'A daughter who you have not even taught how to feed a sick man ...'

'Oh, Agbadi!' Ona gasped.

'Kolanut and palm wine are here,' Idayi said as one of Agbadi's children brought in the wooden tray with refreshments. 'Let us pray to our ancestors.'

Being the oldest man in the courtyard, Idayi said the prayers. He prayed to the almighty Olisa to cure his good friend Nwokocha Agbadi and begged him to give them all good health. Agbadi lay silently on his back on the goatskin, sometimes gazing at the bamboo ceiling, sometimes letting out grunts in agreement with the many prayers being said. For most of the time his eyes were closed, and the sweat on his matted chest had to be mopped with cold water time and time again.

Agbadi had slept so much in the day that, now he was feeling better, he was finding it difficult to sleep the night through. He must have dozed for a while, none the less, for when he opened his eyes, the whole compound was quiet. Cool night air blew in through the open roof window and he could hear his goats grunting. He heard a light breathing nearby on a separate goatskin. Now he remembered – Ona was there lying beside him. He watched her bare breasts rising and falling as she breathed, and noted

15

with amusement how she made sure to stay as far away from him as possible, though in unconscious defiance, like everything else she did, her leg was thrust out so that it was almost touching him. 'The heartless bitch,' he thought, 'I will teach her.' He winced as his still-sore shoulder protested, but he managed to turn fully on to his side and gazed his fill at her. To think that in that proud head, held high even in sleep, and to think that in those breasts, two beautiful firm mounds on her chest looking like calabashes turned upside-down, there was some tenderness was momentarily incredible to him. He felt himself burn.

Then the anger came to him again as he remembered how many times this young woman had teased and demeaned him sexually. He felt like jumping on her, clawing at her, hurting her. Then again the thought that she needed him and was there just for his sake came uppermost in his mind and won against the vengeful impulse. He found himself rolling towards her, giving her nipples gentle lover's bites, letting his tongue glide down the hollow in the centre of her breasts and then back again. He caressed her thigh with his good hand, moving to her small night lappa and fingering her coral waist-beads. Ona gasped and opened her eyes. She wanted to scream. But Agbadi was faster, more experienced. He slid on his belly, like a big black snake, and covered her mouth with his. He did not let her mouth free for a very long time. She struggled fiercely like a trapped animal, but Agbadi was becoming himself again. He was still weak, but not weak enough to ignore his desire. He worked on her, breaking down all her resistance. He stroked and explored with his perfect hand, banking heavily on the fact that Ona was a woman, a mature woman, who had had him many a time. And he was right. Her struggling and kicking lessened. She started to moan and groan instead, like a woman in labour. He kept on, and would not let go, so masterful was he in this art. He knew he had reduced her to longing and craving for him. He knew he had won. He wanted her completely humiliated

16

in her burning desire. And Ona knew. So she tried to counteract her feelings in the only way she guessed would not give her away.

'I know you are too ill to take me,' she murmured.

'No, my Ona, I am waiting for you to be ready.'

She felt like screaming to let free the burning of her body. How could one's body betray one so! She should have got up and run out, but something was holding her there; she did not know what and she did not care. She wanted to be relieved of the fire inside her. 'Please, I am in pain.'

'Yes,' came his confident reply. 'I want you to be.'

She melted and could say no more. She wept and the sobs she was trying to suppress shook her whole being. He felt it, chuckled, and remarked thickly, 'Please, Ona, don't wake the whole household.'

Either she did not hear, or he wanted her to do just that, for he gave her two painful bites in between her breasts, and she in desperation clawed at him, and was grateful when at last she felt him inside her.

He came deceptively gently, and so unprepared was she for the passionate thrust which followed that she screamed, so piercingly she was even surprised at her own voice: 'Agbadi, you are splitting me into two!'

Suddenly the whole courtyard seemed to be filled with moving people. A voice, a male voice, which later she recognised to be that of Agbadi's friend Obi Idayi, shouted from the corner of the open courtyard: 'Agbadi! Agbadi! Are you all right?'

Again came that low laughter Ona loved and yet loathed so much. 'I am fine, my friend. You go to sleep. I am only giving my woman her pleasures.'

Grunting like an excited animal with a helpless prey, he left her abruptly, still unsatiated, and rolled painfully to the other side of the goatskin. Having hurt her on purpose for the benefit of his people sleeping in the courtyard, he had had his satisfaction.

17

She hated him at that moment. 'All this show just for your people, Agbadi?' she whispered. Unable to help herself, she began to cry quietly.

Then he was sorry for her. He moved her closer to him and, letting her curl up to him, encouraged her to get the bitterness off her chest. He felt her hot tears flowing, but he said nothing, just went on tracing the contours of those offending nipples.

Agbadi's senior wife, Agunwa, became ill that very night. Some said later that she sacrificed herself for her husband; but a few had noticed that it was bad for her morale to hear her husband giving pleasure to another woman in the same courtyard where she slept, and to such a woman who openly treated the man they all worshipped so badly. A woman who was troublesome and impetuous, who had the audacity to fight with her man before letting him have her: a bad woman.

Agbadi and Ona were still sleeping the following morning when the alarm was raised by one of the children.

'Wake up, Father, wake up! Our mother is having a seizure.'

'What?' Agbadi barked. 'What is the matter with her? She was all right last night.' Momentarily he forgot himself and made as if to get up; Ona, wide awake now, restrained him. 'Damn this shoulder,' he grumbled. 'But what is the matter with Agunwa?'

'That's what we are trying to find out,' said the reassuring voice of Idayi, who had been keeping vigil over his friend.

'Lie still, Agbadi,' other voices advised.

He watched helplessly as they took his senior wife away to her hut in her own part of the compound. 'Send her my medicine man. What is the matter with the woman?' he fumed.

Soon his friend came from Agunwa's hut and told him, 'Your chief wife is very ill. Your *dibia* is doing all he can for her, but I don't think she will survive.'

'Why, Idayi, why at this time?'

18

'Nobody knows when their time will come. Your wife Agunwa is no exception. The strain of your illness ... since the day we brought you back from Ude, she has watched over you from that corner of your courtyard. She was even here last night.'

'Oh, come, my friend. What are you trying to tell me? She's my chief wife, I took here to Udo the day I became an Obi. She is the mother of my grown sons. You are wrong, Idayi, to suggest she might be sore or bitter just because last night with Ona I amused myself a little. Agunwa is too mature to mind that. Why, if she behaved like that what kind of example would that be to the younger wives?'

'You talk of last night as only a little amusement. But it kept all of us awake. You and your Ona woke the very dead ...'

Goats and hens were sacrificed in an attempt to save Agunwa. When, on the eighteenth day, Agbadi was able to get up and move about with the help of one of his male slaves and a stick, the first place he visited was his senior wife's hut. He was shocked to see her. She was too far gone to even know of his presence.

He looked around and saw two of his grown sons watching him. 'Your mother is a good woman. So unobtrusive, so quiet. I don't know who else will help me keep an eye on those young wives of mine, and see to the smooth running of my household.'

Two days later, Agunwa died and Agbadi sent a big cow to her people to announce her death. Having died a 'complete woman', she was to be buried in her husband's compound.

'Make sure that her slave and her cooking things go with her. We must all mourn her.'

Ona moved about like a quiet wife. She knew that people blamed her for Agunwa's death though no one had the courage to say so openly. That night, after she had given Agbadi his meal and helped his men rub life into his stiff side and shoulder, she curled up to him and asked: 'Would you like me to go now? My father will be worrying, wondering what your people are saying.'

'And what are my people saying, woman? That I took my mistress in my own courtyard, and that I take her every night as I see fit? Is that it? Haven't I got enough to worry about without you adding your bit? Go to sleep, Ona, you're tired and you don't look too well to me. Tomorrow is going to be a busy day. The burial of a chief's wife is not a small thing in Ibuza.'

The funeral dancing and feasting started very early in the morning and went on throughout the day. Different groups of people came and went and had to be entertained. In the evening it was time to put Agunwa in her grave. All the things that she would need in her after-life were gathered and arranged in her wooden coffin which was made of the best mahogany Agbadi could find. Then her personal slave was ceremoniously called in a loud voice by the medicine man: she must be laid inside the grave first. A good slave was supposed to jump into the grave willingly, happy to accompany her mistress; but this young and beautiful woman did not wish to die yet.

She kept begging for her life, much to the annoyance of many of the men standing around. The women stood far off for this was a custom they found revolting. The poor slave was pushed into the shallow grave, but she struggled out, fighting and pleading, appealing to her owner Agbadi.

Then Agbadi's eldest son cried in anger: 'So my mother does not even deserve a decent burial? Now we are not to send her slave down with her, just because the girl is beautiful?' So saying, he gave the woman a sharp blow with the head of the cutlass he was carrying. 'Go down like a good slave!' he shouted.

'Stop that at once!' Agbadi roared, limping up to his son. 'What do you call this, bravery? You make my stomach turn.'

The slave woman turned her eyes, now glazed with approaching death, towards him. 'Thank you for this kindness, Nwokocha the son of Agbadi. I shall come back to your household, but as a legitimate daughter. I shall come back ...'

20

Another relative gave her a final blow to the head, and at last she fell into the grave, silenced for ever. As her blood spurted, splashing the men standing round, there was a piercing scream from the group of mourning women standing a little way off. But it was not their feelings for the dead woman that caused this reaction, Agbadi saw; they were holding Ona up.

'Now what is happening?' Agbadi said hoarsely. 'My friend Idayi, take the burial kolanut and finish the ceremony. I think Umunna's daughter Ona wants to die on me, too. She has been ill all day, I don't know why. I must take her inside.' He limped over to her with his stick as fast as he could.

Ona was lain on a goatskin in Agbadi's courtyard while the medicine man went on praying and performing in the centre of the compound. For a while that night Ona went hot and cold, but before dawn it was clear that although the illness was tiring and weakening her she could bear it. Agbadi's early fear had been that it might be *iba*, the malaria which killed anyone in a short time.

Obi Umunna came in the morning and said to Agbadi without preamble: 'I think there is something in your family killing everyone. First you barely escaped death, then your Agunwa was taken, now my healthy daughter who came to look after you – '

'My friend, if you were not an Obi like me, and not Ona's father, I would tell you a few home truths. If she is ill because of a curse in my household, would it not be right for you to leave her with me until she gets better? I will look after her myself.'

Over the next few days Agbadi's practised eyes noted the pattern of the sickness, and he said to Ona one morning as she sat beside him, 'Ona, the daughter of Umunna, I think I am making you into a mother. You are carrying our love child.'

He said it so lightly that she was too surprised to say a word.

'Well, it is true. What are you going to say to your father?'

'Oh, please, Agbadi, don't take my joy away. You know I like staying here with you, but I am my father's daughter. He has no

21

son. Your house is full of children. Please, Nwokocha the son of Agbadi, your bravery is known afar and so is your tenderness. Don't complicate this for me – the greatest joy of my life.'

'But what of me? You and your father are using me as a tool to get what you wanted.'

'We did not force you, remember,' Ona said, anger rising in her. 'Is it my fault that you decided to treat me as a wife and not a lover? You knew of my father's determination before you came to me. We did not use you. You used me, yet I don't regret it. If you want to regret it, well, that is up to you.'

'So when are you leaving me?' Agbadi asked eventually.

'As soon as I feel stronger. You are getting better every day, ready to go back to your farm.'

'Forget about my farm. Hurry up and get well, and go back to your shameless father.'

'Don't call him names,' she cried, and felt very weak.

'You see, you won't even allow yourself to be a woman. You are in the first weeks of motherhood, and all you can do is to think like a man, raising male issue for your father, just because he cannot do it himself.'

'I am not going to quarrel with you,' Ona declared.

That day, for the first time since the accident, Agbadi went to his farm, much to everybody's surprise. 'I want to see how the work is going,' he replied to questions people put to him.

Ona felt lonely during his absence. But she sent word to her father to come for her the next day.

On that last night, she tried to reason with Agbadi, but he gave her his stiff back. 'All right,' she said in compromise, 'my father wants a son and you have many sons. But you do not have a girl yet. Since my father will not accept any bride price from you, if I have a son he will belong to my father, but if a girl, she will be yours. That is the best I can do for you both.'

They made it up before morning, Agbadi being tender and

loving the rest of the night.

The next day, the women from Obi Umunna's compound came with presents for Agbadi's household. They were all very polite to each other, and Ona was relieved to note that her father had not come; she could not stand another argument between the two men, though she supposed she should regard herself as lucky for two men to want to own her.

Nwokocha Agbadi visited her often in her hut, and slept there many an Eke night when he did not have to go to the farm or hunting. People had thought that after a while he would get fed up with her, but that was not so. Each parting was painful, just as if they were young people playing by the moonlight.

Some days when he could not come to her, she knew he was with his other wives. Being Agbadi, however, he never talked about them to her, and she respected him for it. It was on such a night that she came into labour. She cried quietly as she agonised alone through the long hours of darkness. Only when the pain became unbearable did she enlist the help of the women in her father's compound.

Her baby daughter was very merciful to her. 'She simply glided into the world,' the women around told her.

Ona was dazed with happiness. Agbadi had won, she thought to herself, at the same time feeling pity for her poor father.

Agbadi came the very second day and was visibly overjoyed. 'Well, you have done well, Ona. A daughter, eh?'

He bent down and peeped at the day-old child wrapped and kept warm by the fireside and remarked: 'This child is priceless, more than twenty bags of cowries. I think that should really be her name, because she is a beauty and she is mine. Yes, "Nnu Ego": twenty bags of cowries.'

He called in the men who came with him and they brought enough yams and drinks to last Ona a long time, for custom did not allow him to go near her again until after twenty-five days.

23

Obi Umunna came in and for a while the two men toasted and prayed for the happiness of the new child.

'Did Ona tell you of our compromise? She agreed that if she bore a baby girl, she would be mine, if a boy, he would be yours,' Agbadi said coolly.

'That may be true, my friend. I am not a man who can take seriously talks lovers have on their love mat. She was your guest, and you were a sick man then.'

'What are you trying to say, Umunna? That your daughter should go back on her promise?'

'She is a woman so I don't see why not. However, because she is my daughter, I am not asking her to violate her word. Yes, the baby is yours, but my daughter remains here. I have not accepted any money from you.'

'How much do you want for her? What else do you expect? Is it her fault that you have no son?' Agbadi was beginning to roar like the wild animals he was wont to hunt and kill.

'Please, please, aren't you two happy that I have survived the birth? It seems nobody is interested in that part of it. I made a promise to Agbadi, yes; but, dear Agbadi, I am still my father's daughter. Since he has not taken a bride price from you, do you think it would be right for me to stay with you permanently? You know our custom does not permit it. I am still my father's daughter,' Ona intoned sadly.

Agbadi drew himself up from the mud pavement where he had been sitting and said, 'I have never forced a woman to come to me. Never, and I am not going to start now. The only women I captured were slaves. All my wives are happy to be such. You want to stay with your father? So be it.' And he left alone.

For months, Ona did not see Agbadi. She heard from people that he more or less lived in thick, swampy Ude where game was plentiful. Ona missed him, yet she knew that, according to the way things were, she was doing the right thing.

A year after the birth of Nnu Ego, Obi Umunna died, and Ona cried for days for him, especially as he had gone without her producing the wanted son. Agbadi relented when he heard of it, for he knew how close Ona was to her father.

For over two years, he persisted in trying to persuade her to come and live in his compound. 'You are no longer bound by your father's hopes. He is dead. But we are still living. Come and stay with me. You are all alone here among your extended relatives. Please, Ona, don't let us waste our lives longing for each other.'

'You know my father would not have liked it, so stop talking like that, Agbadi. I refuse to be intimidated by your wealth and your position.'

Yet Agbadi went on visiting his Ona.

Nnu Ego was the apple of her parents' eyes. She was a beautiful child, fair-skinned like the women from the Aboh and Itsekiri areas. At her birth it was noticed that there was a lump on her head, which in due course was covered with thick, curly, black hair. But suddenly one evening she started to suffer from a strange headache that held her head and shoulder together. In panic, Ona sent for Agbadi who came tearing down from Ogboli with a *dibia*.

The *dibia* touched the child's head and drew in his breath, feeling how much hotter the lump was than the rest of her body. He quickly set to work, arranging his pieces of kolanut and snail shells and cowries on the mud floor. He soon went into a trance and began to speak in a far-off voice, strange and unnatural: 'This child is the slave woman who died with your senior wife Agunwa. She promised to come back as a daughter. Now here she is. That is why this child has the fair skin of the water people, and the painful lump on her head is from the beating your men gave her before she fell into the grave. She will always have trouble with that head. If she has a fortunate life, the head will not play up. But if she is unhappy, it will trouble her both physically and emotionally. My advice is that you go and appease the slave woman.'

'Ona, you must leave this place,' Agbadi ordered, 'you have to leave your father's house, otherwise I am taking my daughter from you. She can't worship her *chi* from a foreign place; she must be where her *chi* is until all the sacrifices have been made.'

So Ona finally had to leave her people, not because she allowed her love for Agbadi to rule her actions but because she wanted the safety of her child. As soon as they arrived at Ogboli, Nnu Ego got better. The slave woman was properly buried in a separate grave, and an image of her was made for Nnu Ego to carry with her.

Soon after that, Ona became pregnant again. From the very beginning she was ill, so that it was not a surprise to Agbadi's household when she came into premature labour. After the birth, Ona was weak but her head was clear. She knew she was dying.

'Agbadi,' she called hoarsely, 'you see that I was not destined to live with you. But you are stubborn, my father was stubborn, and I am stubborn too. Please don't mourn me for long; and see that however much you love our daughter Nnu Ego you allow her to have a life of her own, a husband if she wants one. Allow her to be a woman.'

Not long after this, Ona died; and her weak new-born son followed her only a day later. So all Nwokocha Agbadi had to remind him of his great passion for Ona was their daughter, Nnu Ego.

'He who roars like a lion.'

'My sons, you will all grow to be kings among men.'

'He who roars like a lion.'

'My daughters, you will all grow to rock your children's children.'

Nnu Ego looked up from where she was kneeling and filling her father's evening pipe and smiled at him. 'Your friend Obi Idayi is here, Father. I can hear people saying his praise names outside.'

'I hear them too. From the number of voices, it seems there are many people out there, Nnu Ego.'

'Yes, Father, they all come to play in our compound.'

'It sounds as if they are mostly young men.'

She smiled shyly again. 'I know, Father.'

Idayi entered. 'My friend Agbadi, you must do something about this daughter of yours.'

'He who roars like a lion,' Nnu Ego said in salutation.

'You will live to rock your children's children, daughter of Agbadi and Ona. Go, daughter, and bring your father's best drink; and here, fill my pipe, also.'

'Yes, Father.'

'Listen, Agbadi, your outer compound looks as if there is a gathering or something. Let someone marry this girl. She has long passed the age of puberty. You don't want to be another Obi Umunna, do you?'

Both men laughed. 'Stupid man, I can't bear to think of him,' Agbadi said, puffing at his pipe. 'The thing is, Nnu Ego is the only part of Ona that I have. Of course, she isn't arrogant like her mother, but the way she throws her head back when she looks you in the face, her light walk ...'

'I know,' Idayi agreed, remembering the happenings of over sixteen years before. 'It all reminds you of Ona. Hmm ... they don't

27

make women like her any more.'

'No, they don't, my friend. I am glad we had the best of them.'

Nnu Ego came in with the palm wine.

'Where is Idayi's pipe, daughter?'

'Oh, Father, I forgot. I shall go and bring it.'

'Your daughter's mind is not here. She dreams of her man and her own home. Don't let her dream in vain. After all, her age-mates are already having their first and second babies. Stop rejecting young men, Agbadi; let one of them marry her.'

'I have promised Amatokwu that I will think about his son. He is one of those out there.'

'They are not bad people, the Amatokwus. And that son has been a great help to his father during the past year. I don't see why he should not make a good husband for Nnu Ego. She would be the senior wife.'

Nnu Ego brought the pipe, now filled, and said, 'I'll be outside with my friends if you want me, Father.'

'Agbadi, we are getting on,' Idayi sighed. 'Here we are talking about Ona's daughter when it seems only yesterday that I heard Ona screaming as she was being conceived.'

The two men laughed long and deep.

The people of Ibuza were never to forget the night the people of Umu-Iso came for Nnu Ego. Her father excelled himself. He accepted the normal bride price, to show that he gave his blessing to the marriage. But he sent his daughter away with seven hefty men and seven young girls carrying her personal possessions. There were seven goats, baskets and baskets of yams, yards and yards of white man's cloth, twenty-four home-spun lappas, rows and rows of Hausa trinkets and coral beads. Her ornamented cooking-pots and gaudy calabashes were attractively arranged round crates of clearest oils. A new and more beautiful effigy of the slave woman who was her *chi* was made and placed on top of all

Nnu Ego's possessions, to guard her against any evil eye. It was indeed a night of wealth display. No one had ever seen anything like it. (Even today if a new bride is too mouthy about her people, she will be effectively challenged: 'But are your people more generous than Nwokocha Agbadi of Ogboli?')

Agbadi's heart was full to bursting point when, the second day, the people from Amatokwu's compound came to thank him for giving them his precious daughter Nnu Ego. They did so with six full kegs of palm wine. Agbadi smiled contentedly and invited everybody in his own compound to drink.

'My daughter has been found an unspoiled virgin. Her husband's people are here to thank us.'

Each visitor would peep into the kegs of palm wine and shout, 'Oh, the kegs are very full. Nnu Ego has not shamed us. We pray that in less than ten months our in-laws will come and thank us again for the birth of her baby.'

Agbadi and his life-long friend allowed themselves to be really drunk. 'There is nothing that makes a man prouder than to hear that his daughter is virtuous. I don't like visiting families where the wedding kegs of palm wine are half filled, telling everybody that the bride has allowed herself to be tampered with,' Idayi declared.

'When a woman is virtuous, it is easy for her to conceive. You shall soon see her children coming here to play,' Agbadi said with assurance.

Nnu Ego and her new husband Amatokwu were very happy; yet Nnu Ego was surprised that, as the months passed, she was failing everybody. There was no child.

'What am I going to do, Amatokwu?' she cried to her husband, after the disappointment of another month.

'Just make sacrifices to that slave woman, and pay your father a visit. He may have a suggestion to make. Other than that, pray for Olisa to help us all. My father is beginning to look at me in a

29

strange way, too.'

'I am sure the fault is on my side. You do everything right. How can I face my father and tell him that I have failed? I don't like going there these days because his wives always rush out to greet me hoping that I am already carrying a child. You can see the disappointment on their faces.'

'We can only hope.'

After a while, Nnu Ego could not voice her doubts and worries to her husband any more. It had become her problem and hers alone. She went from one *dibia* to another in secret, and was told the same thing – that the slave woman who was her *chi* would not give her a child because she had been dedicated to a river goddess before Agbadi took her away in slavery. When at home, Nnu Ego would take an egg, symbol of fertility, and kneel and pray to this woman to change her mind. 'Please pity me. I feel that my husband's people are already looking for a new wife for him. They cannot wait for me forever. He is the first son of the family and his people want an heir from him as soon as possible. Please help me.'

The story would repeat itself again the following month.

She was not surprised when Amatokwu told her casually one evening that she would have to move to a nearby hut kept for older wives, because his people had found him a new wife. 'My father is desperate. It is now known that your *chi* came from the people down by the river. Their women are said to be very strong. I am sorry, Nnu Ego, but I cannot fail my people.'

Amatokwu's new wife became pregnant the very first month. As the pregnancy became obvious, Nnu Ego shrank more and more into herself. In the privacy of her hut, she would look at herself all over. She would feel her body, young firm and like that of any other young woman. She knew that soft liquid feeling of motherhood was lacking. 'O my *chi*, why do you have to bring me so low? Why must I be so punished? I am sorry for what my father did and I am sure he is sorry too. But try to forgive us.' Many a

30

night she cried tears of frustration and hopelessness.

During the yam harvest Amatokwu, who only spoke to her when it was necessary, said crisply: 'You will go and work with me on the farm today. Your young mate may be having my child any time now. She will stay at home with my mother.'

At the farm Amatokwu kept ordering her about as he would any farm help. She stood in the middle of the farm and said abruptly, 'Amatokwu, remember when I first came to your house? Remember how you used to want me here with only the sky for our shelter? What happened to us, Amatokwu? Is it my fault that I did not have a child for you? Do you think I don't suffer too?'

'What do you want me to do?' Amatokwu asked. 'I am a busy man. I have no time to waste my precious male seed on a woman who is infertile. I have to raise children for my line. If you really want to know, you don't appeal to me any more. You are so dry and jumpy. When a man comes to a woman he wants to be cooled, not scratched by a nervy female who is all bones.'

'I was not like this when I came to you,' Nnu Ego said with a small voice. 'Oh, I wish I had the type of pride they say my mother had,' she cried in anguish.

'Yes, your father could afford to have an Ona as his jewel, when he knew that he had enough sons to continue his line. And your mother ... well, you are not like her. I will do my duty by you. I will come to your hut when my wife starts nursing her child. But now, if you can't produce sons, at least you can help harvest yams.'

Nnu Ego shed tears in her heart all the way home. At home they were greeted with the news that a son had been born to Amatokwu.

'Father, my position as senior woman of the house has been taken by a younger woman,' Nnu Ego would lament on her visits to Agbadi's courtyard, after she had filled his pipe for him as she used to.

'Don't worry, daughter. If you find life unbearable, you can

31

always come here to live. You are so thin and juiceless. Don't you eat enough?'

On her way back from one such visit she promised herself never again to load her father with her own problems. 'The poor man suffers more than I do. It is difficult for him to accept the fact that anything that comes from him can be imperfect. I will not return to his house as a failure, either, unless my husband orders me to leave. I will stay with Amatokwu and hope one day to have a child of my own.'

Nnu Ego's relationship with the other women in the Amatokwu compound was amicable. The younger wife did not keep her new son to herself but allowed Nnu Ego as the senior wife to share in looking after him. Many an evening neighbours would hear Nnu Ego calling the younger woman to come for her crying baby. 'This daughter of Agbadi,' the older women remarked, 'she is so fond of babies and yet they have been denied her.'

The younger wife often stayed in Amatokwu's hut till very late, and the longer she stayed there the more time Nnu Ego had with the baby. On one such evening the baby began to cry for its mother, and Nnu Ego wondered what she should do. 'If I go to Amatokwu's hut, they will say I am jealous because he prefers the young nursing mother to me. All the same it is wrong for him to do so, not giving the new wife a chance to wean her child before calling her into his hut. But I haven't even the courage to enforce our rules since my position as senior wife is now being eroded.'

She looked at the crying child again. Why not breastfeed him herself? The mother wouldn't mind, she wouldn't even know.

Nnu Ego locked her hut, lay beside the child and gave him her virgin breasts. She closed her eyes as contentment ran through her whole body. The baby's restlessness abated and he sucked hungrily, though there was no milk. For her part, she felt some of the fulfilment for which she yearned. Comforted, they both fell asleep.

The new wife was full of apology the next morning for not having come for her baby. 'Sorry, senior wife. I knocked at your door but you must have been sleeping, so I knew that our son must be all right. It's our husband, he just won't let me go.'

'That's quite all right. Here is your baby.'

This became almost the daily pattern and Nnu Ego did not discourage it. On one evening, she noticed that milk was dripping from her still firm breasts, which were responding to the child's regular stimulation. She ran to the effigy of her *chi* and cried once more: 'Why don't you let me have my own children? Look, I am full of milk. I can't be barren or juiceless as my father said. Why are you so wicked to me?'

Before the baby was scarcely a year old, it became clear that the young wife was expecting another child. Nnu Ego took up the boy's feeding in earnest. She would sing and coo to him and say, 'Why did you not come to me? I cried in the night and longed for a child like you – why did you not come to me?'

The notion of just taking the child, who had by now become very attached to her, occurred to Nnu Ego. Many a time on her way to the stream she longed to run away, miles and miles from anywhere. But the thought of her father's displeasure restrained her from the idea. Harming anyone never crossed her mind. All she wanted was a child to cuddle and to love. Allowing this child to suckle as much as it wanted relieved her agony, and when they were both satisfied, he would nestle against her and rest.

On the eve of the day Amatokwu's second wife was giving birth, the pain hit Nnu Ego with such force that she could stand it no longer. When she thought no one was looking, she took the boy and went into her own inner room, forgetting to lock her door. She began to appeal to the boy to either be her child or send her some of his friends from the other world. Not knowing she was being watched, she put the child to her breasts. The next thing she felt was a double blow from behind. She almost died of shock to see her husband there.

The child was snatched from her, and her father Agbadi was summoned. He took only one look at his daughter, then said:

'Amatokwu, I don't blame you for beating her so badly. We will not quarrel, for we are in-laws, but let me take her to my house so that she can rest for a while and I can look after her. Who knows, maybe after the calming effect of her family she will be cool enough inside to be fertile. At the moment, whatever the juice is that forms children in a woman has been dried out of my daughter by anxiety. Let her stay with me for a while.'

Nwokocha Agbadi took his daughter home. Most of his wives, now elderly, were sympathetic and nursed her mentally back to normal. They made her feel that even though she had not borne a child, her father's house was bursting with babies she could regard as her own. Her father renewed his expensive sacrifices to her *chi*, begging the slave woman to forgive him for taking her away from her original home. He told her through the rising smoke of the slaughtered animals that he had stopped dealing in slaves and had offered freedom to the ones in his household. He even joined a group of leaders who encouraged slaves to return to their places of origin, if they could remember from where they came. All those in his own compound who refused to go were adopted as his children; he had seen to it that proper adoption procedure was carried out, in that they were dipped in the local stream and had the chalk of acceptance sprinkled on them. It would be illegal for anyone in the future to refer to them as slaves; they were now Agbadi's children. He made all these concessions for the emotional health of his beloved daughter Nnu Ego.

Nnu Ego, though sorry for bringing such shame to her family, did not cherish the idea of going back to Umu Iso. She noticed, as did everyone, that she was putting on healthier flesh as a result of her new ability to sleep well. Gone was her jumpiness, gone was the dryness which her people never liked in a woman. She was softer and plumper, and relaxed and happy. Her good humour returned and when her peals of laughter rang out Agbadi would jump up from where he was usually lying, thinking that her mother, his Ona, had come back to him.

In Nnu Ego were combined some of Ona's characteristics and some of his. She was more polite, less abusive and aggressive than Ona and, unlike her, had a singleness of purpose, wanting one thing at a time, and wanting it badly. Whereas few men could have coped with, let alone controlled Ona, this was not the case with Nnu Ego.

It was clear, however, that she did not want to go back to Amatokwu's house. She was taking the trouble to look more feminine than usual, Agbadi noticed. That was a quality many Ibuza men appreciated; they wanted women who could claim to be helpless without them. Nnu Ego was not surprised to see men conferring in secret with her father. This time he wanted a man who would be patient with her, who would value his daughter enough to understand her. A man who would take the trouble to make her happy. Feeling this way, he refused all very handsome-looking men, for he knew that though they might be able to make love well, handsome men often felt it unnecessary to be loving. The art of loving, he knew, required deeper men. Men who did not have to spend every moment of their time working and worrying about food and the farm. Men who could spare the time to think. This quality was becoming rarer and rarer, Agbadi found, and sometimes he thought it was actually dying out with his own generation. He would rather give his daughter to an old chief with a sense of the tried, traditional values than to some modern young man who only wanted her because of her family name. Agbadi prayed that he might find the right man soon, for he was well aware of the restless ripeness in Nnu Ego. Nor had he forgotten the last promise he had made to Ona when she was dying and had said to him: 'Our daughter must be provided with a man of her own, if she wants it so, a man to father her children.' Yes, there were signs now that Nnu Ego longed for one.

Agbadi was no different from many men. He himself might take wives and then neglect them for years, apart from seeing that they each received their one yam a day; he could bring his mistress to sleep with him right in his courtyard while his wives pined and bit their nails for a word from him. But when it came to his own daughter, she must have a man who would cherish her.

As usual with such serious family matters, Agbadi conferred with his old friend Idayi about the problem of the right suitor.

'I wish Nnu Ego had been born in our time. When we were young, men valued the type of beauty she has,' he mused.

Idayi smiled knowingly. 'Nevertheless, the fact is, my friend, she was not born then; she was born in her own time. Things have changed a lot. This is the age of the white man. Nowadays every young man wants to cement his mud hut and cover it with corrugated-iron sheets instead of the palm leaves we are used to. You'll just have to accept a man of today, Agbadi.'

There was a pause as they both enjoyed the tobacco-flavoured smoke from their clay pipes.

Then Idayi asked: 'There must be one family you favour among all these people coming to you?'

'Yes, my friend. I would have liked her to marry into the Owulum family, but the man in question is not in Ibuza. He is in a white man's job in a place they call Lagos. They say any fool can be rich in such places. I don't trust men who can't make it here in Ibuza,' Agbadi said. He could not help feeling that only lazy men who could not face farm work went to the coast to work, leaving the land which their parents and great-great-grandparents had worked and cared for. Things like working on ships, the railway, road-building, were beyond his comprehension.

'And how would I know my daughter was being well treated

36

in such a far place?' he concluded.

'It is funny you should mention the Owulums, because the senior son came to see me just last Eke market. Though he didn't spell it out, I imagined he wanted Nnu Ego for himself, and as he already has two wives and many children I did not think it worth bothering to worry you with. But if it is for his brother who is away, I don't see why you shouldn't let Nnu Ego try him.'

From outside came the sounds of goats bleating, children playing, the voices of women singing to their babies; but inside the courtyard there was a long silence, during which Agbadi chewed the edge of his mouth furiously, trying to decide his daughter's future.

'You never know,' said Idayi, 'her *chi* may give her some peace if she leaves Ibuza. I don't think it would be a bad thing for the house of Amatokwu, either.'

'What of the Amatokwus?' Agbadi snapped. 'That marriage should never have taken place. I don't think much of people who illtreat a woman because she has not yet borne a child.'

'You can afford to think that way. The Amatokwus cannot. I would like our Nnu Ego to go away from here so they are not able to know much of her movements – you know, the usual prying and gossiping. They are bound to affect Nnu Ego somehow. Amatokwu's new wife is expecting another child, so I am sure he would welcome the return of Nnu Ego's bride price. He'll need it to pay for another woman, or else at the rate he is going he will kill his present wife.'

'He will get the bride price back. I think you'd better ask the Owulum family to come and see me,' Agbadi said finally.

Some days later, after the arrangements had been made, Agbadi introduced the decision he had arrived at to his daughter. He had a way of broaching important topics casually to his family so as not to alarm them.

'Nnu Ego, my pet child, you know I have been making

37

preliminary arrangements for you to go to another man?'

'Yes, Father, I have noticed the movements of people.'

'I would not agree to let you try again but for the promise I made your mother. You do want a man and family of your own?'

'Oh, very much, Father,' Nnu Ego replied, looking up from the tobacco she was grinding on two pieces of stone for his pipe. 'When one grows old, one needs children to look after one. If you have no children, and your parents have gone, who can you call your own?'

'That is true, my daughter. However, my only fear is that we do not know the man I have in mind. His family here are good, hardworking people, though. This man's name is Nnaife Owulum, and he has been in Lagos for five years. He has saved and sent the bride price, so he must be working hard there.'

'I wish I did not have to go so far away from you, Father; but if you wish it so, so it will be.'

'I think it is better that way. Amatokwu and his family will no longer be able to see you and compare notes.'

'If Olisa wills it, Father.'

'You will be leaving next Nkwo day, then. The first son of the Owulum family will take you to his brother in Lagos. I don't want it noised about, not even among my wives. I know it will be regarded as an odd move. Besides, you had enough publicity the last time you left your father's compound.'

'You do not want me to go and see the people of my new family here in Ibuza?'

'No, my daughter. I think the chief wife of the older Owulum brother – they call her Adankwo – knows, and from what I have heard of her she is a good senior wife and has been saying prayers for you. I don't want you to see them yet.'

A slightly pained look momentarily passed over Nnu Ego's face, but she cheered herself by saying lightly: 'Maybe the next time I come back, I shall come with a string of children.'

'That is our prayer, and I am sure it will be like that,' Agbadi said in all seriousness.

It was with pride that Nwokocha Agbadi returned the twenty bags of cowries to his former son-in-law and he even added a live goat as a token of insult. He had not waited to listen to Amatokwu's protestations that he had not sent Nnu Ego away. However, the goat was too tempting for Amatokwu to refuse, though by the time he sent people to thank his former in-laws, he learned that Nnu Ego had left for Lagos.

'Let her go,' he consoled himself, 'she is as barren as a desert.'

The journey from Ibuza to Lagos took Nnu Ego and the elder Owulum brother four days, travelling in overloaded mammy lorries that carried various kinds of foodstuffs as well as passengers; people, live hens, dried fish and all were packed into the same choking compartment. Like herself, the senior Owulum was a bad traveller and, worse still, did not seem to know where they were going. He knew only that they were on their way to Lagos, but whether it was to the west or east of Ibuza he could not tell. When they came to Benin and had to get off the lorry, poor brother-in-law thought they had arrived. A group of laughing traders teased him, 'Yes, this is Lagos – if you turn that corner you'll be there.' But he was soon put right, for they were in fact just transferring to another lorry. The incident was almost repeated at Oshogbo, though the brother-in-law could not be blamed for hoping their journey was over; they were by now extremely tired and travel-sore, and had been so long on the road that Nnu Ego herself imagined they must be near the end of the earth. They changed to the last lorry, and when they did eventually arrive at Iddo in Lagos, brother-in-law would not trust what anyone said. He had to be assured by the driver as well as the other passengers before he believed they had finally reached their destination.

He came out of the lorry with the slowness of an old man, the muscles of his arms beginning to knot in anticipation of being made fun of again. But this time he had been told the truth. He pulled Nnu Ego along, and they showed the address they wanted to a food-seller at the lorry station who directed them correctly to Yaba.

So it was that Nnu Ego arrived in Lagos and was led by her new brother-in-law to a queer-looking house. They had to wait on the veranda while a woman neighbour identifying herself as Cordelia, the cook's wife, went to tell the prospective husband Nnaife, who was attending to the washing of his white master and mistress, that his people were there and that it looked as if he had been brought a wife.

'A wife!' he said, pretending to be surprised at the mere idea. 'Are you sure?'

'She looks like a wife. She has things wrapped up, like somebody who is not just here for a visit but to stay.'

Nnaife was so pleased at the idea that he hurried with his ironing, almost burning himself with the coal pressing-iron. He whispered the news to the cook and the steward. Since they were all Ibos, though Nnaife was the only one from western Iboland, they knew that there was going to be a to-do that evening. They were excited to hear of the arrival of a new person; so far was it from Lagos to their homeland – it took several days to make the journey, and only very few enterprising people attempted it at the time – that anyone who spoke any dialect remotely connected with Ibo was regarded as a brother or sister. They also knew that palm wine would flow aplenty till the small hours of the morning. So they all hurried with their work, some singing, others whistling. It was indeed a piece of good news.

The white master, Dr Meers, worked at the Forensic Science Laboratory in Yaba. He and his wife both wondered what the excitement was about but could not bring themselves to ask.

Soon afterwards, Nnaife went up to the Madam and said, 'I go, madam.'

'Yes,' she replied in the cultured, distant voice which she invariably used when addressing the native servants. 'Yes, Nnaife, I shall not need you till the morning. Good night.'

'Good night, madam. Good night, sah,' Nnaife said to the master, who was pretending to be too engrossed in the paper he held in front of him to be aware of what was going on about him.

Dr Meers peered over the paper, smiled mischievously and

answered, 'Good night, baboon.'

Mrs Meers straightaway went into a torrent of words, too fast and too emotionally charged for Nnaife, who stood there like a statue, to understand. He gaped from husband to wife and back again, wondering why she should be so angry. The woman went on for a while, then suddenly realised that Nnaife was still standing by the door. She motioned with her arm for him to go away. He heard Dr Meers laugh and repeat the word 'baboon'.

Women were all the same, Nnaife thought as he made his way to his own part of the compound, determined to ask someone in the near future what the word 'baboon' meant. Not that he was the type of man who would have done anything had he known its meaning. He would simply shrug his shoulders and say, 'We work for them and they pay us. His calling me a baboon does not make me one.'

If the master was intelligent, as it was said all white men were, then why did he not show a little of it, and tell his wife to keep quiet? What kind of an intelligent man could not keep his wife quiet, instead of laughing stupidly over a newspaper? Nnaife did not realise that Dr Meers's laughter was inspired by that type of wickedness that reduces any man, white or black, intelligent or not, to a new low; lower than the basest of animals, for animals at least respected each other's feelings, each other's dignity.

By this time Nnu Ego and her escort were very tired. The cook's wife, the woman who had gone to inform Nnaife of their arrival, welcomed them with pounded yam and okazi soup. They were not used to this type of soup, but the novelty of it and the fact that they were so hungry and tired took its strangeness away. Nnu Ego was grateful for it, and was just falling asleep with a full stomach when in walked a man with a belly like a pregnant cow, wobbling first to this side and then to that. The belly, coupled with the fact that he was short, made him look like a barrel. His hair, unlike that of men at home in Ibuza, was not closely shaved; he left

42

a lot of it on his head, like that of a woman mourning for her husband. His skin was pale, the skin of someone who had for a long time worked in the shade and not in the open air. His cheeks were puffy and looked as if he had pieces of hot yam inside them, and they seemed to have pushed his mouth into a smaller size above his weak jaw. And his clothes – Nnu Ego had never seen men dressed like that: khaki shorts with holes and an old, loose, white singlet. If her husband-to-be was like this, she thought, she would go back to her father. Why, marrying such a jelly of a man would be like living with a middle-aged woman!

She saw out of the corner of her eye the two men embracing, clearly glad to see each other. She heard the senior Owulum referring to the other as Nnaife, and, looking up, she saw that this newcomer indeed had a tribal mark identical with that of his brother. It could not be! This could not be the man she was to live with. How could two brothers be so unalike? They had similar foreheads, and the same kind of gestures, but there the similarities ended, for otherwise the two men were as different as water and oil. She felt like bursting into tears, like begging the senior Owulum to please take her home; but she knew that even though her father was the best of fathers, there was such a thing as overstaying one's welcome. This man was welcoming them. He was taking in her wooden box and her other things which had been wrapped in a home-made net for her with so much care by her father's wives. At first Nnaife had greeted her only shyly with a single word, 'Nnua ' – Welcome. The senior Owulum glanced at her for a second, concerned at her obvious disappointment but his increasingly enthusiastic brother did not give him a chance to worry for long. He more or less steered him away from Nnu Ego who followed them inside and sat huddled in a chair, as if she was suffering from cold.

Nnaife could tell that Nnu Ego did not approve of him. But he could not help the way he was made, and what anyway was she going to do about it? In his five years in Lagos he had seen worse situations. He had seen a wife brought for an Ibuza man in Lagos running away at the sight of her future husband, so that friends had to help the poor bridegroom catch the runaway bride. At least Nnu Ego did not do that. Very few women approved of their husbands on the first day. It was a big joke to the men, women from home wanting to come to Lagos where they would not have to work too hard and expecting a handsome, strong figure of a husband into the bargain. Women were so stupid!

The cooks and stewards and many of the Ibuza people living in that area came to congratulate Nnaife, and to remark that they had sent him a 'Mammy Waater', as very beautiful women were called. Nnu Ego held herself tight, trying bravely to accept the greetings and not to imagine what her father would say had this man come in person to ask for his daughter. She fought back tears of frustration. She was used to tall, wiry farmers, with rough, blackened hands from farming, long, lean legs and very dark skin. This one was short, the flesh of his upper arm danced as he moved about jubilantly among his friends, and that protruding belly! Why did he not cover it? She despised him on that first night, especially when much later people began to take their exaggerated leave.

He demanded his marital right as if determined not to give her a chance to change her mind. She had thought she would be allowed to rest at least on the first night after her arrival before being pounced upon by this hungry man, her new husband. After such an experience, Nnu Ego knew why horrible-looking men raped women, because they are aware of their inadequacy. This one worked himself into an animal passion. She was sure he had never seen a woman before. She bore it, and relaxed as she had been told, pretending that the person lying on her was Amatokwu, her first sweetheart of a husband. This man's appetite was insatiable, and by morning she was so weary that she cried with relief and was falling asleep for the first time when she saw him leave the room to go to do his job as the white man's servant. She was so grateful to open

44

her eyes and see him dressing rapidly and talking in a low voice to his brother who was sleeping only a few yards away. She felt humiliated, but what was she to do? She knew she must have cried all night long and that the older Owulum had been there listening, congratulating his brother in his heart. She was used to her long wiry Amatokwu who would glide inside her when she was ready, not this short, fat, stocky man, whose body almost crushed hers. What was more, he did not smell healthy either, unlike men in Ibuza who had the healthy smell of burning wood and tobacco. This one smelt all soapy, as if he was over-washed.

When he had finished dressing he said, 'There is enough yam for all of us for some time. I shall tell the women next door to take you to the market and you can buy meat and make soup. I shall be back for the afternoon meal. I hope you slept well.'

'Oh, yes, she did,' replied Nnaife's brother, smugly, wanting her to realise he knew all that had happened in the night. She would have to put up with things. She would rather die in this town called Lagos than go back home and say, 'Father, I just do not like the man you have chosen for me.' Another thought ran through her mind: suppose this man made her pregnant, would that not be an untold joy to her people?

'O my *chi*,' she prayed as she rolled painfully to her other side on the raffia bed, 'O my dead mother, please make this dream come true, then I will respect this man, I will be his faithful wife and put up with his crude ways and ugly appearance. Oh, please help me, all you my ancestors. If I should become pregnant – hm ...' She nursed her belly, and felt her rather sore legs. 'If I should ever be pregnant.' She smiled wistfully at the whitewashed ceiling, and as she watched a house lizard scuttled from a crack to the slightly open windows. She stared until she fell into a light sleep.

In her exhaustion, she dreamed that her *chi* was handing her a baby boy, by the banks of the Atakpo stream in Ibuza. But the slave woman had mocking laughter on her lips. As she tried to

45

wade across the stream to take the baby from her, the stream seemed to swell, and the woman's laughter rang out in the dense forest. Nnu Ego stretched out her arms several times, and would almost have touched the baby, had not the stream suddenly become deeper and the woman risen to a higher level. 'Please,' Nnu Ego cried, 'please let me have him, please.'

At first her voice was pleading, but after she had been tantalised like this many times, she screamed at the woman, 'Have you not tortured me enough? I did not kill you! Oh, give me my child, give me my child.'

She was being shaken by someone. It was Nnaife's brother.

'New wife, what is all this shouting for? You are having a bad dream. Wake up, wake up, it is only a dream.'

She opened her eyes, startled. 'Do you think I shall be tempted to take other people's babies in this town? I dreamed that I was doing so ...'

'No, you will not. You are tired and over anxious, that's all. Don't go to that market today; we shall use the fish and the yams we brought.'

'But your brother's friends will come to eat the food cooked by a new wife – suppose they realise that it's only fishy soup and no meat?'

'I will tell them that I like only fishy soup.' He smiled sympathetically. 'You are very tired and my brother was very greedy. You must forgive him. You see, he did not believe his luck. He wanted to make sure you wouldn't run away. You know you are beautiful, and the daughter of a famous man. Learn to respect him. It may be difficult, but you will see your hopes fulfilled. I shall come and visit you again when you are really 'mad'.'

'Mad? Brother-in-law, did you say mad?'

He walked away to his side of the room with slow deliberation. She did not notice his shoulders twisting slightly in amusement.

46

This type of man, thought Nnu Ego as she watched him, did not belong to a soft place like this. He belonged to the clear sun, the bright moon, to his farm and his rest hut, where he could sense a nestling cobra, a scuttling scorpion, hear a howling hyena. Not here. Not in this place, this square room painted completely white like a place of sacrifice, this place where men's flesh hung loose on their bones, where men had bellies like pregnant women, where men covered their bodies all day long. Yes, he would go back to where his people had lived for five, six, seven generations without any change at all. How did his younger brother called Nnaife come to find this place in the first instance? And if she should go mad in a town like this, where would she find a medicine man?

'If you think I shall go mad, brother-in-law, I'd like to go back with you. But please drop me at Ogwashi, where my grandparents came from; I don't want to be a disgrace to my father any more.'

Nnaife's brother now laughed out loud throwing back his shaven head, and explained to her in a kind voice: 'New wife, I don't mean that kind of madness. I mean the kind that goes like this – ' he crossed his arms, couched his shoulders as one would when holding a small baby and rocked his arms – 'cootu, cootu! Ha, ha, ha! Cootu, cootu, cootu!'

Then Nnu Ego laughed too. She returned to the raffia mat bed and did not dream any more, understanding what he was saying: that women talk and behave like mad people with their infants who are too young to make sense of any such noises.

Before her brother-in-law left a few weeks later, he prayed that she would not be a failure. Nnu Ego thanked him, and through him she sent twenty thousand messages to her father, to say how happy she was, how handsome her husband was ... She kept repeating this over and over again, like a child frightened of being left alone. The senior Owulum did his best to assure her that her father would never forget her in his prayers. He told her that things were beginning to look all right already, though she did not at the time know what he meant.

She soon realised that her brother-in-law had guessed correctly. The changes that came about in her were so gradual that at first she did not attribute them to anything like pregnancy. As her suspicions intensified, she was too confused even to tell her husband. Perhaps she was only imagining things, having delusions. She found that she was feeling slightly ill and dizzy, but she would hide it, and when Nnaife had gone to work she would close the door, take out their small mirror an examine herself. Had she changed all that much? Her breasts – how big were they before? Was that tingling itch she felt in them not there before? Had her belly really become bigger? She could not tell for sure. The more positive she became, the more afraid she was.

Her husband Nnaife would get up at six in the morning by the clock the master and his wife had given him. He would then pull on his khaki shorts, eat the night's left-over food, and dash to Dr Meers's part of the compound to start doing their washing. He used two giant tin bathtubs, grey and big enough to take up to three people at the same time. He would sit on a kitchen stool by the first bath and wash all manner of articles, towels, women's nightdresses and what-have-you. Then, in mid-morning, he would move to the second bathtub and start the rinsing. Intermittently, he had to fetch water from the garden pump, carrying a tin bucket in each hand. After the day's washing had been hung up to dry, he would go into the pantry and fill the pressing-iron with coal. So regularly timed was his daily progression that one could tell the hour of the day by what he was doing. They gave him the grand title 'Nnaife, the washerman'. So good was he at his job that, for a small consideration, the master's friends often borrowed him. He only had half a day off in the week and that was on Sundays, when he worked till two o'clock in the afternoon. So he had little time to take notice of Nnu Ego, and she did not look or ask for any attention from him. She had come to accept him as one of the inevitabilities of fate.

She had at first rejected his way of earning a living and had asked him why he could not find a more respectable job.

Nnaife had scoffed and told her that in a town people never minded what they did to get money, as long as it was honest. Did she not think the work easier and much more predictable than farming? But every time she saw her husband hanging out the white woman's smalls, Nnu Ego would wince as someone in pain. The feeling would cut deeper when, with sickening heart, she heard Nnaife talking effusively about his treatment of dainty clothes and silk. The man was actually proud of his work, she realised.

On Sunday afternoons, when he was free, they would walk from Yaba to Ebute Metta and then to Lagos island, where the Ibo community held their own Christian services. Nnu Ego did not understand what Christianity was all about but, like any bride brought from home, she simply followed in her husband's footsteps. They would return on a bus which for her was a great treat, that coming home in style.

On the first Sunday of every month, Nnaife would take her to the Ibuza family meeting, also on Lagos island. Most of their people lived in the older part of the town near their places of work at the dockyard. The few in domestic service lived a little outside the town, in the quieter and newer parts, with their white masters.

She learned early in their married life to economise, since Nnaife earned little. After going to the market on Saturdays, she would buy soda soap, wash all their clothes and, with a towel tied round her waist, hang them out in the sun. She would then lock herself indoors and, however much the other wives in the compound called her, she would not emerge until their clothes were dry. Then she would fold and press them with her *odo* handle, and put them under their pillows to make them smoother, ready for the next day.

One Sunday she toyed with the idea of telling Nnaife that

she would like to stay at home, just for a change. After all, not only did church mean little to her, it was becoming monotonous attending week after week.

She left Nnaife's food on their one table, placed the hand-washing bowl with water in it conveniently near for him and, contrary to her nature and to custom, sat and watched him eat.

After a few mouthfuls Nnaife looked up. 'You stare at me as if you don't want me to eat the food you cooked. You know a wife is not allowed to do that.'

'That applies in Ibuza, not here,' Nnu Ego said.

'Well, whether we're in Ibuza or not, I am still your husband and still a man. You should not sit there staring at me.'

'A man, huh? Some man.'

'What did you say? Did I not pay your bride price? Am I not your owner? You know, the airs you put on are getting rather boring. I know you are the daughter of Agbadi. Pity he didn't marry you himself and keep you by his side forever. If you are going to be my wife, you must accept my work, my way of life. I will not have it any other way. You must understand that. So go out and gossip with Cordelia, and let me finish my food in peace.'

Nnu Ego stood up angrily and declared: 'If you had dared come to my father's compound to ask for me, my brothers would have thrown you out. My people only let me come to you here because they thought you were like your brother, not like this. If things had worked out the way they should have done, I wouldn't have left the house of Amatokwu to come and live with a man who washes women's underwear. A man indeed!'

Nnaife was hurt, but despite it he looked at Nnu Ego as if he had never seen her before. Why, the woman was changing! She had been beautiful when she came here, but surely not this beautiful – that high forehead carrying the tribal marks of a chief's daughter, the still thin body which somehow seemed to emphasise the flabbiness of his own, that looping neck ... why was she holding her

50

neck so stiffly? It must be the hairstyle she was wearing, too tightly plaited. And those breasts, didn't they look rather large? Nnaife tried to remember how they had looked when his wife first arrived, but could not; all he knew was that they were now bigger. Yes, something was happening to her. Anyway he was not going to allow Nnu Ego to keep comparing her life with him with her life with her former husband.

'Pity your ideal Amatokwu almost beat you to death because you did not bear him a son. Look at yourself – you look pregnant to me, and you were not like that when you came here. What else does a woman want? I've given you a home and, if all goes well, the child you and your father have been wanting, and you still sit there staring at me with hatred in your eyes. The day you mention Amatokwu's name in this house again I shall give you the greatest beating you have ever had. You spoilt, selfish woman! You who put Amatokwu's manhood in question so that he had to marry again quickly and have many children in quick succession. Now you come here, where I did not particularly press you to be pregnant in the first month, and you talk this foolishness.'

'You are not only ugly but you are a shatterer of dreams. I imagined that when I told my husband of my coming child I should tell it nicely ...'

'Yes, maybe by the moonlight, or on your goatskin by the fireside.'

'I will not listen to your nonsense,' Nnu Ego cried, feeling very sorry for herself. That it should all come to this.

'Well, if you are pregnant – and believe me, I hope to God you are – there is still one problem. What will they say in the church? We have not been married there. If I do not marry you in church they will remove our names from the church register and Madam here will not like it. I may even lose my job. So keep it quiet, will you? Ubani the cook had to marry his wife in the Catholic church to save his job.'

All the time he was saying this, a sick sensation was turning round and round inside Nnu Ego's head. That she had to keep such a joyous thing as this quiet because of a shrivelled old woman with ill-looking skin like the flesh of a pig! If Nnaife had said it was because of Dr Meers, Nnu Ego might have swallowed it; but not for that thing of a female whom she would not dream of offering to an enemy god. Oh, her dear mother, was this a man she was living with? How could a situation rob a man of his manhood without him knowing it?

She whirled round like a hurricane to face him and let go her tongue. 'You behave like a slave! Do you go to her and say. "Please, madam crawcraw-skin, can I sleep with my wife today?" Do you make sure the stinking underpants she wears are well washed and pressed before you come and touch me? Me, Nnu Ego, the daughter of Agbadi of Ibuza. Oh, shame on you! I will never marry you in church. If she sacks you because of that, I shall go home to my father. I want to live with a man, not a woman-made man?'

Nnaife laughed cynically and remarked: 'I wonder what good father would take his pregnant daughter back into his home, just because his son-in-law's job doesn't suit her? Your father is well known for his traditional principles. I'd like to see his face when you tell him you don't like the second husband he has chosen for you, especially since your *chi* has consented to the marriage by making you pregnant. If you were not pregnant, it might be more understandable. But not now that the gods have legalised our marriage, Nnu Ego the daughter of Agbadi. As I said earlier, you have to do what I say. Your father cannot help you now.'

'You are not even happy to see me pregnant – the greatest joy of my life!'

'Of course I am happy to know that I am a man, yes, that I can make a woman pregnant. But any man can do that. What do you want me to do? How many babies are born in this town every day? You're just looking for an excuse to pick a quarrel. Go and pick one with your friend Cordelia. Leave me alone. Remember, though, without me you could not be carrying that child.'

Amid the heat of her emotion, a calmer voice said to her, 'Yes, without what he has, you could never become a mother.'

She started to cry then. Bitter, angry and frustrated sobs that set her whole body ashake. Nnaife stood there, his hands hanging by his sides. He did not know what to think, how to react. He could only say, 'If I lose my job, who will feed you and the child? And the other children you are going to have for me?'

Her lot was not worse than those of her Ibo neighbours, the cook's wife and the wife of the steward. Even those girls from Ibuza who now lived on the island with their husbands told her many a time that she was lucky not to be married to a man working in the docks. The dock workers would go away for weeks and weeks, leaving their young wives to have babies on their own, with no help except that given by neighbours. They had told her the story of a girl called Ngboyele whose husband was working at a dock in Port Harcourt: she had her first baby in the night, and she never stopped bleeding until she died. She and her child had been buried ten days before her husband Okeibuno returned. It took the man a long time to recover from the shock.

When Nnu Ego later confided in Cordelia, the wife of Ubani, she had laughed at her moanings about her husband and had said to her, 'You want a husband who has time to ask you if you wish to eat rice, or drink corn pap with honey? Forget it. Men here are too busy being white men's servants to be men. We women mind the home. Not our husbands. Their manhood has been taken away from them. The shame of it is that they don't know it. All they see is the money, shining white man's money.'

'But,' Nnu Ego had protested, 'my father released his slaves because the white man says it is illegal. Yet these our husbands are like slaves, don't you think?'

'They are all slaves, including us. If their masters treat them

53

badly, they take it out on us. The only difference is that they are given some pay for their work, instead of having been bought. But the pay is just enough for us to rent an old room like this.'

'Will it never end?' Nnu Ego asked.

'I don't know, my friend. I don't know if it will. It has been going on for ages. I don't think it will ever end,' Cordelia finalised, shaking her head.

The monthly meetings on the island with her fellow Ibuza wives did Nnu Ego a great deal of good. The other women taught her how to start her own business so that she would not have only one outfit to wear. They let her borrow five shillings from the women's fund and advised her to buy tins of cigarettes and packets of matches. A tin of cigarettes cost two shillings, and she then sold the cigarettes singly for a penny each; as there were thirty-six in each tin she made a profit of a shilling on a tin. The same thing applied to boxes of matches. She would buy a carton of twelve boxes for one shilling and sixpence and then sell each box for two pence, making a profit of sixpence on each carton. She was so thrilled with this that, as the other more experienced women had foretold, she had no time to be lonely or worry about her husband's humiliating job, or bite her fingers about her coming child.

Yes, she was pregnant. She also now had some money of her own and she started paying back her loan to the women's fund. Some of the women sold lappas and Nnu Ego was able to buy one outfit for herself, paying two shillings every month. By the time she had been in Lagos for six months, she had bought herself another complete outfit with a headtie to match, and had paid off her five shillings' loan.

Like other husbands and wives in Lagos, Nnu Ego and Nnaife started growing slightly apart, not that they were that close at the start. Now each was in a different world. There was no time for petting or talking to each other about love. That type of family awareness which the illiterate farmer was able to show his wives, his household, his compound, had been lost in Lagos, for the job of the white man, for the joy of buying expensive lappas, and for the feel of shiny trinkets. Few men in Lagos would have time to sit and admire their wives' tattoos, let alone tell them tales of animals nestling in the forests, like the village husband who might lure a favourite wife into the farm to make love to her with only the sky as their shelter, or bathe in the same stream with her, scrubbing one another's backs.

In Lagos a wife would not have time. She had to work. She provided the food from her husband's meagre housekeeping money, but finding the money for clothes, for any kind of comforts, in some cases for the children's school fees, was on her shoulders.

Nnu Ego soon slipped into this pattern of living, so much so that on the night she came into labour she made sure she had her evening market first. With her husband still asleep she slipped out and went to the cook's wife next door. Between them they managed to stifle her labour cries, and Nnu Ego agonised for hours there in the back of their shared kitchen so as not to wake their sleeping husbands and the Madam in the main building. It was only after the baby was born that Nnaife would be woken from his masculine slumber.

Nnu Ego thanked the Owerri woman who helped deliver her little boy, and the latter said, 'We are like sisters on a pilgrimage. Why should we not help one another?' Then she had laughed, and continued: 'I see you have given your husband a son. It's not very common for people to have sons for the first baby. You are very lucky.'

Nnu Ego smiled weakly. 'I know what you mean. Girls are love babies. But, you see, only now with this son am I going to start loving this man. He has made me into a real woman – all I want to be, a woman and a mother. So why should I hate him now?'

'No reason,' replied her friend and helper. 'I must wake them up now to begin their labour pains by drinking palm wine.'

'Yes, you do that. At home in Ibuza, when a wife is in labour the husband becomes restless. But these our men here sleep through it all,' Nnu Ego observed.

Cordelia nodded. 'They stopped being men long ago. Now they are machines. But I love Ubani. I was married into his family when I was only five. His mother brought me up, and I had grown to like and respect him long before he sent for me. I guess that's why I keep having girls.'

'You will have a boy one day, I am sure of it. Call the men to enjoy their triumph.'

The men duly started celebrating with palm wine and cigarettes from Nnu Ego's stock, and the celebration went on till dawn.

In the morning, the white woman asked the men what the matter was with them and they told her the good news. The Madam promptly brought out a lot of old babies' clothes which she had brought with her from her last visit to England. Nnu Ego was grateful, for even though they were old they were clean, and so beautiful and soft were they that she forgot her pride and accepted them gladly. She forgot that in her culture only slaves accepted worn outfits for a newly-born baby: every child had the right to his own first hand-woven *npe* cloth to be wrapped in, after he had been washed from the banana leaves. But Nnu Ego was so tempted by this new softness that she told herself that it did not matter very much. After all, who knew her in Lagos? She was just a mother among so many thousands of others. It did not matter.

Nnu Ego spent all her meagre savings the day her baby was named. Nnaife bought her a new abada cloth, the first he had ever bought her with his own money, and they had a piece made up for the baby as well. Everyone ate and drank to their hearts' content, for people had brought small gifts to help the new parents in entertaining their guests.

When Nnu Ego felt stronger, she went back to her petty

trading. As soon as Nnaife left in the mornings to go to Dr Meers's compound, she would wash her baby, put him on her back and rush to catch the early workers on their way to work. They bought many matches and cigarettes from her. Then she would come home to feed her child and lay him down to sleep while she hurried through her housework. In the afternoon her husband came in for lunch, and later she would 'back' her baby again in time for the evening rush of workers.

There were beginning to be changes in their one room. They now had attractive mats on the floor, they had polished wooden chairs and new patterned curtains. And Nnu Ego no longer had to wait for her only outfit to dry before going out whenever she washed it; now she had two others. She accepted Nnaife as the father of her child, and the fact that this child was a son gave her a sense of fulfilment for the first time in her life. She was now sure, as she bathed her baby son and cooked for her husband, that her old age would be happy, that when she died there would be somebody left behind to refer to her as 'mother'.

Then one morning, the morning when this story started, when Nnu Ego came to put her baby on her back before going to her stall at the railway yard to sell her wares, she saw him, her baby Ngozi, lying there where she had laid him only a short while before, dead. Stone dead.

She did not scream; she did not call her husband. She simply left the room, walking gingerly backwards, until she whirled round like a fierce hurricane and ran.

5 A FAILED WOMAN

Nwakusor was returning home from working all night on the ship that docked along the marina in Lagos. He was an Ibo of medium height and slight build, and though it was difficult to determine his age from looking at him, with the knowledge that he had been a docker for ten years one could have guessed that he was between his mid-thirties and the age of forty. He was now noticeably tired; his eyes were bloodshot, his feet heavy. But he had one consolation: he was going home to catch up with some sleep before the evening shift. He did not wish to look beyond his quiet rest and cooling bath. With such sweet thoughts in his mind, he climbed on to his rickety bicycle, black with age, and faced the formidable task of setting it to work its way up the hill to Ebute Metta, where he lived with his sad-eyed wife.

He laboured painfully from the island to the mainland. The weather was damp and so dewy that all shapes seemed indistinct. Even the graceful palm trees and coconut palms that guarded the shores of Lagos like faithful sentries were vague this morning. Looking across the lagoon, Nwakusor could see mist rising from the bluey waters and melting into the moving clouds. To think that in a few hours this very place would be steaming from direct heat! By the time he got home, in any case, his wife Ato would be ready to go to her fish stall in Oyingbo market. It was not that he wished to avoid her, it was just that he was not in any mood to listen to her inconsequential prattling.

The Lagos bridge was restricted on both sides by intricate iron uprights, painted red and with spear-shaped points, and a narrow tarred road wound itself between these fence-like iron works. Near Tabalogun, it was necessary for Nwakusor to cycle from the wider road to the narrow part of the bridge joining the island to the mainland.

Still full of thoughts of his bed, and puffing away ominously at the same time, he was jolted into the present by angry shouts and screams.

'If you wish to die, why do you want me to be your killer, eh?'

Nwakusor looked up to see a kia-kia bus swerving dangerously to his left in order to avoid hitting him. As usual at that time in the morning, the ordinary buses were almost impossible to get, so all varieties of private vehicles cashed in on the high demand. They were dubbed with the name 'kia-kia bus', meaning literally 'quick quick bus', for the advantage of this kind of transport was that once loaded it would never stop until it reached the island, and several trips could be made each morning, while the bus owned by the white man's company would go from stop to stop, slogging slowly like a duck up and down the Lagos bridge. The quicker the owners of these mini-buses went, the more money they would collect, for clerks and messengers working on the island preferred to go by them, even though a full kia-kia bus meant six to ten passengers hanging on at each window, another dozen or so by the door, some even clinging to the roof. It was one of these buses that was now almost knocking Nwakusor down.

The shouting driver, like Nwakusor, was sweating in the morning mist. This mini-bus seemed to be exceptionally tightly packed and, looking at the driver, one could not be blamed for thinking that it was his own physical energy that was propelling the vehicle along and not the power produced by any kind of petrol. The man was gasping breathlessly. He had swerved so dramatically that some of the passengers hanging outside the bus had to jump down to save themselves from injury. There were screams and the squeaking of brakes. Nwakusor realised that he had had a narrow escape from death. Instinctively like the precariously hanging passengers, his feet sought solid ground. He stood there breathless and confused. He looked about him wildly while his mind began to register the extent of the danger he had been in a minute before.

'Well?' thundered the driver, looking offended and demanding an apology. He shook an angry fist in the air at the same time. 'If you don't know what to say, at least take your ancient bundle of old iron off the road. I still want to make use of my life. Next time you are looking for a killer, please, in the name of Allah, take yourself somewhere else. Please move out of my way.'

Nwakusor, who was too shocked to protest, did as he was told, picking up his ancient bike from where it had fallen, twisted but still workable, and his shrivelled and shaky self with it. 'I am sorry,' he said, ignoring the laughing passengers who by now had recovered from their shock and were cheering the driver's uncouth language. Nwakusor would have replied in like manner, but he was too shaken to want to play the game of abuse. Moreover, his Yoruba was not good enough; he would lose such a contest. So he decided to be apologetic, seeing that it was all his fault. And he was tired; the driver saw this, and stopped his verbal fight.

'I am sorry, driver, I have been working all night, and my mind is still asleep, believe me.'

The driver smiled widely at this. It was not every morning that drivers were treated politely, and in fact one of the tools of their trade was their ability to reduce anybody to tears with pointed tongue. Still, he would not deny his passengers the joy of seeing him win once more.

'The life is yours, man. But next time you're tired of it, stay out of the road and out of my way. You can strangle yourself in your room. It's less spectacular, but at least wouldn't put an innocent man in trouble.' With that, he careered round a sharp corner, roaring his bus and its loudmouthed passengers towards the island.

Nwakusor, judging from the way his legs still shook, knew it would be better to walk, even though he could have manipulated the bicycle back into action. Only the front wheel was a little bent and he could have straightened that out had he the inclination.

People who did not know what had happened passed him and wondered whether he was mad, to be simply rolling his cycle along the sidewalk, taking up so much space, when he could be riding it, arriving at his destination sooner and saving himself the effort of having to say 'sorry, sorry' to everyone he collided with. It was getting busy on the pavements siding Carter Bridge at this time of the morning. He knew that people tended to prejudge others without knowing the reasons for their unorthodox behaviour, but he did not have the time to go about justifying his actions. As long as he did not hurt anybody, and he arrived home safely, he did not much care what other people were thinking.

As the sun came out it infused a kind of energy into Nwakusor's exhausted body. He even began to accept that being alive on a day like this was a privilege, and he told himself to start enjoying it. He was like someone who had a valuable gift and who for a long time had not appreciated its value: it was only when the gift was about to be taken away from him that he realised what he had been taking for granted. He became appreciative. But it was a private appreciation. If he were to stop any of these hurrying people and tell them of it, they would think that he had suddenly taken leave of his senses. Indeed, he did not appear all that sane, in his dirty work clothes, wheeling an antiquated machine, and smiling benignly at vacancy.

He was debating with himself whether it was not about time he remounted, when he saw a crowd on the other side of the bridge. It was a group of early workers, market women and labourers on their way to the Ebute Ero market, all babbling in a kind of excitement. Their voices were tense and feverish, tinged with awe, like those of people watching a human sacrifice, he thought; not that he had ever seen such a sacrifice, but he had heard of people who had witnessed such an uncommon sight. They were all talking nervously, yet they stood away from a person whom Nwakusor could not make out. Was it a man or a woman?

He peered in between the traffic and deduced that the person looked more like a woman.

She was not old; in fact, judging from her straight back and agile body, she must be rather young. But she was behaving in a curious way, almost as if she was doing some sort of acrobatic dance. Nwakusor wanted to look at closer quarters. He blasted the unceasing traffic, but his eyes never left the scene. He was extra careful after the shock he had earlier, not wishing to be knocked down just because he was going to look at a woman who was either mad or doing some kind of juju dance for her god. He was going to take his time. One shouldn't be near death twice on the same morning.

His impatience was far from diminished as he saw from where he stood what the woman was actually trying to do. She was trying to jump into the lagoon! 'Good Lord,' Nwakusor thought, 'look at me jubilant for being given another opportunity to live longer, and see this foolish woman eager to end her own life when her Maker is not yet ready for her. How uneven the whole business of living is ... Oh, blast this traffic!' One would have thought that the unending business was being staged to tantalise him. Soon there was a little gap, and he ran, bicycle and all, across the road.

As he approached the other side, there was a roar from the crowd as the woman floored a man who was trying to wrestle with her and free her from the railings which she was climbing in order to facilitate her leap to death. To be floored by an opponent in wrestling meant defeat, but to be laid flat by a woman was more than a defeat, it was a humiliation. The crowd, while eager to be at their places of work, appreciated this free entertainment, though none of them wanted the woman to achieve her suicidal aim, not when they were there anyway. No one wanted to start the day with such an incident on their conscience. Another man tore himself from the crowd in an attempt to save her, but though the woman did not floor this one, she fought fiercely and expertly, so that both of them were panting, and the fear of everybody was that the man might give in and say, 'After all, it's her life.' However a thing like that is not permitted in Nigeria; you are simply not allowed to commit suicide in peace, because everyone is responsible for the other person. Foreigners may call us a nation of busybodies, but to us, an individual's life belongs to the community and not just to him or her. So a person has no right to take it while another member of the community looks on. He must interfere, he must stop it happening.

It was while watching the fight and the way she was warding off her opponent that Nwakusor realised that this woman whose face was still hidden from him was not a Yoruba woman. She was from his village, where women were taught to wrestle like men, to learn the art of self-defence. She turned her face in the struggle and Nwakusor saw Nnu Ego, unbelievable though it was. It took him less than a second to pinch himself and rub his hands over his face to convince himself that he was not dreaming. As if he needed a double reassurance, he shouted hoarsely:

'Nnu Ego! Nnu Ego, the child of Agbadi's love, Nnu Ego! What are you doing? What are you trying to do?'

She stopped abruptly in her fight. She looked up at the bystanders, her eyes roaming over their heads and not on their faces. She was shocked. Someone in this crowd knew who she was! She had bargained on the fact that Lagos was such a big place, with people of so many different races and backgrounds that it was very unlikely that anyone would know her. She had known she would probably be opposed by some pedestrians on the bridge, but she had calculated that she would arrive there before it got too busy. She was wrong. Though it was still misty and a little dampness lingered from the night before, yet the morning had a dazzling brightness from the young sun which drew people from their sleeping places and on to the open road.

Nnu Ego's hesitation gave Nwakusor the chance he needed.

63

He had not made a mistake. It was Nnaife's wife, all right. Acting instinctively, he threw his cherished antiquated machine to one side where it crashed with a pathetic jangle of old pieces of rusty metal. Like an agile cat, pouncing on an unsuspecting mouse, he rolled himself almost into a round shape and leapt towards Nnu Ego. They both fell on the cemented ground. Nwakusor's grazed knee started to bleed immediately. Nnu Ego got up quickly, trying to tear herself away like a lunatic, but now there were more people willing to help Nwakusor. The first man who had tried unsuccessfully to restrain her undaunted came forward again and held her tightly by the wrist.

Nwakusor, breathing heavily, gasped in Ibo, 'What are you trying to do to your husband, your father, your people and your son who is only a few weeks old? You want to kill yourself, eh? Who is going to look after your baby for you? You are shaming your womanhood, shaming your motherhood.'

For the first time since Nnu Ego had seen her child there on the mat, tears of shock and frustration flowed down her cheeks. Who was going to give her the energy to tell the world that she had once been a mother, but had failed? How would people understand that she had wanted so desperately to be a woman like everybody else, but had now failed again? *Oh, God, I wish these people, though they mean well, had simply let me be.* Her heart was pounding in pain, and bitterness welled from the same heart into her mouth. She tried several times to talk, but her voice produced no sound. She could only shake her head negatively at Nwakusor's angry tirade, trying to tell him that he was wrong.

Another Ibo woman, carrying a large basket of yams on her way to the market, was not satisfied with Nwakusor's verbal chastisement. She stepped forward and slapped Nnu Ego on one side of her face, adding, 'You mean you have a baby at home yet you come here disgracing the man who paid for you to be brought into this town? I don't know what our people are becoming; as soon as

64

they step near the coast they think they own themselves and forget the tradition of our fathers.'

So angry was this woman that she had put all her energy into the slap and its sting went home, momentarily blinding Nnu Ego.

Then Nnu Ego cried, put so much force into the use of her voice that the sound broke through, and it sounded roughly like that of a man:

'But I am not a woman any more! I am not a mother any more. The child is there, dead on the mat. My *chi* has taken him away from me. I only want to go in there and meet her ...'

It was then that people understood the reason for her irrational behaviour. Even some of the men had tears of pity in their eyes. Pieces of advice and consolation poured from people she had never seen before and would never see again. Many took the time to tell her their own stories. Even the woman who had slapped her told her that out of six pregnancies she only had two children alive, yet she was still living. She reminded Nnu Ego that she was still very young, and said that once babies started coming, they came in great numbers.

'She is not mad after all,' the woman took it upon herself to inform the crowd in her imperfect Yoruba. 'She has only just lost the child that told the world that she is not barren.'

And they all agreed that a woman without a child for her husband was a failed woman. It was left to Nwakusor, who had saved a life, to lead Nnu Ego home safely to her husband Nnaife.

Cordelia, the cook's wife, was warming a bowl of corn porridge breakfast for her two young children. There was enough of it for her husband Ubani too who, though he did all manner of fries and bakes for the Meers, did not like English food; he said it made him feel queasy, somehow. So despite the sweet smell emanating from the main kitchen Ubani would sneak a few minutes to come to their room for some hot African pap. Cordelia was hurrying to satisfy her hungry children and make sure that Ubani's share was left at the ready.

She was not too preoccupied, however, to notice that she had not seen Nnu Ego all morning. They were the same age and they were neighbours, and although like all good neighbours they might occasionally be jealous of each other's possessions or pass gratuitous remarks about one another, yet their basic friendliness remained unchanged. The two families shared the same veranda, which was attached to their rooms and opened into Dr Meers's back yard; this small outer building where they lived was typical of the accommodation provided for African servants which their white masters always referred to as the 'boys' quarters'. Though they belonged to different parts of Iboland – Nnaife came from the west and Ubani and Cordelia from the east – the fact that they spoke the same language and had the same cultural background cemented the intimacy of the cook and the washerman. When the women quarrelled, their husbands would take sides, but eventually common sense would prevail and they decided that it was not worth excommunicating each other. There was far more to be gained by communication: 'If the tongue and the mouth quarrel, they invariably make it up because they have to stay in the same head.'

So although Nnu Ego and Cordelia might have their argu-ments, the men never allowed them to go too deep. In fact the truth of it was that while the women bickered and gossiped about each other, the men usually patched things up on pay days, declaring their loyalties and drowning any differences in palm wine. On the whole the two couples co-existed well; they went into each other's rooms without formal invitation, they joined naturally in one another's conversation, and in general lived together like members of one large family.

Cordelia saw as she made her many trips to and from the kitchen that her friend's door was ajar. Nnu Ego could not have gone to buy cigarettes so early, and anyway she never went without saying anything. Cordelia did not recall having heard Ngozi this morning, either. He was growing to be a very demanding baby and his morning cries were unmistakable. But Nnu Ego could not be far away, since she had left her door open. Cordelia made a mental note to look in later, when her own demanding babies' needs had been met. In her haste, thoughts about her friend were temporarily pushed to the back of her mind.

Soon the children were busy lapping their pap like kittens, and Cordelia made a last journey to the kitchen for Ubani's share. Since he was not in yet, she felt justified in leaving his bowl by Nnu Ego's door while she checked inside. She carefully placed the hot bowl on the floor and, without straightening her back, peeped into the room. 'Nnu Ego, where the goodness are you? And look, leaving your baby asleep on the mat ...'

Suddenly she felt a kind of chill. Something was not quite right here. Why was the child lying like that? Why did he look so stiff, and his legs so lifeless? She called her friend again, now in a low voice, purring like a cat, but Nnu Ego was not there. As she progressed softly into the room Cordelia sensed that all was far from well.

She felt herself pulled into the middle of the room and, still stooping as though in involuntary prayer, she peered into the face of the baby.

'You are dead,' she said in a whisper. 'Mary, Mother of God! You are dead, Ngozi, you are gone!' She crossed herself; she and Ubani were devout members of the Catholic church and lived by its laws. She walked back stealthily, as if she had killed the child herself, and, by the door, she let out a scream: 'Nnu Ego, where are you? Your beautiful baby is gone!' She shouted this twice, and then she covered her mouth, not wanting to over-react, as her children came up to her wanting to know what the trouble was. Her whole body shook like one convulsed, still she managed to shepherd her children away from Nnu Ego's room.

In her haste, she upset the pap she had left by the door. The heat of it burned her bare feet and she did not have time to nurse them. One of her children pointed out that she had upset their father's breakfast, but she ignored the child, and led them to another part of the compound to play.

Her first thought was to run to Nnaife and tell him, and then to her husband. But where was Nnu Ego? she wondered again as she made her way to the white man's quarters. Then she stopped short, for right there in front of her, just a few feet away from where she stood on the wet grass, was Nnaife, stooping in his work, his concentration so deep that the song he was whistling was completely tuneless. It would be like a sacrilege to disturb such complete and personal bliss. No, she would go and tell her own husband first; he would know how to break the sad news to Nnaife. But to still her pounding heart and answer him calmly when he greeted her, as she knew he would, was going to be a difficult task.

She breathed very deeply, her hands clutched in front of her as if in prayer, her eyes averted, and she blurted out, to prevent him speaking first: 'It looks as if it's going to be a clear morning!'

'Hello, good wife, did you sleep well? You miss your husband already?' He laughed. 'Eh, but he left you only about an hour ago.'

'I know, he has taken some of my housekeeping money.' Cordelia lied, forcing herself to make a sound that was meant to be laughter, but which sounded croaky even to her own ears.

Nnaife wondered to himself what the matter was. Cordelia did not sound her usual cheerful self. Aloud he said, 'Go on, don't keep him off his job for too long. You don't want our employers complaining, do you, good wife?'

Cordelia felt sorry for Nnaife. He was such an easy-going, generous, simple man. Why then should this happen to him? First, he had a wife who neither respected nor cared for him until after the birth of his son. Now this had happened.

Ubani saw her approaching and frowned. He had told her repeatedly not to come for him unnecessarily. He wiped his hands on his massive apron and came out and stood by the kitchen door. One look at her told him that something was very wrong. 'What is it?' he prompted, looking anxious himself.

He frowned deeply as his wife told him what had happened.

'Oh, Jesus Christ! This is terrible. Are you quite sure? I mean ... I'm sorry. You haven't told him yet?'

Cordelia shook her head negatively.

'Then go back and, as quietly as you can, close their door. And look round for your friend. She probably has not seen the dead child. You say you haven't seen her all morning? Maybe she has seen him. Poor woman. I hope she is not doing something stupid. I don't like it. I don't like it at all.'

'You mean she may try to harm herself?'

'That may be being over-dramatic. Just go. Keep calm, and surreptitiously look about for her without raising any alarm until I have told Nnaife. God, this is really awful.'

'Oh, poor woman,' she said, hugging herself. Her mind went back to the picture of Nnu Ego having this baby only a month ago: how she had agonised in the kitchen, how painful it had been, being a first child, and how pride had not let her call Nnaife ... 'Please, Mary the Mother of God, why did you let this happen to my friend?'

'Go home, Cordelia,' Ubani's voice reached her. 'Remember, God giveth and God taketh away. We are His, and He treats us the way He feels. You never know, maybe behind all this there is something smiling for your friend.'

Cordelia nodded wordlessly, hot tears running down her cheeks. She walked back to their quarters and was made the more aware of her friend's loss by her two-year-old calling, 'Mother, Mother, I want another bowl of pap.'

Ubani, a thickly built man with a large head, looked out of the window of his kitchen, to see his friend working away and whistling as he rubbed at an over-washed sheet. So engrossed was he in his work that Ubani felt it a sin to disturb him, just as his wife Cordelia had felt earlier. And what a bad disturbance too! But he must be bold, and whatever happened it must be kept a secret; none of them wanted to be involved with the law. The local municipal would want to know how the child died. It was actually illegal then for anyone to die at home: this law had been passed to discourage people taking their sick children to the native medicine men. So when something like this happened, people tended to keep it very quiet. Nnaife must be told, they must look for Nnu Ego, and she must be forced to realise that in Lagos one was not allowed to show grief openly in such circumstances. They would all be in trouble.

Ubani hurried his washing up, and left the drying to his young nephew Dilibe, who had been staying with them in Lagos two months. He too was now employed by their master Dr Meers, and the little he earned in the glorified post of 'small-boy' – everybody's servant – helped towards his expenses. His uncle was working hard at seeing the right people who could fix Dilibe up in a proper position with a pension, either at the railways or the docks. This young man could read and write, and with a good 'dash' – a kind of approved bribe – given to the right people such a young man would go a long way. But meanwhile, he had to work to save for the dash. Ubani knew that the fatter the dash, the quicker his nephew would make headway, and he was determined to help him. Once Dilibe was well placed, part of his money would flow if not to Ubani then to his children.

'Make sure the plates and things are dry and shiny before you put them away into their right drawers.'

'Yessir!' replied the young man eagerly, pleased and rather surprised at being left in charge of such an important establishment as the Big Kitchen. The cooking-place in the boys' quarters where they made their native African food was referred to as the little kitchen. But this was the one from which the Master's food was prepared, and it had to be well kept and cleaned. Dilibe realised the depth of his responsibility and was grateful for being entrusted the job. He did not ask why it was important for his uncle to leave his kitchen so early in the morning. Like most youths he could only think of himself. He was going to use this opportunity to show his uncle that not only was he good enough to take care of the Big Kitchen, he could do even better, if given the chance; had he not youthfulness on his side as a plus?

Ubani guessed what he was thinking from his keenness and smiled sadly. He might have laughed but for the unsavoury task ahead of him. All young people were the same: they never imagined they would get old. Why, not so long ago he had thought that way himself. He had dreamed that he would make so much money from the white men by the time he was thirty he would be able to go back to his home town in Emekuku Owerri, where he would live as his grandparents had lived on the farm. In his dream there was no place like this one he found himself in, here where babies badly wanted by their parents died before they had lived at all. Yes, life could at times be so brutal that the only things that made it livable were dreams.

He stood for a while watching Nnaife's concentration. It was not much to ask, really, the chance to work and earn enough to provide for a family and to be happy doing it, like this man. Still, it could not be helped; he had to be told. Nnaife was not unaware of Ubani standing there and saying nothing. So he decided to say it for him.

'It's going to be a beautiful morning. You know what they say, beautiful mornings seldom make bad days.' Nnaife spoke without raising his face to his friend.

He guessed that something was wrong somewhere, but it never occurred to him that it could be in his own family. First, he had seen Cordelia go up to her husband, now Ubani was here standing like a statue unable to utter a word. Well, he was going to continue talking banalities until Ubani was ready to tell him what the matter was. He was not going to hurry him; protective men like Ubani could feel very touchy about their families.

Then suddenly his friend spoke in a rough voice, tremulous and very unlike his.

'Can you possibly have a break?' He was looking away, too, avoiding Nnaife.

Nnaife stopped the movement of his hands, hands that had grown agile in years of squeezing and unsqueezing clothes in soap-suds. He looked at Ubani, and saw that he was trying to hide something; in fact, it was the first time he had ever seen this Ibo man from the eastern interior looking perplexedly into nothingness. Nnaife tried to catch his eyes but they were as elusive as those of a new wife on the first morning in her husband's house. He stood up from his washing. What could be so serious in life as to warrant this lost look? To soften the sharpness of the situation he said, 'I can't come with you right now. I have to hang out these wet sheets otherwise they will not catch the early sun. And Madam knows when they have not, because the sun bleaches them all white.'

'Oh, damn the Madam! Sorry, friend, but man cannot live by bread alone.'

Nnaife did not miss the urgency in his tone. For the first time, his mind went to his own family, but he soon dismissed the worrying thought: had he not seen them this morning before starting work?

By way of reply he jokingly remarked, 'Preaching and living the gospel on a Friday? Or have you become Moslem?'

Ubani did not answer. He walked towards the boys' quarters, with Nnaife following him, still uncertain of what to expect and beginning to tremble with impatience and suspense:

'What is it? Another quarrel between our wives?'

Ubani shook his head.

The sun was already coming out, drying the damp grass. Birds chirped loudly under the roof of the veranda, circled their nests which hung rather precariously on the branches of the mango trees in the compound. Nnaife noticed that the nuts of the palm trees bordering their compound were ripe: he must cut the bunches down soon, for the birds were already hovering around them. Ubani's children were sitting at the edge of the raised cemented part of the veranda, digging the balding part of the grass and singing tunelessly to themselves. On a morning like this, when everything looked so natural and normal, Nnaife could not believe anything could be so wrong that he would not be able to bear it. His friend must be over-dramatising the issue.

But where was Nnu Ego? He could see no sign of her. He saw Cordelia standing between the wooden poles that held the veranda roof up, looking at them rather speculatively.

'I wonder where my wife is at the moment – away to sell at the market, perhaps?' It was more a remark to elicit reassurance than a question.

Ubani said nothing, just went on briskly towards the house, his head bowed.

'You won't mind coming into our room.' Ubani then said. 'I don't think your wife is at home. She does not expect you at

73

this time of the morning.'

'No, I'm not in the habit of coming home at odd times. I wish you would be kind enough to tell me what all this hide-and-seek is about.'

Ubani's room was badly lit, and on such a bright, clear morning the dimness struck one rather forcibly. To worsen the situation, Cordelia had decided to place their bed by the only window and as the bed was curtained off, a great deal of daylight was also cut off with it. She was sitting huddled behind the curtain, hugging her bended knees as if in acute pain.

'You haven't been beating her so early in the morning, the mother of your children?' Nnaife asked.

He was the more disturbed when Cordelia, unable to hold herself any longer, started to whimper, trying hard at the same time to control her feelings.

Ubani shook his head sadly. Then he told Nnaife, told him that the son he was so proud of was there lying on their mat, stone dead. Ubani said many things by way of comfort. He advised his friend to trust in God, he quoted instances where worse things had happened, and finally begged his friend to wake up, to make a move.

Nnaife sat there glued to the straight-backed chair, looking in front of him and yet seeing nothing in particular. It was incredible, unbelievable, what Ubani was saying. It had little to do with him, or had it?

Ubani said to his wife. 'Bring me a half glass of that *ogogoro* for him.'

Cordelia moved, and then Nnaife felt a small glass of native gin being pushed into his dead-like hands. He was forced to drink the hot stuff in one quick gulp. His hands started to shake, and Ubani took the glass from him.

'Look, Nnaife my friend, if you behave like this, what of your wife?'

A kind of life seemed to be forced into him with that statement.

'Yes, where is my wife, and where is Ngozi?' he asked eventually, waking up from his dream and wanting to know which part of it was actually real.

'Ngozi ... his body is lying there in your room. Let us go in. But his mother – we don't know where she is. I decided to break the sad news to you first, so we could then plan the best thing to do,' Ubani said apologetically.

Nnaife led the way into their room and saw the dead child. He knew then that he had not been dreaming. He moved and spoke mechanically.

'I wonder if Nnu Ego knew about the child,' he mumbled, staring hypnotically at the dead infant, as if by not taking his eyes of his son the stiff limbs would start to quiver with life as he had seen them do only a few hours before when he was being given his early feed. Nnaife answered his own question: 'I think she must have seen the child and in her sorrow has run away from me.'

'If that is the case we must search for her now. Few women are rational when hit by such a shock. She may over-react, and God knows what she will do,' said Ubani, looking grim.

'Oh, my God! Poor woman. She endures me only because of this child, you know. She thinks I'm ugly. She hates me, she has always hated me.'

'Nonsense, my friend,' Ubani tried to console him. 'How can a woman hate a husband chosen for her by her people? You are to give her children and food, she is to cook and bear the children and look after you and them. So what is there to hate? A woman may be ugly and grow old, but a man is never ugly and never old. He matures with age and is dignified.' His own wife Cordelia had begun to weep in sympathy with her bereaved friend.

'Please accept my condolences, Nnaife,' Ubani went on, 'and you must stop talking like a woman. Not everyone is lucky with their first child, and I am sorry. But now you have to make Nnu Ego pregnant again very soon,' he urged. 'You'll see, this will soon be something of the past.'

7 THE DUTY OF A FATHER

Nnu Ego pulled herself out of her negative thoughts. She must go and put her house in order, prepare the midday meal. Three months after Nwakusor had rescued her from the Carter Bridge, she found it so much easier to dream of all that might have been than of what might still happen. Many a time she regretted being saved: 'If only that wretched beggar-man had not stopped me, I would have been under the Lagos waters long before Nwakusor showed up.' She had to face the fact that not only had she failed as a mother, she had failed in trying to kill herself and had been unable even to do that successfully.

One of the advantages of being far away from home, she knew, was that her husband's people could not register dissatisfaction with her by just getting him a girl next door as a surprise bride, neither could they easily interfere to persuade him to make a decision about her, knowing as they did that Nnaife always dithered like an old man. Nnu Ego found herself comparing him with Amatokwu. That native Ibuza man. That African. She imagined Amatokwu being in this situation with her. He would have mourned aloud with her. He would have handed her to the female members of his father's compound and those old women would have comforted her with stories of the babies they themselves had lost. They would have got her ready to share his mat again a few days after it had happened and he would make her forget as soon as possible. Yes, Amatokwu measured up to the standard her culture had led her to expect of a man. How would he react if he were forced by circumstances to wash for a woman, a skinny shrivelled-up one with unhealthy skin? He would surely refuse. That was the sort of man to respect, Nnu Ego thought. Yet why was she thinking of him more often these days? Was it because grass is always greener yonder?

She wished she could get rid of the ache that hung so heavily in her chest. She wished she had someone to help her deaden it, she wished her father were here to talk it away, but ... Somebody was calling her. Was it her imagination or was it real? Was she going completely mad now?

'Nnu Ego!'

The voice could not be that of her husband who had only just left to go and begin his work, after his usual insensitive remark to her that 'Life must go on, you know.'

Well, whoever it was would soon find her, Nnu Ego said to herself without getting up from where she was sitting, staring at her blank whitewashed wall.

'Three months is a long time to mourn for a child who was only four weeks old,' Nnaife had said that morning.

'What do you know about babies?' she had asked him. 'If I had had him at home in Ibuza, I would never have come to this town.'

Ignoring the statement, Nnaife had said: 'Sometimes I think they deliberately brought me a mad woman. The things you say sometimes – does it make you happy to hurt other people? I did not kill your child. I gave you the child. He was mine too, remember?'

'Yes. Yours too. What do you know about him?'

Nnaife had decided to discontinue the argument. He hurried as he pulled on his khaki shorts and dashed out to work. So he would not now have come back again. Why, she had not even got up from where she was sitting then.

Now she could hear the voice clearly. It was a woman's voice and if her childhood friend Ato had not gone home to see her people, she would have said that the voice was Ato's. But it could not be. Curious, she got up and peeped out of her door, only to see Ato laughing. The peals of laughter reverberated in Nnu Ego's brain, as something out of place, out-of-the-ordinary. How dare

Ato look so happy, laugh with such naturalness, as though she did not know that her Ngozi had died three months before? Ato came closer still laughing and lifting her feet unnaturally high to clear the dewy grass.

'Oh, you people living with the white men. I never can make out which room or house belongs to which cook or which washerman. So I had to call you from the street. Oh, my *chi*, it's so nice to see you! I am really very happy to see you, Nnu Ego, the daughter of Agbadi. Please take that lost look from your face. If you wear a look like that for long, do you realise what people are going to say? They are going to say, "You know the beautiful daughter of Agbadi, the one his mistress had for him, the one who had a woman slave as her *chi*, the one who tried to steal her mate's child, the one who tried to kill herself and failed on purpose so as to get sympathy – well, she is now completely mad." You know our people, you would not be the only one to suffer; your father would never live it down. All your many sisters would find no husbands, because it would be said that madness runs in the blood. Do you want all that to befall your people?'

'Of course not,' Nnu Ego said, smiling a little.

'Then take that mad look from your face, and let it go for ever. Do you want me to leave?'

'Oh, Ato, I am glad you came. I thought I was hearing things. I did not know that you were back yet. That was why, when I heard your voice, I said to myself, "It cannot be. Ato is at Ibuza.' How is your good husband and my saviour, Nwakusor?"

'I have not seen him since I returned. He has gone to sea.'

Nnu Ego led her into their room, which was unswept; the curtains had gone grey from lack of timely washing and the whole atmosphere was disorderly. Ato, knowing how clean and meticulous her friend normally was, tactfully said nothing. But she was not going to let her wallow in a loss which had happened three long months previously. Agbadi had begged her only a few days before not to indulge Nnu Ego in this, but to let her see the danger she was running into; to explain to Nnu Ego that the dividing line between sanity and madness was a very thin one.

'My God, Nnu Ego, you frighten me, standing there immobile like a witch. Aren't you happy to see anybody? Is it true what they say, that you behave like some side-track bushes do, closing up when people come near? All because you lost a child? People say you have even stopped coming to the meetings. Well, that is very serious. God forbid that anything should happen to you here, but if it did, who would look after you if not your people, and yet you don't attend the meetings? Nnu Ego, the daughter of Agbadi, what has gone wrong with you?'

Nnu Ego smiled, feebly and apologetically. 'Ato, you must forgive me. I sometimes forget myself. I just stand for ages thinking and thinking. You know, it happens even in the market, and I worry that people may think I am mad. Even Nnaife calls me a mad woman sometimes.'

Ato laughed again, this time really startling Nnu Ego who had not heard such laughter for a very long time. 'He can talk, that fat fufu dough of a man. If he calls you mad, tell him to look in the mirror!'

Nnu Ego could not help laughing almost as loudly as her friend. 'No, he is a man, and you know men are never ugly.'

'I know,' Ato confirmed. She became serious again. 'Let him sleep with you. Please don't let your people down.' She started to laugh again. 'Even if you don't find him a good lover because of his round stomach, you may find him loving. Many men can make love and give babies easily but cannot love.'

'I know, loving and caring are more difficult for our men. But Nnaife is very loving; you see, he copies the white people he works for. He is not bad in the other way, too ... I just did not know him before – no, I don't mean that, I didn't dream I would end up marrying a man like him.'

'Neither did I dream of marrying a man who would stay away months at a time. You know something, they say men who work on the ships have mistresses wherever they land.'

'Oh!' Nnu Ego exclaimed, covering her mouth. 'Your husband would never do a thing like that. Never. The women overseas, they have a different colour from ours, pale like pigs – how can our men stand them? And what do these women see in our men?'

'Well, I don't care really. They say their men are not very strong.'

'That may be so. The one we have here smokes all the time. Always coughing, and looking ill. Still, they spoil their women. I don't think I like that either.' Nnu Ego stopped short, surprised at hearing herself talk and gossip like other women. It pleased her and she told her friend Ato so.

'I know, I can see that. It makes me feel as if I've been useful and not just saying wicked things about other people. Your father will be glad to know you are well again, and I shan't leave you until you laugh like this all the time.'

'That would be another kind of madness. How is my father? I still haven't got over the fact that you are back from home so soon. And you coming to see me almost straight away.'

'No, I didn't stay long. You know my mother was ill, but she is better now. The journey doesn't take long these days. Instead of going by boat via Port Harcourt, we went and returned by the mammy lorry and bus. It only took four days.'

'I came by the same route,' Nnu Ego added. 'The lorry went on and on and I thought we would never get there.'

'Oh, so you know what I'm talking about.' She brought out a parcel well wrapped in plantain leaves and gave it to Nnu Ego. 'I think it is a chunk of bush meat which your father roasted for you himself. He said that at least we all know you are not barren, and that you should let him know as soon as you become pregnant again so that you can come home and have sacrifices made for you, for the safety of your child. But how can you have a child when you don't sleep with your man?'

Nnu Ego was eagerly untying the wrapped meat. She stopped in between her movements and asked. 'How do you know that Nnaife and I sleep apart?'

'You forget that like you I was brought up in a large compound and have seen neglected wives all my life. You have the same look in your eyes, seeking something yet not knowing what.'

'Really?' Nnu Ego looked unconvinced; however she was not going to argue, for the size of the rump of the bush pig that came into view was far bigger than one could have judged from the covering of the plantain leaves. 'Oh, my poor father. He gave me almost a whole pig, enough to make us many, many pots of soup. What of my mothers, his wives, and my sisters and brothers? I do miss them all.'

'They are well. Your big mother said I should tell your husband to hurry up and do his work because her arms are itching for a baby to rock.'

They both laughed and Nnu Ego said, 'Oh, those people, is that all they think about?'

On his way to hang up some sheets, Nnaife passed quite near to their room, and he heard laughter. Now she must really have gone completely mad, he thought. He came nearer and heard voices – Nnu Ego actually talking and laughing, incredible! Who could she be laughing with at this time? He went in, for he could not believe his ears, but his eyes lit up with relief at what he saw.

'Ah ... I heard voices, so I came in. Do you want me out?'

Ato laughed, but Nnu Ego was taken aback. She looked almost as if she was sorry for being so happy. Then she began enthusing to Nnaife as if they had just been married: 'Look, look at what our father at home has sent us. A big chunk of bush meat which he dried by the fire himself.'

'Really!' There was a ring of nostalgia in Nnaife's voice when

82

he asked of the welfare of the people at home. At the end of the pleasantries, he said, 'You are not sending your friend and age-mate home to the island without feeding her, are you?'

'Oh, Nnaife, I am not going to do that. We have been talking about so many things that we forgot food. But we shall soon go and cook. Don't forget to come home for your mid-afternoon meal.'

'No, I will not forget. Ato, is your husband back?'

'No, we are expecting his ship in a few days.' She shrugged her shoulders. 'Though when they say a few days, it may be a few weeks.'

Nnu Ego detected a note of regret in Ato's voice, and said to herself, 'So I'm supposed to be lucky to have Nnaife here with me all the time.'

'Go back to your work, Nnaife, or do you want to listen to the wicked things we have been saying?'

'No. I'd rather not, otherwise I might hear nasty things not meant for men's ears.'

When months later, Nnu Ego fell into that tired sleep often characteristic of early pregnancy, she dreamed she saw a baby boy, about three months old, who had been left by a stream. She had wondered to herself why this child should be so abandoned. He was half covered with mud, half with mucus from his nose and mouth. She shuddered when she came closer to pick him up. He was very dark with the type of jet blackness of her father, but chubby and extremely dirty. She did not think twice, but picked the child up and decided to wash him clean by the stream and then wait for his mother. His mother did not come, and Nnu Ego dreamed she put him on her back, as the child was sleepy. Then in her daze she saw the woman slave, her *chi*, on the other side of the stream, saying. 'Yes, take the dirty, chubby babies. You can have as many of those as you want. Take them.' She had laughed and her laughter was ghostly as she disappeared into the grove of thick forest that bordered the stream.

Nnu Ego opened her eyes suddenly and exclaimed, 'Oh, my God, not again!'

'What is it?' Nnaife asked anxiously. Nnu Ego had cooked him a meal and while sitting watching him eat it she had fallen asleep in the chair. 'I say, what is the matter?' Nnaife asked again in between mouthfuls. 'If you are so sleepy, the bed is there; you don't have to sit here, nodding like a child. You will soon fall off that chair, the way you are going.'

Nnu Ego looked straight at her husband with a look so penetrating and direct that Nnaife could have sworn that what she said immediately afterwards was a statement from her dream: 'It's all right – ' she spoke in a low voice – 'I've just picked up another child from the side of a stream, in my dream.'

'Yes?' Nnaife asked incredulously. 'You mean you sat there on that chair and saw yourself picking up a child? Whose child? And by what stream?' He shook his head in perplexity, as Nnu Ego stared at him.

She found it difficult to explain it to him. This she knew was a bond between her and her *chi* and her coming child. Nnaife had little to do with it. He was just the father. She was going to carry a new man-child. The more she looked at Nnaife, the more she knew that he would never understand. He lacked imagination. Most hurtful of all was her guess that he laughed at her behind her back, maybe with his friend Ubani over a keg of palm wine.

She sat there ignoring him completely. She was now wide awake, and though she felt weak physically, her imagination was far from weak. In her mind's eye, she could see a handsome young man, black and shiny of skin like carved ebony, tall, straight and graceful like the trunk of a palm tree, with no fat anywhere but strong bones set inside his perfect body. The man had proud carriage, with his jaw jutting forward like the edge of a sharp rock.

She was not sure whether he was a farmer or a successful business-man in the country's biggest market, that of Otu in Onitsha. All she knew was that this perfect figure of a man she saw in her mind's eye was not a washerman, washing women's clothes. And he was not a ship-worker, neither was he a labourer, cutting grass somewhere. But he was her son. Her grown-up son. Her certainty of expecting a man-child injected new life into her flagging spirit. She was sure this son of hers would live next door to her, whatever profession he chose, as a good son should live near his parents and look after them. And she would see to the growth and welfare of his children and wives. The compound in Ibuza would be one bustling with animals – goats, hens and pigeons – and humans: wives, grandparents, relatives and friends. She would tell stories of her life in a crazy town called Lagos and warn them never to go to such a place in search of a demeaning kind of living.

She smiled into space, and moved her tips in a quiet prayer: 'Please God, let this child stay with me and fulfil all these my future hopes and joys.'

Nnaife was sitting there picking his teeth. He saw the smile and frowned. There was no point in his asking her about it; she would only sidetrack the question. So he stood up, walked out on to the veranda and called Ubani who had by then also finished his evening meal. Nnu Ego could hear them laughing and exchanging the evening's gossip.

She cleared the table, and as she did so debated with herself. 'The other baby, Ngozi, was very clean and was taken away from me. But this one was so dirty that he looked abandoned. Was that why my *chi* was laughing, laughing at me because I have been left with a dirty child? I don't mind. Dirty boy babies don't remain dirty when they have been washed; and after about twenty years of care and love, they become men. That is what my child is going to be. A man who will command respect. Yes, respect.'

She wrote to her father and told him what she had noticed,

that she was going to have another child. He sent messages back in reply to say that the oracle foretold that it would be a boy, who would go far in modern learning but who in so doing would attract a lot of jealousy. All the required sacrifices for him had been made to take away any evil eye people might cast on him so that instead he would be loved by many. Agbadi sent charms for Nnu Ego to wear as a kind of protection around her neck and special home-made soap for bathing as part of the ritual.

And as her father had predicted, all went well. Even the birth of the boy was painless. She was overjoyed.

Months afterwards, when Nnu Ego looked at the child she was holding, she saw that, whereas the first one had looked like her, this one had more of Nnaife in him, especially the slightly bloated face, but with this baby it was so tender and yet firm that one would have thought he was a girl, and he had the very fair colour of her own skin.

Her only regret was that for this baby she could not afford a naming ceremony like the one they had given Ngozi. She had not felt inclined to do any kind of trading after Ngozi's death, and throughout the term of her second pregnancy she had been so apprehensive that something would happen to make her miscarry that she took things easy, concentrating solely on having the child safely. She had reminded herself of the old saying that money and children don't go together: if you spent all your time making money and getting rich, the gods wouldn't give you any children; if you wanted children, you had to forget money, and be content to be poor. She did not remember how this saying had originated among her people; perhaps it was because a nursing mother in Ibuza could not go to the market to sell for long, before she had to rush home to feed her baby. And of course babies were always ill, which meant the mother would lose many market days. Nnu Ego realised that part of the pride of motherhood was to look a little unfashionable and be able to drawl with joy: 'I can't afford another outfit, because I am nursing him, so you see I can't go anywhere to sell anything.'

One usually received the answer. 'Never mind, he will grow soon and clothe you and farm for you, so that your old age will be sweet.'

Meanwhile with a few kegs of palm wine and some kolanuts, friends and a few neighbours gathered and named the new child. There was no heavy cooking and no special outfits were worn, but they all enjoyed themselves till morning.

Nnaife, fully saturated with drink, announced to his friends that although their first baby was thrown into 'the bush' – the term for a burying place – this one, he was sure, was going to live and be a man. Most of the Ibos present agreed with him that the name Oshiaju, meaning 'the bush has refused this', was appropriate.

Though Nnaife was not skilled at speaking Yoruba, the language commonly used in Lagos, he had made a lot of palm-wine friends among the Yoruba people, and on that evening one of these friends said, 'You Ibos think you are the only ones with such names. We have our own version, and I will give it to the boy.' Suiting his actions to his words, he marched up to the mother and child, gave them two shillings and said, 'Your name is "Igbo ko yi", which also means "the bush has refused this".'

So weeks later when Nnu Ego sang and rocked her new child Oshia on her knees, she was more confident. The voices of all the people who knew them had said she deserved this child. The voices of the gods had said so too, as her father had confirmed to her in his messages. She might not have any money to supplement her husband's income, but were they not in a white man's world where it was the duty of the father to provide for his family? In Ibuza, women made a contribution, but in urban Lagos, men had to be the sole providers; this new setting robbed the woman of her useful role. Nnu Ego told herself that the life she had indulged in

87

with the baby Ngozi had been very risky: she had been trying to be traditional in a modern urban setting. It was because she wanted to be a woman of Ibuza in a town like Lagos that she lost her child. This time she was going to play it according to the new rules.

She would sometimes ask herself how long she must do it. In Ibuza after the child was weaned, one could leave him with an elderly member of the family and go in search of trade. But in Lagos there were no elderly grandparents. Then she would scold herself: 'Nnu Ego, the daughter of Agbadi, don't be greedy. Manage with Nnaife's income and look after your child. That is your duty. Be satisfied with his earnings. Let him do his duty.'

It was a wet day in July, 1939. How heavy the rain was that day; it seemed as if all the taps in the sky had been turned on by the hand of whoever makes the weather. In no time the compound belonging to Dr Meers, the streets, the whole neighbourhood, became a mass of miniature rivulets. One could hardly believe that only a few hours before this same area had been completely dry land. Water poured from the sky, dimming the sun that was struggling to come out, until the earth could absorb no more, and people thought the earth itself was oozing water as well. Most of the trees in the compound, after hours of bowing and rising to the force of the howling wind, lost their branches. Meanwhile, it continued to rain.

Nnaife did not like such weather. There would be no place for him to dry his washing and he knew the Madam would be displeased. In the illogical way of women, she would thump into the ironing-room blaming him, talking in that strangling voice of hers, as if he, Nnaife, had sent the rain. He quickly squeezed out as much water as he could from the washing by hand, and filled the iron with coal. At least he was going to see to it that his employers had something dry to wear, even if there was no sun to bleach the clothes white. He settled his mind to this occupation, telling himself that he was going to spend the rest of the day in this way. The rain could go on pouring, until it became like the flood in the Bible, but right here he was going to keep his corner dry.

He could hear the shuffling feet of the Madam: she was still in her house shoes and had not changed into her walking shoes that clap-clipped all over the place, Nnaife noted mentally. He quickly stopped whistling. She did not come straight to him; she went to the kitchen first, and talked to her cook and her 'small boy' there. Nnaife heard her laughing in a low, patronising way, displaying the attitude which white people adopted towards their servants in the colonies. In any case, judging from the way Ubani was grunting, much like an angry pig, he either did not like what the Madam was telling him or he did not understand, though there was no reason why he should not understand, since the Madam was speaking pidgin English. Nnaife could tell that much from the rise and fall of her voice, but he was not near enough to hear what she was saying. She was shuffling in his direction – now he could hear it, yes, she was coming to him.

His heart began to beat fast. He decided to start whistling again so that the Madam would not guess that he was aware of her approach. When he saw her, he pulled himself up straighter, his sagging stomach nicely tucked into his khaki shorts, and ironed his washing with such a flourish one might have believed the whole world belonged to him.

Mrs Meers stood there by the door, not unaware of the show this man was putting on specially for her. She did not speak, but listened to the noisily cheerful and unconcerned way Nnaife whistled 'Abide with me', as if the tune was one of his native victory songs. Then she decided to put him out of his suspense, otherwise he would burn the whole house down, the way he was swishing the heavy coal-iron.

'Ehem! Naaaa-fy.'

The woman was never able to pronounce his name properly. At first it used to annoy him, but later he shrugged his shoulders; after all, she was not one of his people and it gave him a kind of secret delight to have proof that the white people, with all their airs, did not know everything. If anyone had pointed out to him that neither did he pronounce the Meers's name properly, that his version sounded like 'Miiaass' to his employers, he would have said. 'But I am only a black man, and I don't expect to know everything.' He was one of the Africans who were so used to being told they were stupid in those days that they started to believe

90

in their own imperfections.

'Naafi!' drawled Mrs Meers. She was a comparatively young woman, though the intense heat and sun of the tropics had given her an aged look. Her grey eyes were sunken, and Nnaife was always uneasy when she talked to him, for not only must he watch her lips to catch what she was saying, he had to watch those eyes right inside her head. It was like watching the eyes of a cat.

'Yes, Madam!' he replied, his head bowed in submission.

'We de go back to England!'

Nnaife looked up, rather sharply, stared boldly into her eyes. This was no laughing matter, not a matter to be shy about. What was she talking about? He knew the meaning of her words, yet they did not make sense to him. It was only a few months since she and her husband Dr Meers had returned from their annual leave. Were they going on leave again? Nnaife would not be able to afford it, because when the master went on leave, they, the servants, were only paid a month in advance, and if the master decided to stay away for three months as most of the colonials did, then they had to fend for themselves. Nnaife had not recovered from the financial loss incurred during the Meers's last leave. So why were they going again? The Madam was still talking, noting the shock on his face.

'No be this week, but na week after this one,' she added.

His heart was beating furiously again. He decided he was going to ask a question, and though he knew it would be regarded as impertinent of him, he would rather that than have to face Nnu Ego at home and tell her he did not know why the Meers were going or for how long they would stay in England.

'Another leave?' he gulped, fear clinging to his throat.

'No, no leave. England de fight the Germans.' She smiled again, as if that would explain everything.

Nnaife stopped his ironing, putting the still glowing coal-iron in its cradle and thinking. Well, if that was so, what had it got to do with them?

'But why Master?' he persisted. 'Why 'im de go England? 'Im be no fight-fight man. Why, Madam?'

There were many things he wanted to ask, but his knowledge of English was limited, and Mrs Meers knew and thanked her stars for that because she did not want to have to answer many questions. Now she was sure that they would be leaving the coast of West Africa, she wanted the servants to remember them with affection. Yet the social distance must be maintained, behind the decorum of a meaningless smile. As if as a double reassurance, she repeated with a touch of finality tinged with slight pity:

'No be dis week, but na week after next. Those them sheets, don't bother to iron them. Make you and your missus keep them.'

She did not shuffle back, she walked back briskly, like somebody who, having dreaded an unpleasant task, was grateful that she had finished it. She said nothing to Ubani on her way to their living quarters.

When she had disappeared, Ubani and Nnaife stared at each other. The unspoken question was, 'What are we going to do?'

The rain went on falling as if determined to shed openly the tears which the two men could not shed.

Dr Meers paid them off and before he went back to defend his country he told his bewildered servants that they could stay on in the 'boys' quarters' until a new master came. Nnaife was given a generous reference: it said he was a devoted servant, that he knew how to bleach sheets white, knew the correct amount of blue to add to a shirt and that he never overstarched his master's khaki shorts. Nnaife was assured that the piece of paper would get him a new job.

'But, Nnaife, that paper alone won't employ you, will it?' Nnu Ego asked. 'You must have a master first. All I see all over the place are soldiers of different races – some white with round-shaped faces, others with eyes sunk into their heads. Are they to be the new masters? Why are they all here in Lagos?'

'There is a war going on. I have told you before. The new master could be an army man. I only hope he turns up soon, as our money is running out.'

'I had thought Oshia would be going to school, starting after Christmas. Now we have little money to buy even food,' Nnu Ego despaired.

Nnaife started to smile as if in a dream. He was staring at the wall opposite, not at his wife. 'So you see, Nnu Ego the daughter of Agbadi, that washing the white woman's underclothes was what was able to keep us alive. Only now do you know its value, when even that is taken away from me.'

'Why bring that up? Is it because I mention Oshia's schooling? Every woman is dissatisfied on first arriving in this town, so why taunt me with it? You didn't make a very pretty picture when I came, you know.'

Nnaife went on laughing; with that mirthless type of laughter, Nnu Ego could never tell whether he was in sympathy with her or mocking her. She had stopped trying to understand the man. Sometimes he was clever enough, but often he adopted such a stupid attitude, especially when she brought up some important topic, that it seemed his only way of facing up to a difficult situation. She knew that if she did not do something about their present condition, Nnaife would be content to wait hopefully for a new master forever, even though there was absolutely no sign of one ever arriving.

'Nnaife, since we are not sure when the new person will be here, can I use part of the money we have left to buy some stocks of cigarettes and matches and start my little business again?' she asked. 'We can't lose, and it will give me something to do.'

'And what of Oshia? Do you want to lose him as you lost Ngozi, while you're looking for money? Who is going to take care of him when you go out to sell your stuff?'

'Listen, Nnaife, at times I don't know what to make of you ...'

'We've heard that too often, so don't say it again. I'm not an ideal husband, I am not like your father, I am not like your former husband. Oh, I know all about that. But, woman, you have to look after your child. That at least is a woman's job.'

'Ngozi was only four weeks old when he died in his sleep. Oshia is old enough to let me know his wants. I would prepare his morning meal and yours too before leaving the house. All you'd have to do is keep an eye on him.'

'What if a new master comes tomorrow, eh?'

'When the new master comes, we'll make a plan for that. He hasn't come yet, has he?'

'But Ubani and Cordelia are happy to wait for the new master. They and their three children are managing well,' Nnaife challenged.

'Cordelia is a good woman, but I am not Cordelia. I don't know how they manage. Anyway don't forget that Ubani's young relative Dilibe is working to help them out. And you never know, Ubani may be looking for another job.'

'I don't think so.'

'How do you know? People don't tell others everything about their lives, do they? I shall start tomorrow morning, Nnaife. I won't put you to any discomfort, you'll see.'

Weeks passed and no one came to take Dr Meers's place. Nnu Ego had another stall in the market and some afternoons she would take Oshia with her, though most mornings he remained with his father. Nnaife did not like this arrangement and grumbled about it, but there was nothing he could do. Not only did life in Lagos rob him of his manhood and of doing difficult work, now it had made him redundant and having to rely on his wife. He would find any excuse to pick a quarrel with Nnu Ego. One evening when

94

they were in the middle of an argument there was a knock on the door.

'Come in, it's open,' Nnu Ego said in a tired voice.

'Oh, it's you, Ubani,' said Nnaife.

'You sound as if you don't want me to come in, my friend.'

'Why not take a seat.'

Nnu Ego took her cooking things and left the men to their conversation, glad that Ubani had come at the right time to avert a big row.

In the kitchen which she shared with Cordelia, she noticed that her neighbour seemed to be clearing her things. Nnu Ego did not want to pry into what she was doing because there had been so much bickering between the two families lately. The fact that the men were unemployed did not improve matters. However, all of a sudden Cordelia coughed and announced:

'Oshia's mother, do you know we are moving away in two days?'

'What? What are you talking about? Moving where? Aren't you waiting for the new man?'

'No, my friend. I've wanted to tell you for days, but you were still cross about the last little tiff we had, and I didn't know how to bring up the subject.'

'Oh, forget that. We've always squabbled, so it's nothing new. Friends always do,' Nnu Ego said, laughing slowly. 'I bet the men pray we quarrel often, since they usually settle our differences with palm wine. My Nnaife looks for any opportunity to buy himself some.'

'And Ubani is always a willing guest. But we can't go on living this way. Ubani has got a job with the railways. He'll be working as a cook there.'

'You are very lucky, Cordelia. Do you know, Nnaife still believes that Dr Meers's praise holds good, even though the man has certainly forgotten all about us, and we don't know if anyone is ever coming to take his place.'

'I think Ubani made his decision quickly as he knows I am not gifted in trading like you. Nnaife knows he can always rely on you. I think that's it.'

'You think so? I think it's that he resents me going out at all. Oh, that man, I really don't know what I'm going to do about him.'

'You can't do anything. That's the way he is made. He's one of those people who don't worry about things till they are very imminent.'

'Hmm. I wish you luck. You'll be living in the railway compound, only a few miles from here?'

'Yes, it's not far. We shall see each other at the Zabo market.'

'And you'll be close enough for me to call on you and let you know when the almighty new master comes,' Nnu Ego said sarcastically.

They laughed as they each took the evening meal they had been cooking in to their families.

Nnaife's face was a picture of sadness. It was obvious that Ubani had been telling him of his new job, but Nnu Ego knew better than to bring up the subject.

After the Ubanis left, a few days later, Nnaife said: 'Do you know, Nnu Ego, that I could get a good job in the army?'

Nnu Ego hurriedly cleared away the bowls from which they had just finished a meatless meal, which was all she could afford with the little profit she made out of her trading.

'Is that so?' she asked. 'Have you forgotten that it is a curse in Ibuza for a respectable woman to sleep with a soldier? Have you forgotten the customs of our people completely, Nnaife? First you washed a woman's clothes, now you want to join people who kill, rape and disgrace women and children, all in the name of the white man's money. No, Nnaife, I don't want that kind of money. Why don't you start looking for proper work? You don't make any effort.'

'What do you imagine I sit here thinking about day and night? Please don't annoy me. I have taken enough insult from you.'

Nnu Ego knew it was time to drop the topic. Nnaife was not given to much thinking, and to have arrived at this conclusion about joining the army must have cost him a tremendous effort. It was a consolation to know that he thought about their position at all.

They were now the only family living in the compound, a compound in which the grass had grown till it almost swallowed up the servants' quarters. The gardeners and 'small-boys' had left one by one, to join the army, to become labourers or to return to their villages. And still there was no master. That night Nnaife and Nnu Ego clung to each other in sheer desperation, and she seemed to draw strength from this man whom she had never respected. After five years of living with him, she was used to him; listening in the dark to his snores, she coiled inside with shame, remembering some of the evil things she had once thought of Nnaife. Her new Christian religion taught her to bear her cross with fortitude. If hers was to support her family, she would do so, until her husband found a new job. Meanwhile they had to keep body and soul together somehow. The mere idea of having to move out of this room and pay rent somewhere else sent a cold shiver through her body.

She rolled over on their grass-mattressed bed and called softly to Nnaife, as the early light began to break.

'I shall be going to the island this morning. The ship arrived last night and I want to find out if I can get some cartons of cigarettes on the black market from the sailors.'

Nnaife was wide awake now, staring at the ceiling of their one-room home. This aspect of his wife's trade was illegal and could land her in trouble if she were caught. But what was he to do? Ask her to stay? What about food for them? He had paid the last of the money from Dr Meers to a clerk at the docks who was to see if he could get Nnaife a post as a washerman, or as anything, however menial, on a ship. However, so far the clerk had had no success whatsoever. Nnaife could not go back to Ibuza and admit failure. He was used to living in Lagos, even though it was difficult. There were many of their people there without jobs, and some had been like that for years, so he was not the only one. But this illicit buying of cartons of cigarettes from sailors who had stolen them from their ships ... It was impossible for him to make a moral judgement. He could see that there was no way out. It was either that or starvation.

'Just be very careful. I don't trust these sailors,' he whispered.

Their hushed tones were because Oshia loved going to the island with his mother and if he should guess that she was going to the wharf there was bound to be a scene. So while he still slept, Nnu Ego made ready to leave, saying, 'I shall be back before noon if all goes well.'

She went by foot to save money, though she intended to return by bus if she was successful. But at the quayside that morning she was not lucky. In fact she had almost given up hope of getting what she wanted when she saw the sailor, a gangling young man with a funny walk. She had seen his likes before on previous visits and knew he could guess what she wanted without their exchanging any words. He beckoned to her to follow him to the cabin below, where he showed her what he had to sell. There were many cartons but most of them were soaking wet. It would take her a long time to dry them. However, that was better than going home empty-handed, especially as the young sailor was asking only a tenth of the price.

Nnu Ego ran with her purchase, her heart thumping with excitement at her luck. By the time she reached the bus stop, she was giddy with joy. She reckoned that the money she would make would feed them for a whole month. She added and subtracted mentally, with the result that by the time she got home her head was swimming as if she would die.

'Welcome, welcome!' Oshia shouted as he saw her wading through the overgrown grass to their door.

She smiled weakly in return.

'Look, Mother, look what we found in the big house. It plays! Look!'

Nnu Ego looked dazedly at the old guitar that had obviously seen better days. Nnaife pretended he had not heard her return and went on making noises on the ancient thing.

'Where did you get that from, Nnaife?'

'You heard your son. There was nothing I could do to amuse him, so we went into the big house to see what we could find. And we found this. We've been busy cleaning it all day. Now I have something to amuse Oshia with.'

'And amuse yourself. I hope it won't stop you looking for a job, Nnaife the son of Owulum, because it is important for you to get one soon, now.'

'Why, isn't that a big bundle of cigarettes you are carrying? That will last us some time, will it not?'

'Yes, it will last us for some time, not forever. I am not even well enough to dry them out. I am ill with a child, Nnaife. So you have to think fast. You always need something to push you into action – well, here it is: another child is on the way.'

'What type of *chi* have you got, eh? When you were desperate for children she would not give you any; now that we cannot afford them, she gives them to you,' he exclaimed, his large head lolling to one side. In fact it seemed to have shrunk in size since he had cropped his hair closely to save the cost of haircuts.

'Well, what do you propose to do? Leave me and go back to your father?'

'You know very well I cannot do that. Do I have to make a song and dance of it? Get up and go look for a job. Go on! Get on with it! Do you want me to tell you what I really think?'

'If you don't stop that screaming I will hit you. Madam would not – '

'Ah, ha, Madam has gone to her country. They are never coming back. Get up!'

Nnaife lost his temper and banged the guitar he was holding against her head.

Nnu Ego began to scream abuse at him: 'You are a lazy, insensitive man! You have no shame. If you hit me again, I shall call the soldiers in the street. Haven't you any shame?'

Nnaife made to go for her again but held back when Oshia started to howl with fear. He turned to look at the frightened child and in that split second Nnu Ego lifted the head of the broom and gave Nnaife a blow on his shoulder. She ran past him, pulling the howling Oshia along.

'Go and get a job, you! Who is your father that you can come here and beat me, just because we are far away from anywhere?'

Nnaife did not chase her. He sagged down on a chair rubbing his shoulder. 'If I stay here with this mad woman, I will kill her,' he muttered to himself. Going behind their curtained bed, he took out his work clothes – the khaki shorts he had not worn for a long while, the khaki shirt that had been specially made to match but which he seldom wore as it was so hot. Thus equipped, he shouted in the direction where Nnu Ego had hidden with Oshia:

'I'm not coming back until I find a job; and if I don't find a job, I will join the army. So if you don't see me again, then I am dead. And, believe me, my *chi* will never give you or your god-forsaken father any peace. I swear!'

'Just go and look for a job,' Nnu Ego shouted back. 'That is all I ask, nothing more.'

Nnaife had a faint idea of where he was going; as far as he was concerned, his talk about joining the army was just a bluff, which would have paid off if it scared Nnu Ego a little. He smiled to think of how worried she would be.

He had been told there were many European residences at Ikoyi on the island of Lagos, and that was where he was headed to see if there was anything there for him to do. He would not even have minded being hired on a daily basis as long as he could bring something home, anyway until the clerk who had accepted his five-pound 'dash' fulfilled his promise to find him a post. Ubani was fortunate to have got a new job so soon after Dr Meers left. It was a small consolation to Nnaife at least to be leaving the house, just like any man who tells his wife, 'I am going to work.' He had never had to say that, because his work had been in the same compound as his home. Now he felt like other men, even though he was setting out at one o'clock in the afternoon when most men would have done the greater part of the day's work. Still he felt better, knowing that the food he left would feed his family in the evening: he was going to make sure that he came back late, too late for any kind of meal. He changed the penny he had in his pocket for four farthings and with one he bought a piece of kolanut which he chewed thoughtfully on the way, like a goat. Walking to Ikoyi was tiring; it was almost ten miles from the part of Yaba he had left.

His enquiries at many of the gates yielded him nothing. At first he asked the servants, most of them Ibos like himself, if there were any jobs going in their masters' compound. They did not know, and he had the feeling that even if they had known they would not have told him. But he was not going home without definite news for his wife and son. He was now very weary and hungry and he was sure it was showing in the way he walked. Fortunately he saw a ripe mango, whereas all the ones he had seen previously were green ones. How this one came to be ready to be eaten and not picked by someone else before he came on the scene, he did not know. But he was thankful for it; the juice quenched his thirst and its spongy flesh filled him somewhat. He was busy enjoying it just like a schoolboy would, when he saw a group of white men going into Onikan park to play golf. He followed them at a distance, still sucking the mango. One of the men took notice after a while, looked back, said something to the others, and they laughed. However, Nnaife was not to be deterred. He was going to talk to them and no amount of jeering was going to intimidate him.

They ignored him for a while, and when they got to Onikan, Nnaife settled on the cool grass. He needed to rest his tired legs. Unbidden, he started helping them to pick up the balls. Some boys from nearby St Gregory's school came to do the job, but one look at Nnaife's bloodshot eyes sent them scurrying like a group of frightened mice, and from a distance they taunted him and called him 'grandad the ball-picker'.

The man who had turned round before now came up to Nnaife and asked, 'Is there anything we can do for you? If not, just go and go quickly before I call the police.'

The others heard him and guffawed. One of them said, 'Fancy threatening someone with the Lagos police, when a pound given to the right person would set you free anyway.' They laughed again.

'No, no, sah! No police, sah! Na work me de find. I be washerman, sah! Look!' Nnaife showed the reference Dr Meers had given him to the man, who obviously felt sorry for him.

'I knew you were after something, the way you were following us,' he remarked in undertones – not that Nnaife would have been able to decipher his upper-class English public-school accent, though even if he had understood the man, he would not have said anything. Do beggars ever have any choice?

'Listen, old boy,' the man called to one of his friends.

Nnaife, catching the word 'boy', thought he was being addressed and replied, 'Yessir!'

This amused the man and he laughed, throwing his cap behind his head. 'No, not you. Not you at all,' he continued laughingly. His friend eventually turned round from one of the swings he was giving the ball to ask what the fuss was about.

'This man here, judging from this,' he shook the piece of paper in the air, 'is the best washerman in the country, and listen, old boy, he wants to be employed.'

'Really? Must we be his employer? Why us?' He stood up and gave Nnaife a searching look. 'I don't like the look of him.'

'He's hungry, that's all,' replied the first man, who still held Nnaife's reference.

'What! Hungry, with a stomach like that!'

'It's palm wine, I think, too much of it,' put in the third man, who was lankier than the rest of them. He was approaching his friends, his curiosity much aroused. 'He probably has a family, otherwise we could take him with us tomorrow to Fernando Po.'

'Hm,' drawled the first man. 'That would be a good idea. Let's ask him if he would like to go.'

'Yes, you do, I can't speak that stuff they call English, that 'canary' English.'

'Pidgin English, old boy, pidgin English.'

The second man talked to Nnaife, and it was decided that he should join them at the wharf the following day. He told them that although he did have a family, his wife and child would be delighted to see him employed again. Yes, he said, he was an Ibo. The Europeans were happy about this because it had long been an accepted thing that Ibo men made good domestic workers. Nnaife thanked them profusely, and something in the way he did so told the first man that he had no money and maybe would like to give his family some before leaving for Fernando Po.

He called the others and said, 'Look, this man has been retrieving our balls all evening. He deserves something, and, by Jove, I think he needs it.' They each searched their pockets and, having made sure they left enough money for drinks at the Island Club on their way home, gave Nnaife the huge sum of two dollars (as four shillings were then called).

Nnaife's heart was singing. He quickly disappeared and could even afford to go home by bus. On reaching the Loco Market, he bought a small bag of rice, a large tin of herrings and some fruit, costing him less than a shilling altogether.

At home, Nnu Ego was now so ill that all Oshia had had to eat was a little garri left over from their afternoon meal. She was relieved to know that Nnaife was back, but how was she going to cope if he went away on the morrow? Eventually they agreed that it was better than his staying here, eating up the little reserves they had. 'At least,' Nnaife added, 'I'll be taking my stomach away with me, and you won't have to worry about buying soap to wash my clothes.'

'You're taking away the help you can give as well,' Nnu Ego said in a tired voice.

To Nnaife, this was something new, almost an accolade. So he was of help to Nnu Ego? These last days he had felt he was more like a stone tied round her neck. He never knew that she needed him. Not that this had worried him unduly, for after all he was a man, and if a woman cared for him, very good; if not, there would always be another who would care. Yet it was so convenient, so tidy, if the woman who cared for a man happened to be either his mother or his wife. He felt sorry for Nnu Ego in a way, she had so far had a rotten deal; but judging from how close to Oshia she was sitting, Nnaife knew that if there was a choice between him and Oshia, the mother would jump for her son. Still, he was leaving them four shillings; by the time they had finished spending that, he hoped she would have recovered enough to sell the cigarettes she had bought for almost next to nothing.

They ate well that night, even though Nnu Ego did not feel like joining in much. Nnaife made a large soup that would last them for days, as long as she could get up and have it heated regularly. He made her promise to look after herself and to visit the other Ibuza people on the island and the few living in Yaba.

Tentatively, Nnu Ego asked when he would be coming back, but Nnaife did not know. All he knew was that he was being employed. He was happy that he did not have to negotiate for wages: he was confident he would be paid, because he liked the men, and they looked like people from good stock. There was something about them, especially the one who had first approached him, that made him trust them completely and prefer them to Dr Meers. These men looked you straight in the eye, and did not avoid your stare. That to Nnaife was proof that they would find it very dishonourable to lie, so he was sure he would be paid adequately, that they would not cheat him.

Nnu Ego worried all night, at the same time trying to hide her anxiety over him, and though she could hardly sleep most of the night, ironically, as soon as the first cocks in the compound started to announce the beginning of another day, she fell into a troubled sleep.

The sun cut itself through the little opening in their window, and across their bed. Its early heat fell on her face and she opened her eyes gradually, wondering where she was, and why she was not out selling her morning wares. She reminded herself that Nnaife had gone to work, but it took her a few minutes to realise that he had not just gone to wash clothes in the compound, that he had gone to Fernando Po. Where was this town with such a strange name? The name had a kind of music in it, but how strange it sounded. 'Please, Fernando Po, treat him well,' she prayed.

Nnu Ego was in her kitchen heating some beans one evening when Oshia dashed in, his eyes as round as saucers.

'Mother, Mother, there are "solders" in the compound. They have big lorries.'

'Soldiers? I knew it would happen one day, now that Nnaife is not here and Ubani lives far away. I wonder what they want?' She was going to peep through the kitchen window when a short European barged in through the open door. There were two big fierce-looking dogs in his wake barking furiously at Oshia, who ran and hid himself behind his mother. Nnu Ego begged the man in her halting pidgin English to please stop the dog from frightening her 'pikin'.

The man got the message and barked just like the dogs, 'Sit and behave yourselves!'

This surprised mother and child so much that for a while they were lost in admiration for this man who could make such fierce-looking dogs obey him.

Then he barked at Nnu Ego, 'Your husband – the child's father, hm?'

Nnu Ego did not understand him and she started to talk in her own language. The man looked out and called to another person in the compound. This one was black but also in army uniform and he acted as interpreter, speaking to Nnu Ego in a strange kind of Ibibio dialect. It was made clear to her that the senior members of the British army stationed in that part of Lagos needed houses like this one. She must pack her things and move. When her husband turned up they would tell him where she was if she would leave her address. All this was said in a very loud voice as if Nnu Ego and Oshia were completely deaf.

She shook with fear and anger while Oshia tugged at her lappa as if he would pull it off her. They soon marched away, their horrible dogs with them.

'They have gone now, Oshia, leave my lappa alone. We must move from here, and God help us.'

'It's our house, Mother. Father won't be able to find us when he comes back. Are we going to live like the Hausa beggars in the streets?'

'No, we will not live like Hausa beggars, we'll look for a place to stay, and if we can't find a place, then we'll live with our friends

106

until your father returns.'

Staying another night in her present place did not appeal to her at all. Not with men who barked like that. Only God knew what they could do to a woman. And those snarling dogs ... no, she would not sleep another night there.

Signs advertising 'Rooms to let, apply within' were so rampant at the time that even Nnu Ego who could neither read nor write could recognise them for what they were. She found a small room in Little Road where the rent was four shillings a month and had to be paid in advance.

The Yoruba landlord asked where her husband was because he did not cherish the idea of having in his house a single Ibo woman who might turn out to keep the company of bad Ibo men. Nnu Ego was then forced to tell the story of her misfortune, and though the man did not trust any Ibo person, he believed Nnu Ego for there had been similar cases where he worked in the Nigerian Railway Department. Many junior messengers had lost their jobs because the masters they were serving returned to Britain to join up.

Nnu Ego left Oshia with the other tenants in the new compound and dashed down to the railway yard to enlist the help of Cordelia. Ubani was still working so he could not come with them, but he advised:

'Nnu Ego, be very careful. You know your condition.'

'Thank you, I will. I'll be so happy when I have moved from that house. It's not the same. It has all changed, and those army men were the last straw.'

The two women dashed out into the evening to start shifting the few pieces of furniture that adorned the room where Nnu Ego and Nnaife had lived for over five years. After they had made three trips, Ubani was free to join them. He helped them lift the heavy things. The three of them moved the bed, chairs, cooking pots and mattress. Last of all they brought the squawking hens and their newly laid eggs. Nnu Ego boiled some of these and she and her friends ate them as they relaxed in front of the veranda of her new home, ruminating about their past life in Dr Meers's compound.

'It will be nice to live among people again,' Nnu Ego remarked to her friends.

'I know what you mean,' said Cordelia. 'Life can be pretty lonely in white men's compounds. No one talks to you and you must not make noise. It is not so bad for us now because the cooks and stewards in the railway compound live together.'

'I am surrounded by people. Almost like Ibuza.'

'You and your Ibuza,' Ubani laughed. 'You can never duplicate such a life here. But your new neighbours look very friendly. They are not Yorubas, I see.'

'The landlord is a Yoruba man, but all the tenants are from other parts of the country.'

'Then you will not be lonely. The Yorubas are nice, too, it's just that I don't think they think well of us Ibos.'

'Especially if you don't understand their language,' Cordelia said.

'I know ...'

As the days passed, it became clear that she was going to have her next baby without the help of Nnaife. His ship had been delayed. Ato, whose husband Nwakusor was in another ship, had told her during the last Ibuza meeting that rumour had it that the Japanese and the Germans were fighting the British, and that because of this Nnaife and many others working on ships could not come home.

'But, Ato, on whose side are we? Are we for the Germans or the Japanese or the other one, the British?'

'I think we are on the side of the British. They own Nigeria, you know.'

'And Ibuza too?' Nnu Ego asked not believing a word.

'I don't know about that,' Ato confessed.

She was at home nursing her now extended stomach inside her one-room apartment when Oshia burst in, crying with sheer anger and frustration. The boy felt humiliated. The tarpaulin shirt she had bought for him months previously was torn on both sides, revealing his large belly above rather thin legs. All Oshia seemed to have now, she thought as she watched him banging his head against the door, were head and this unhealthy-looking stomach. What was she to do? The child was being fed regularly, though if one had told her that garri in the morning, garri in the afternoon and garri in the evening all days of the week, was not proper nutrition for a growing child, she would have felt very hurt. She knew no other way to feed a child, and the sad thing was that Oshia was lucky to get even enough garri to fill his belly.

Nnu Ego knew that someone had annoyed her son. She could only watch him work out his emotion in this way. She could not go out to see who had so angered Oshia: apart from the fact that she was too tired, she had washed the only decent outfit she possessed and now had to sit indoors, on their only chair, to wait for it to dry. Her other outfit was too gaudy for everyday wear; she kept it in case the time came when she had to sell it to the Fulani wanderers who came knocking at people's doors asking for old things to buy.

'What is the matter?' she asked at last when she saw that Oshia's temper was not so violent. 'Come, son, and tell your mother. Tell ...'

He did not go to her, but he lifted his tear-stained eyes, rubbed some of the wetness away, unknowingly making a greater mess of the already dirty face. Perspiration ran down both sides of his head forming two more snake-like lines to add to those made by the tears. 'They asked me to go away,' he blurted out.

'Who asked you to go away?'

'Them!' He pointed towards the door. 'They wouldn't let me

eat of their sarah.'

'You mean the landlord's people? I thought their little boy Folorunsho was your friend?'

'He isn't my friend any more. They told me to go away.'

'Well, Oshia, you can't force people to invite you to their *sarah*.' But she sighed, knowing that *sarahs* were unofficial parties where food was free for all, especially children; they were usually given by women who wanted babies who were invariably told by the native doctors that the only way they would conceive was if they fed other children. Nnu Ego could see in her mind's eye what must have happened. The other children would have been in smart clothes with neat haircuts, looking very healthy and clean; her Oshia looked like a tramp compared with them: it would have cost her good money which she could not spare to wash his tarpaulin. She imagined his mouth watering at the sight of the heaps of boiling rice, akara, goat's meat; she imagined him sitting down in anticipation with the other children ...

'I was about to dip my hands into the rice when Folorunsho's mother came and pulled me up. She said I should get up. I hate the Yorubas. She said I wasn't invited.'

'Maybe there was a mistake,' Nnu Ego said, and she knew that Oshia was watching her closely. She brightened up for his sake. 'Don't worry, son. When we have money you'll go to school like the other children. All Ibuza people in this town send their boys to school. Why should you be the exception? Do you know that you're the most handsome of them all? You have the look of an Arab or a Fulani, and those horrid people can't take that away from you. When we get enough money and dress you up nicely, you'll see what I am saying. Remember, son, that you are a very handsome boy.'

Oshia stopped crying and listened attentively to his mother's voice. Her reassuring words made an impression on him that remained during the long wait for Nnaife to return from Fernando

Po; for if his mother said he was handsome, Oshia thought, then it must be true.

9 A MOTHER'S INVESTMENT

The light had been turned out in the one room that served as bedroom, playroom and sitting-room for Oshia and his mother. The night was hot, and he had slipped off the mat which his mother had carefully spread for him, on to the cool cement floor. He felt the coolness on his bare skin, and would have fallen asleep with this comfort but for the fact that an enterprising ant bit his bare thigh. The bite stung like fire and he screamed in pain. Normally such a scream would have woken his mother, who knew all about such bites. Oshia screamed again and rubbed the spot furiously, feeling its slight swelling. If it had been daylight, he would have seen the ant scurrying fast into a corner to hide. Knowing that the ant would be near, he beat about him in anger and agony. Yet his mother did not answer. He got up and went to the bed behind the curtain, still rubbing his burning thigh, to find her. But her bedclothes were thrown about in disorder as if there had been a fight, and she was nowhere to be seen.

He screamed with all the power in his lungs, 'Mother!' He yelled again and again. How dare she leave him by himself on such a night? It was not completely dark: he could see the light of the moon, cutting into their room like a knife of fire, but the knife was not very big. He felt really sorry for himself, as if nobody had ever in the history of mankind been so badly treated. He stopped his wailing and could hear voices, then the sounds of footsteps hurrying along the cemented corridor to their room. The person opened the door, carrying a hurricane lamp, and came in.

Oshia sighed with relief at seeing Iyawo, the wife of an Itsekiri man living next to them. Iyawo, a Yoruba word meaning 'new wife', was the name given to a woman without any children. She was a tall, thin person with close-cropped hair and tribal marks by the corners of her eyes. Iyawo Itsekiri and her husband, a handsome fierce-looking Urhobo man who worked somewhere in Apapa, had two rooms, one for sitting and eating, and another for sleeping. Oshia was always going into Iyawo's house to help her make cassava into a tapioca-like stuff called 'kpokpo garri'. Iyawo would in return give him a big bowl of it and whenever her husband came home Oshia and his mother were given tails of pigs and sometimes the feet, for where the husband of Iyawo Itsekiri worked these pigs were being killed every day. Sometimes Oshia dreamed of working in a place like that so that they would never buy any more meat, but just eat away.

Now Iyawo was smiling in a kind of sickly way. Why was she smiling like that when he was in such an agony?

'My mother isn't here – where is she?' he demanded, his anger almost choking him.

Instead of answering, Iyawo put the lamp on a table nearby and, still smiling foolishly, said in a voice like that of one saying prayers that his mother was asleep by the fire in the kitchen, because she was tired, and she was tired because he, Oshia, had just had a baby brother.

'A brother!' he said in disbelief. Where did people get brothers from? Was it because of this brother that his mother was not with him to rub the spot that the ant had bitten? Anyway, at least he would have somebody to play with tomorrow. But now he wanted his mother.

Iyawo told him that it would be a while before he could play with his brother, and that he should go to sleep, because his mother would be resting for a while yet. Iyawo would not even allow him to see her, insisting that he would do so in the morning. Tired of arguing, and seeing that she was determined to have her way, Oshia resentfully allowed her to rub coconut oil on the bite and, feeling very hard done by, went to sleep. He dreamed of how he and his brother were going to fight and overpower weaklings like Folorunsho, how they would make the biggest trap and catch all the crabs in the whole of Yaba, how they would wear smart clothes and go to the best school, and all the while his brother would do whatever he said because, according to Iyawo, he was much smaller than Oshia.

But Iyawo never told him that his new brother was that small! He could not even talk, he had not even a single tooth, and his colour was like that of a pig. Nnu Ego gave him all her attention, and kept telling Oshia to be a big boy, because now he was the big brother. He hated the 'big brother' part of the whole thing, and the fact that his mother and her friends were making such a fuss over this tiny brother of his. Oshia felt neglected and would throw tantrums about everything. If he screamed, they would tell him to stop being a child, whereas if the baby brother screamed as he was always doing, they would coo and fuss over him and his mother would put him to the breast. Sometimes Oshia would give an ear-piercing yell, to attract attention but also for the sheer joy of it, since it upset the adults so.

Their poverty was becoming very apparent and Oshia was constantly hungry. He was lucky if he had a good meal a day. His mother had not been able to go out to evening market since the birth of his brother, so she would make a display stand outside the house, with cans of cigarettes, boxes of matches and bottles of kerosene, and ask Oshia to sit beside them. If there were any customers, he would shout for an adult to sort out the intricacies of change and money.

After sitting by the avocado pear tree for a long time, watching people come and go, while his mother attended to the new brother, he felt so tired that he could not keep awake. In his daylight sleep, he wished he were out in the gutters, catching crabs. At least they made a good and filling meal. He smiled in his afternoon sleep, but his beautiful dream was cut short by a neighbour called Mama Abby who was fond of wearing red clothes.

'Wake up, Oshia, you have fever. Where is your mother?

114

Mama Oshia, come!' she called to Nnu Ego, addressing her in the customary manner for a woman with a male child. 'Your son is talking in his sleep in the afternoon. You'd better come.'

Oshia was a little surprised to see his mother strapping the baby brother behind her back and hurrying up. He saw her weeping as they took him into the coolness of their room. He heard her say desperately, 'I hope it's not *iba*.'

Iyawo Itsekiri stood by the door with one of her palms under her chin, watching Nnu Ego worriedly running about for her son. She guessed that the boy was suffering from something not too remotely connected with food, but who was she to raise her voice?

In any event, Nnu Ego had nothing to give Oshia but the kpokpo garri from the day before. The truth of the matter was that he had had enough of kpokpo garri. He had had it yesterday, and the day before that. He wanted some pepper soup, he told his mother. Taking the few pennies she had in the house, Nnu Ego rushed to Zabo market and bought a small piece of calf meat to make him some pepper soup. However, not having had this type of luxury for so long, Oshia's system refused it. He vomited over and over again, and when by the third day he still had no appetite it seemed inevitable to Nnu Ego that her son was going to die. People recommended one thing, and she would prepare it; they recommended another, and she would get that. She sold all her clothes at a fraction of their cost to the Fulani street-walkers, telling herself that if her sons should live and grow, they would be all the clothes she would ever need.

'Oshia, do you want to die and leave me?' she called softly to him.

The poor boy would shake his head.

'Then stop this sickness. I have nothing else to give you. Please stay and be my joy, be my father, and my brother, and my husband – no, I have a husband though I don't know whether he is alive or dead. Please don't die and go away too.'

115

Whenever his mother started to cry, Oshia, realising that she took his asking for something in particular as a sign that he was improving, did his best to put on a steady voice and say, 'Mother, please give me some water, I'm thirsty.'

Nnu Ego would fetch it gladly, but no sooner had he drunk it than it would come out again, in one direction or another. He could keep nothing down. Oshia was becoming a bag of bones encased in what looked like a piece of yellowing dry skin, and Nnu Ego herself was looking ill.

Iyawo Itsekiri cooked a delicious yam stew the following afternoon. Alone in the kitchen, she thought of this likeable Ibo woman with her two sons, one on the verge of dying. The mother herself was not far off from death, for the little flesh she had on her was being sucked away by the new baby at her breast. Iyawo made a lot of the stew, hoping that she would be able to tempt both Nnu Ego and Oshia, for she still suspected that malnutrition and not malaria was the main cause of the boy's illness. Why otherwise had his stomach become so huge and the hair on his head light brown instead of its normal black?

With a beaming smile, showing her perfect teeth to the full, Iyawo Itsekiri carried in the yam hotpot, into which she had added chunks of pork, and lashings of palm oil and fresh onions, so much so that the sick child could smell the vegetable aroma even before she entered the room. She placed the food on a tray made from the bamboo plant common in Lagos. She was nervous inside, not because mother and child might refuse but because she did not want them to feel she was feeding them or telling them in effect that lack of food was all that was ailing them. Iyawo guessed that after they paid the monthly rent to the landlord, they could have little or nothing left for food, but Nnu Ego never complained. If you made the mistake of pitying her, she would tell you what her two sons were going to be when they grew up; for anybody who had no 'two sons', or who only had daughters, or who had no children at all like Iyawo Itsekiri, it was better to keep quiet. Mellowed by the constant beatings of her husband, she had become apathetic and she was always cautious, and doubly sensitive.

'I shall go to my room and get some spoons,' she said, partly in truth but partly to give Nnu Ego time to think over whether she and her son were going to accept the food or not.

Iyawo Itsekiri's fears proved quite unfounded. Oshia did not wait to be invited. He crawled from the mat on which he was lying, and at his efforts to reach the bowl of porridge his mother wept – he was like a moving carcass. But he refused her help, and reached the wooden tray just as Iyawo brought in the spoons. All of them, with the exception of the baby who was peacefully sleeping on the bed, pounced on the stew. Nnu Ego swore that she had never tasted any so tasty.

'Even when we were well-off, working for the white man, we never bought yams like this. This is so good. Thank you, Iyawo. I hope God will hear your prayers and give you your own children.'

'Amen,' replied Iyawo. Then she burst out giggling as the seemingly cured Oshia rolled himself on to his mat and fell asleep.

'So it is hunger that was taking my son away from me!' Nnu Ego exclaimed. She looked at him reflectively for a long time.

Iyawo noticed that Nnu Ego was beginning to doze like her son. 'I will leave you to it now. My husband will be home at four today and I must go and cook for him.'

'Thank you, God's messenger. You are the greatest doctor I have ever seen. You diagnosed our illness in your head and, without bothering us, you prepared the medicine and applied it to us. And in less than an hour we are all well.'

'Well, God works through us all. Keep the rest of the porridge. Don't give him any more today. Heat it up tomorrow.'

Nnu Ego nodded. 'We don't want to have to start worrying about indigestion instead of dysentry, or whatever it was he was suffering from. Once more, thank you.'

When she woke to the demands of her baby, she felt Oshia and knew that he was going to live. She promised herself that when he got better, she would go back to Ibuza with her two children. She would never lack in her father's house. When Nnaife returned, these kind neighbours would tell him where to find her. The following day, it being clear that all she needed was food and a little kindness, everybody gave her what they could and the greatest help was that the landlord told her to disregard paying rent for that month. That would be a whole four shillings saved! She would be able to start her trading again, when Oshia was really well. Mama Abby said to Oshia, 'When you get better, I'll take you on a day trip to the island. So hurry up and get better.'

With the sharp edge of their poverty blunted, Oshia regained his strength fast and was soon unrecognisable as the sack of bones people had almost given up for dead less than two weeks before. On the day of his outing with Mama Abby, he was to put on his best outfit, made from a kind of khaki material which his mother had bought ten months previously when Dr Meers was leaving. Brushing the now too small suit, she recalled how Nnaife had declared her to be the most illogical woman ever: 'Look at us, just look at us – we have little money for food, very little hope of a new job,' he had said, 'and the small profit you get from your petty trading you use in buying expensive cloth to make a new suit for a four-year-old who knows nothing about life and contributes nothing towards his upkeep.'

She sighed as she shook the wrinkles out of that suit. There was no time to iron it now, for Oshia was urging her to hurry up or else Mama Abby might change her mind about taking him to the island. Nnu Ego smiled at his impatience. As he dressed Oshia talked incessantly, his mother agreeing with everything, until all of a sudden he stopped, looking with dissatisfaction at the sleeve of his jacket.

'It's too short, almost at my elbow,' he pouted.

His mother did not know what to make of this self-consciousness, this new self-awareness that was emerging.

'Well, haven't I been telling you that you're going to grow up to be really tall?' she said lightly. 'A tall, handsome man, like an Arab ...'

'A tall Arab.' He brightened, catching his mother's spirit. 'And when my father returns, I shall get a new suit – a big one that will cover my arms properly, and we'll even have to fold it back.'

Nnu Ego burst out laughing and there were tears in her eyes. She hoped fervently that the predictions of the medicine men came true. She would hate to disappoint this enthusiastic little fellow.

Mama Abby's brown eyes were aglow when she saw how excited Oshia was, for his happiness was proving infectious. Her own son Abby was already sixteen and at a good school in Lagos. Her other child, a girl called Bena, had had to get married very early and was never forgiven for bringing such disgrace to her family; so Mama Abby had no young grandchild to look after. She would insist on calling Oshia 'our son'.

'I see that our son is quite ready,' she beamed. 'What a nice suit!' She stood and looked at him with an exaggerated air of reflection.

Putting her baby to her breast Nnu Ego said gratefully, 'I do thank you for taking all this trouble over him, Mama Abby.'

The older women laughed. 'You know I'm no better off than you, but at least a man pays my rent.' Her husband, Abby's father, was a European who had been in the Nigerian colonial service; he had gone home after Abby was born, leaving Mama Abby fairly well provided for. The wise woman saved all the money to use for her son's education. She herself had white blood in her; she came from the Brass area, the rivers region of Nigeria whose people had had longer contact with foreigners than those from the interior: some places were so full of fair-skinned people that one might be in a world where whites and blacks had successfully intermarried and produced a nation of half-castes. By now Mama Abby had passed child-bearing age, though she would die rather than admit it to anybody. She had the slim figure of a girl and had learned the art of looking every inch a lady. She still moved with the upper crust of society, but she preferred to live fairly cheaply in rented accommodation and spend most of her money on her only brilliant son, for that would secure her a happy old age. The days when children would turn round and demand of a parent, 'If you knew you couldn't afford me, then why did you have me?' had not dawned. So Abby's mama, though a woman whom many righteous would frown upon their wives associating with, bought her way into respectability through her son, who was destined to become one of the leaders of the new Nigeria. In Nnu Ego's case her husband was not there to tell her whom to talk to and whom not to. She had to eat, and she needed friends. She was like a beggar, and since when did beggars have a choice? Moreover, Mama Abby was nice, in a harsh, forced way; but, none the less nice and responsible.

"Bye-'bye, see you soon!' shouted Oshia, putting his trusting hand into Mama Abby's willing one. As they neared the door, Oshia freed himself and made a dramatic dash back through the curtain, reappearing with his hat. 'I almost forgot that,' he panted, biting his tongue, shyly.

Nnu Ego heard him shouting goodbye to all and sundry in the yard as they made their way to the bus stop.

She was going to make the best use of a day like this, when Oshia was not at home, after feeding the baby, whom she still would not name until her husband arrived, and whose birth she would not announce to her father, lest a name be sent from Ibuza before Nnaife had the chance to see his son. But she knew she could not wait for ever; the child was now six weeks old and everybody simply called him 'Baby'. She washed him, and with the money she had saved from the rent went out in search of a place to buy cigarette cartons on the black market. She was surprised at what changes had taken place in the year since she had last had enough capital to invest in a whole carton. Now, look as she might, she could only see soldiers in khaki uniforms strolling along the marina. There he was no friendly sailor to ask her if she wanted to buy any surplus from the ship. Unbelieving, she took a ferry and crossed over to Apapa wharf, but the story there was the same. There was a shortage of cigarettes. She had to go home, stopping only at the John Holt's store to buy a small carton at the legal price. She would have to think of something else to sell. The joy of trading in cigarettes had been that she would buy them at about half the market price and after sales make a huge profit, the profit which went into feeding her family. She felt very sorry for herself now. How was she going to manage? Well, if things continued as they were, she would have to go back to Ibuza before the rent was due.

Having made up her mind, she walked with confidence carrying her day's purchases on her head. She beamed happily as she saw Abby's mother and Iyawo Itsekiri laughing conspiratorially, for no reason she could see. Perhaps Oshia had behaved badly today, she worried to herself.

Aloud she asked Mama Abby, 'How did it go then – the outing, I mean?'

'Oh, that,' Mama Abby drawled, as if her question was unimportant. 'That went very well, I think.'

She suspected that her two friends were trying to hide something from her, some kind of surprise. Whatever it was, it must be something they thought would be good news for her, judging from the way both were smiling.

'Go in,' gestured Iyawo Itsekiri, wedging her palm under her chin as usual and pointing with her other hand. 'Your son is as pleased with himself as a king. Go in.'

'Well, thank you very much. I will go in and feed this one.

Then I'll come out and have a chat. Oh, look,' she pointed as she approached the wide steps that led into their own veranda. 'He has put on the lights all by himself. You must have really done something to him today.'

But it was not just Oshia who was in the room. She could hear the twanging of the old guitar, which she had brought with her when they moved, just for sentimental reasons, not because she liked it much or because Nnaife was good at playing it at all.

Now as she stood outside their door she could hear the sound of that very guitar and, judging by the music coming from it, whoever was playing it was far from an expert; what was more, Oshia was singing with the person. She looked back at the women who had helped her in the past months and she saw the message on their faces. They were happy for her. Nnaife was back and alive! He had polished up his guitar-playing a little, probably indulging himself in the art while working on the ship. It must be true!

Her heart raced with excitement as she walked in into their one-room apartment to say '*Nnua*, welcome home,' to her husband Nnaife, and to say to him, 'Look, I had another son for you while you were away on the great seas.'

Humans, being what we are, tend to forget the most unsavoury experiences of life, and Nnu Ego and her sons forgot all the suffering they had gone through when Nnaife was away.

The first important thing to attend to was the celebration at which they would give their new child a name. All the Ibuza people living in Yaba, Ebute Metta and in Lagos island itself were called to the feast. Palm wine flowed like the spring water from Ibuza streams. People sang and danced until they were tired of doing both. To cap it all, Nnaife brought plentiful supplies of the locally made alcohol called *ogogoro* which he discreetly poured into bottles labelled 'Scotch Whisky'. He assured Nnu Ego that he had seen the white men for whom he worked on the ship drinking this whisky. Nnu Ego had asked wide-eyed, 'Why do they call our *ogogoro* illicit? Many of my father's friends were jailed just because they drank it.'

Nnaife laughed, the bitter laugh of a man who had become very cynical, who now realised that in this world there is no pure person. A man who in those last months had discovered that he had been revering a false image and that under white skins, just as under black ones, all humans are the same. 'If they allowed us to develop the production of our own gin, who would buy theirs?' he explained.

However Nnu Ego's long stay in Lagos and her weekly worship at St Jude's Ibo church had taken their toll. She asked suspiciously, 'But our own gin, is it pure like theirs?'

'Ours is even stronger and purer – more of the thing. I saw them drink it on the ships at Fernando Po.'

So on the day his baby boy was named, Nnaife served his guests with lots and lots of *ogogoro* and his guests marvelled at the amount of money he was spending, for they thought they were drinking spirits which came all the way from Scotland. They did not think of doubting him, since most ship crew members brought all sorts of things home with them. Their masters, not able to buy these workers outright, made them work like slaves anyway, and allowed them to take all the useless goods which were no longer of any value to them. They were paid – paid slaves – but the amount was so ridiculously small that many a white Christian with a little conscience would wonder whether it was worth anybody's while to leave a wife and family and stay almost a year on a voyage. Yet Nnaife was delighted. He was even hopeful of another such voyage. But on the day of his child's naming ceremony he spent a great portion of the money he brought home. He and his family had been without for so long that the thought of saving a little was pushed into the background.

Nnu Ego, that thrifty woman, threw caution to the winds and really enjoyed herself this time. She bought four different kinds of outfit, all cotton from the U.A.C. store. One outfit was for the morning, another for the afternoon, when the child was given the name Adim, Adimabua meaning 'now I am two': Nnaife was telling the world that now he had two sons, so he was two persons in one, a very important man. She had another outfit for the late afternoon, and a costly velveteen one for the evening. This was so beautiful that even those women who had been her helpers in time of want looked on enviously. But she did not care; she was enjoying herself. Not to be outdone, Oshia and his father changed their clothes as many times as Nnu Ego. It was one of the happiest days of her life.

A month after that, Oshia started to attend the local mission school, Yaba Methodist. This made him very proud, and he didn't tire of displaying his khaki uniform trimmed with pink braid. Nnu Ego sold off the spoils from her husband's ship over the next few months, and with this they were able to live comfortably.

Nnaife was developing a kind of dependence on his battered guitar. He would sing and twang on the old box, visiting one friend

124

after another, and not thinking at all of looking for another job. 'They promised to send for me,' he said. 'They said as soon as they were ready to sail again they would send for me.'

Nnu Ego was beginning to realise something else. Since he had come back, Nnaife had suddenly assumed the role of the lord and master. He had now such confidence in himself that many a time he would not even bother to answer her questions. Going to Fernando Po had made him grow away from her. She did not know whether to approve of this change or to hate it. True, he had given her enough housekeeping money, and enough capital in the form of the things he brought from Fernando Po, but still she did not like men who stayed at home all day.

'Why don't you go to Ikoyi and ask those Europeans if they have other domestic work for you, so that when they are ready to sail you will go with them?'

'Look, woman, I have been working night and day non-stop for eleven months. Don't you think I deserve a little rest?'

'A little rest? Surely three months is a long time to rest? You can look for something while you are waiting for them.'

If Nnu Ego went further than that he would either go out for the rest of the day or resort to his new-found hobby, the twanging of Dr Meers's old guitar. She decided to let him be for a while. After all, they still had enough money to pay for the rent. She also made sure of another term's fees for Oshia. She was now able to have a modest permanent stall of her own, at the railway yard, instead of spreading her wares on the pavement outside the yard. Oshia was helping, too. After school, he would sit by his mother's stand in front of the house, selling cigarettes, paraffin, chopped wood, and clothes blue. His mother would let him off to go and play with his friends as soon as she had finished washing and clearing the day's cooking things from the kitchen.

On one such evening, she sat with her neighbours in front of the house by the electric pole which provided light for yards around the house. Adim, Oshia's little brother, was now four months old, and he was propped up with sand around him to support his back, so he would learn how to sit up straight. He kept flopping on the sand like a bundle of loosely tied rags, much to the amusement of all. Nnu Ego had her stand by her, with her wares displayed, and Iyawo Itsekiri had started selling pork meat in a glass showcase. Another woman from the next yard had a large tray full of bread, so in the evenings the front of the house at Adam Street looked like a little market.

The women were thus happily occupied when they heard the guitar-playing Nnaife coming home. This was a surprise because when he went out these days he would not return until very late, sometimes in the early hours of the morning.

'Look,' Iyawo Itsekiri pointed out to Nnu Ego, who was trying to make sure she was not seeing things. 'Look, your husband is early today. Is something wrong?'

'Maybe he has decided to make use of his home this evening, for a change. And look at the group of friends he has with him. Are they going to have a party or something? Even our old friend Ubani is with them. I haven't seen him for a long time.' With this statement, Nnu Ego forgot her husband's inadequacies and rushed enthusiastically to welcome their friends. They were equally glad to see her. Nnaife didn't stop twanging his guitar throughout the happy exchanges. Nnu Ego showed off her children and Ubani remarked how tall Oshia was growing and told Nnu Ego that his wife Cordelia would be pleased to know that he had seen them all looking so well.

'Oh, so you didn't tell her you were coming here tonight?'

'Few men tell their women where they are going,' Nnaife put in, trying to be funny.

'I did not tell Cordelia that I would be seeing you all because I met your husband by accident in Akinwunmi Street, having a nice evening with some of his friends, so we all decided to come here and see you.'

126

There was a kind of constraint on the faces of their visitors, she thought, though Nnaife did not seem to notice anything, but she was becoming uneasy. None the less, she said airily, 'Please come in, come inside. Oshia, you mind the stand. I shall not be long.'

Nnu Ego noticed that only Ubani was making an effort to talk. The others, Nwakusor, Adigwe, and Ijeh, all men from Ibuza living around Yaba, looked solemn. Well, there was little she could do to alleviate their glumness, though she was going to try. She gave them some kolanut and brought out cigarettes and matches. Nnaife added his ever-present *ogogoro*, and soon the gathering resembled a party. After the prayers, Nwakusor gave a small tot of *ogogoro* to Nnaife, and another to his wife. When he urged them to drink it, Nnu Ego sensed that something was very wrong. These men were there to break bad news. All the same, like a good woman, she must do what she was told, she must not question her husband in front of his friends. Her thoughts went to her father, who was now ageing fast, and her heart pounded in fear. She started to shiver, but drank the home-made alcohol with a big gulp. She coughed a little, and this brought a smile to the faces of the men watching her. Nnu Ego was a good wife, happy with her lot.

Nwakusor cleared his throat, forcing furrows on to his otherwise smooth brow. He addressed Nnaife in the full manner, using his father's name Owulum. He reminded him that the day a man is born into a family, the responsibilities in that family are his. Some men were lucky in that they had an elder brother on whose shoulders the greater part of the responsibility lay. His listeners confirmed this by nodding in mute assent. It was an accepted fact.

'Now, you, Nnaife, until last week were one of those lucky men. But now, that big brother of yours is no more ...'

Nnaife who all this time had kept his old guitar on his knee, waiting for Nwakusor to finish his speech so that he could start one of the songs he had learned during his short stay at Fernando

Po, threw the instrument on the cemented floor. The pathetic clang it made died with such an echo of emptiness that all eyes hypnotically followed its fall, and then returned to Nnaife, who let out one loud wail. Then there was silence. He stared at his friends with unseeing eyes. As Nnu Ego recovered from the shock of the loud guitar the news began to register. So that was it. Nnaife was now the head of his family.

'Oh, Nnaife, how are you going to cope? All those children, and all those wives.' Here she stopped, as the truth hit her like a heavy blow. She almost staggered as it sank in. Nnaife's brother, the very man who had negotiated for her, had three wives even when she was still at home in Ibuza. Surely, surely people would not expect Nnaife to inherit them? She looked round her wildly, and was able to read from the masked faces of the men sitting around that they had thought of that and were here to help their friend and relative solve this knotty problem. For a time, Nnu Ego forgot the kind man who had just died; all she was able to think about was her son who had just started school. Where would Nnaife get the money from? Oh, God ... She ran out, leaving her baby on the bed.

She ran into Mama Abby who with many others was wondering what the noise and crying was about. Nnu Ego blurted out the first thing that came into her head: 'Nnaife may soon be having five more wives.'

Seeing that her friends were in suspense, Nnu Ego went on to explain: 'His brother has died and left behind several wives and God knows how many children.'

'Oh, dear, are you bound to accept them all?' asked Mama Abby, who knew little of Ibo custom. 'You have your own children to think of – surely people know that Nnaife is not in a steady job?'

'Maybe he'll be asked to come home and mind the farm,' said one of the curious women.

They all started talking at the same time, this one telling Nnu Ego what to do, that one telling her what not to do. The voices jangled together, but Nnu Ego thanked the women and went back inside to her menfolk. Her husband was being consoled by his friends, who had poured him another glass of *ogogoro*. Nnu Ego was asked to bring more cigarettes from her display stand, with a vague promise of repayment by someone. Many neighbours and friends came in, and they held a small wake for Nnaife's brother.

Ubani was the first to take his leave. But before he did so, he called Nnu Ego and Nnaife out into the yard, as their room was filled with people who had come to commiserate with the bereaved family and stayed for a glass of gin or whisky and a puff of tobacco. The air outside was fresh, and the sky was velvety black. Stars twinkled haphazardly against this inky background, and the moon was partly hidden. Ubani told them that he could fix Nnaife up at the railways as a labourer cutting the grass that kept sprouting along the railway lines. Unless he wanted to go back to Ibuza, Ubani suggested he come the very next day.

Nnaife thanked him sincerely. No, he said, he would not go to Ibuza. He had been out of farming practice for so long that he would rather risk it here in Lagos. At home there would be no end to the demands his family would make on him. He had more chance of living longer if he didn't go into what looked like a family turmoil. Of course he would be sending money to the Owulum wives, and would see that their sons kept small farmings going. But he would help them more by being here in Lagos. He would definitely go with Ubani the next day to take up the job if they would accept him.

Ubani assured him that they would; he himself now cooked for the head manager of the whole Nigerian Railway Department and his work was permanent. He was employed by the Railway Department and not the manager himself, so that whenever he decided to leave he would simply be transferred to a new master. Ubani laughed bitterly. 'I talk like an old slave these days, grateful to be given a living at all.'

'Are we not all slaves to the white men, in a way?' asked Nnu Ego in a strained voice. 'If they permit us to eat, then we will eat. If they say we will not, then where will we get the food? Ubani, you are a lucky man and I am glad for you. The money may be small, and the work slave labour, but at least your wife's mind is at rest knowing that at the end of the month she gets some money to feed her children and you. What more does a woman want?'

'I shall see you tomorrow, my friend. Mind how you go with these Hausa soldiers parading the streets.'

Nnaife was given a job as a grass-cutter at the railway compound. They gave him a good cutlass, and he would wear tattered clothes while he cut grass all day, come sunshine or rain. The work was tiring, and he did not much like it, especially when he saw many of his own people making their various ways into the workshop every morning. However, like Ubani, he was working for the Department and not for a particular white man, and he intended using that as his basis for getting into the workshop.

One thing was sure: he gained the respect and even the fear of his wife Nnu Ego. He could even now afford to beat her up, if she went beyond the limits he could stand. He gave her a little housekeeping money which bought a bag of garri for the month and some yams; she would have to make up the rest from her trading profits. On top of that, he paid the school fees for Oshia, who was growing fast and was his mother's pride and joy. Adaku, the new wife of his dead brother, would be coming to join them in Lagos, and after some time the oldest wife Adankwo, who was still nursing a four-month-old baby, might come too. Ego-Obi, the middle wife, went back to her people after the death of Nnaife's brother Owulum. The Owulum family said that she was an arrogant person, and she for her part claimed that she was so badly treated by them when her husband died that she decided she would rather stay with her own people. In any case, she was not missed; first, she had no child, and secondly she was very abusive.

130

Adaku, on the other hand, had a daughter, she was better-looking than Ego-Obi, and she was very ambitious, as Nnu Ego was soon to discover. She made sure she was inherited by Nnaife.

Nnu Ego could not believe her eyes when she came home from market one afternoon to see this young woman sitting by their doorstep, with a four-year-old girl sleeping on her knees. To Nnu Ego's eyes, she was enviably attractive, young looking, and comfortably plump with the kind of roundness that really suited a woman. This woman radiated peace and satisfaction, a satisfaction that was obviously having a healthy influence on her equally well-rounded child. She was dark, this woman, shiny black, and not too tall. Her hair was plaited in the latest fashion, and when she smiled and introduced herself as 'your new wife' the humility seemed a bit inconsistent. Nnu Ego felt that she should be bowing to this perfect creature – she who had once been acclaimed the most beautiful woman ever seen. What had happened to her? Why had she become so haggard, so rough, so worn, when this one looked like a pool that had still to be disturbed? Jealousy, fear and anger seized Nnu Ego in turns. She hated this type of woman, who would flatter a man, depend on him, need him. Yes, Nnaife would like that. He had instinctively disliked her own independence, though he had gradually been forced to accept her. But now there was this new threat.

'Don't worry, senior wife, I will take the market things in for you. You go and sit and look after the babies. Just show me where the cooking place is, and I will get your food ready for you.'

Nnu Ego stared at her. She had so lost contact with her people that the voice of this person addressing her as 'senior wife' made her feel not only old but completely out of touch, as if she was an outcast. She resented it. It was one thing to be thus addressed in Ibuza, where people gained a great deal by seniority; here, in Lagos, though the same belief still held, it was to a different degree. She was used to being the sole woman of this

131

house, used to having Nnaife all to herself, planning with him what to do with the little money he earned, even though he had become slightly evasive since he went to Fernando Po – a result of long isolation, she had thought. But now, this new menace ...

What was she to do? It had been all right when this was just a prospect. Not hearing anything definite from home, she had begun to tell herself that maybe the senior Owulum's wives had decided against coming. For she had sent messages to Ibuza to let Nnaife's people know that things were difficult in Lagos, that Lagos was a place where you could get nothing free, that Nnaife's job was not very secure, that she had to subsidise their living with her meagre profits. She could imagine this creature hearing all about it and laughing to herself, saying, 'If it is so bad, why is she there? Does she not want me to come?' Yes, it was true, Nnu Ego had not wanted her to come. What else did Nnaife want? She had borne him two sons, and after she had nursed Adim there would be nothing to hold her back from having as many children as they wanted. She knew this kind of woman: an ambitious woman who was already thinking that now she was in Lagos she would eat fried food.

Nnu Ego knew that her father could not help her. He would say to her, 'Listen, daughter, I have seven wives of my own. I married three of them, four I inherited on the deaths of relatives. Your mother was only a mistress who refused to marry me. So why do you want to stand in your husband's way? Please don't disgrace the name of the family again. What greater honour is there for a woman than to be a mother, and now you are a mother – not of daughters who will marry and go, but of good-looking healthy sons, and they are the first sons of your husband and you are his first and senior wife. Why do you wish to behave like a woman brought up in a poor household?' And all this for a husband she had not wanted in the beginning! A husband to whom she had closed her eyes when he came to her that first night, a husband who until

132

recently had little confidence in himself, who a few months ago was heavy and round-bellied from inactivity. Now he was losing weight because of working hard in the open like other men did in Ibuza, Nnaife looked younger than his age, while she Nnu Ego was looking and feeling very old after the birth of only three children. The whole arrangement was so unjust.

She tried desperately to control her feelings, to put on a pleasant face, to be the sophisticated Ibuza wife and welcome another woman into her home; but she could not. She hated this thing called the European way; these people called Christians taught that a man must marry only one wife. Now here was Nnaife with not just two but planning to have maybe three or four in the not so distant future. Yet she knew the reply he would give her to justify his departure from monogamy. He would say: 'I don't work for Dr Meers any more. I work as a grass-cutter for the Nigerian Railway Department, and they employ many Moslems and even pagans.' He had only been a good Christian so long as his livelihood with Dr Meers depended on it. It was precisely that work, when they had seen each other every day and all day, that had made her so dependent on Nnaife. She had been in Lagos now for more than seven years, and one could not change the habits of so many years in two minutes, humiliating as it was to know that this woman fresh from Ibuza was watching her closely, reading all the struggles and deliberations going on in her mind. Adaku, however, was able to disguise any disgust she felt by wearing a faint smile which neither developed into a full smile nor degenerated into a frown.

Like someone suddenly awakened from a deep sleep, Nnu Ego rushed past her and, standing by their door with the key poised, said hoarsely, 'Come on in, and bring your child with you.'

Adaku, tired from her long journey, bit on her lower lip so hard that it almost bled. Without saying a word, she carried the sleeping child into the dark room, then went back to the veranda to bring in her things and, as expected of her, Nnu Ego's groceries. She had prepared herself for a reluctant welcome something like this; and what alternative did she have? After mourning nine whole months for their husband, she had had enough of Ibuza, at least for a while. People had warned her that Nnu Ego would be a difficult person to live with; yet either she accepted Nnaife or spent the rest of her life struggling to make ends meet. People at home had seen her off to Lagos with all their blessing, but this daughter of Agbadi so resented her. Nnu Ego was lucky there was no Ibuza man or woman to witness this kind of un-Ibo-like conduct; many people would not have believed it. Adaku did not care, though; all she wanted was a home for her daughter and her future children. She did not want more than one home, as some women did who married outside the families of their dead husbands. No, it was worth some humiliation to have and keep one's children together in the same family. For her own children's sake she was going to ignore this jealous cat. Who knows, she told herself, Nnaife might even like her. She only had to wait and see.

Nnaife was delighted at his good fortune. Beaming like a child presented with a new toy, he showed Adaku, as his new wife, round the yard. He pointed out this and that to her, and he bought some palm wine to toast her safe arrival. He took her daughter as his, and vowed to his dead brother that he would look after his family as his own. He called Oshia and introduced the little girl Dumbi to him as his sister. Oshia, who suspected that his mother did not like this new sister and her mother, asked:

'When will they go back to where they came from, Father?'

Nnaife reprimanded him, calling him a selfish boy and saying that if he was not careful he would grow into a selfish man who no one would help when he was in difficulty. Nnaife put the fear of the Devil into Oshia by telling him a story which he said happened on the ship, of a white man who died alone, because he was minding his own business.

Nnu Ego who was busy dishing out the soup while this tirade was going on, knew that half the story was not true. She felt that Nnaife was being ridiculous and, rather like a little boy himself, was trying to show off his worldly knowledge to his new wife. Nnu Ego was the more annoyed because the latter was making such encouraging sounds, as if Nnaife was recounting a successful trip to the moon.

'For God's sake, Nnaife, was there anything that did not happen on that ship you sailed in so long ago?' She expected the others to laugh, but her son Oshia was so taken in by his father's stories that he strongly disapproved of his mother's interruption and protested indignantly:

'But it is true, Mother!'

'Some strange things do happen on those ships that sail on the big seas, and the men do see peculiar sights. This is well known even in Ibuza,' Adaku put in, uninvited.

Nnu Ego stopped in her movements. She knew that if she did not take care she would place herself in a challenging position, in which she and Adaku would be fighting for Nnaife's favour. Strange how in less than five hours Nnaife had become a rare commodity. She ignored Adaku's remark as unanswerable but snapped at her son:

'What type of a son are you, replying to your own mother like that? A good son should respect his mother always; in a place like this, sons belong to both parents, not just the father!'

Nnaife simply laughed and told Oshia not to talk like that to his mother again, adding with a touch of irony, 'Sons are very often mother's sons.'

Again in came that cool, low voice, which Nnu Ego had been trying all day to accept as part of their life, at the same time as telling herself that the owner of the voice did not belong, or that, if she did, her belonging was only going to be a temporary affair – but Adaku, the owner of that disturbing voice, seemed determined to belong, right from the first:

'In Ibuza sons help their father more than they ever help their mother. A mother's joy is only in the name. She worries over them, looks after them when they are small; but in the actual help on the farm, the upholding of the family name, all belong to the father ...'

Adaku's explanation was cut short by Nnu Ego who brought in the steaming soup she had been dishing out behind the curtain. She sniffed with derision and said as she placed a bowl on Nnaife's table: 'Why don't you tell your brother's wife that we are in Lagos, not in Ibuza, and that you have no farm for Oshia in the railway compound where you cut grass?'

They ate their food in silence, Nnu Ego, Adaku and the two children Oshia and Dumbi eating from the same bowl of pounded yam and soup. Nnu Ego's mind was not on the food and she was acting mechanically. She was afraid that her hold on Nnaife's household was in question. She took every opportunity to remind herself that she was the mother of the sons of the family. Even when it came to sharing the piece of meat for the two children, one of the duties of the woman of the house, she pointed out to Dumbi that she must respect Oshia, as he was the heir and the future owner of the family. Their few possessions – the four-poster iron bed which Nnaife had bought from his journey to Fernando Po and the large wall mirrors – were things of immense value to Nnu Ego, and if her son never grew up to be a farmer, she wanted to make sure that whatever there was should be his. She knew again that she was being ridiculous because no one challenged her; it was a known fact. However, she felt compelled to state the obvious as a way of relieving her inner turmoil.

After eating, Nnaife looked at her reflectively and said: 'The food is very nice; thank you, my senior wife and mother of my sons.'

It was Nnu Ego's turn to be surprised. Her husband had

136

never thanked her for her cooking before, to say nothing of re-minding her of being the mother of his two boys. What was happening to them all?

Nnaife was still studying her from his chair; the other members of the family were eating sitting on the floor.

'You see, my brother's death must bring changes to us all. I am now the head, and you are the head's wife. And as with all head wives in Ibuza, there are things it would be derogatory for you to talk about or even notice, otherwise you will encourage people to snigger and cause rumours to fly about you. No one wanted my brother's death. And do you think, knowing him as you did, that he was the sort of man to let you and Oshia beg if anything had happened to me?'

Nnu Ego could think of nothing apposite to say. She was a trifle disconcerted. To try and be philosophical like Nnaife might tempt her to ascribe profundity to the ordinary. None the less, she was intrinsically grateful to him for making what must have been a tremendous effort.

She was determined to attack with patience what she knew was going to be a great test to her. She was not only the mother of her boys, but the spiritual and the natural mother of this household, so she must start acting like one. It took her a while to realise that she was stacking the plates used for their evening meal and taking them out in the kitchen to wash.

'I should be doing that,' Adaku cooed behind her.

Nnu Ego controlled her breath and held tight her shaking hands. Then she spoke in a voice that even surprised her: 'But, daughter, you need to know your husband. You go to him, I'm sure he has many tales to tell you.'

Adaku laughed, the first real laughter she had let herself indulge in since arriving that morning. It was a very eloquent sound, telling Nnu Ego that they were going to be sisters in this business of sharing a husband. She went into the kitchen still laughing as Mama Abby came in.

'Your new wife is a nice woman. Laughing with so much confidence and happiness on the day of her arrival.'

'A happy senior wife makes a happy household,' Nnu Ego snapped. She suspected that her unhappiness at Adaku's presence was by now common knowledge and she was not going to encourage it further. After all, Mama Abby had never had to live as a senior wife before, to say nothing of welcoming a younger wife into her family. To prevent her saying anything further, Nnu Ego added: 'I must go and see to our guests.'

She hurried in and, to take her mind off herself, busied herself entertaining people who came throughout the evening to see the new wife. Nnu Ego fought back tears as she prepared her own bed for Nnaife and Adaku. It was a good thing she was determined to play the role of the mature senior wife; she was not going to give herself any heartache when the time came for Adaku to sleep on that bed. She must stuff her ears with cloth and make sure she also stuffed her nipple into the mouth of her young son Adim, when they all lay down to sleep.

Far before the last guest left, Nnaife was already telling Oshia to go to bed because it was getting late.

'But we usually stay up longer than this, Father.'

'Don't argue with your father. Go and spread your mat and sleep; you too, our new daughter Dumbi.'

The neighbours who had come to welcome the new wife took the hint and left. Did Nnaife have to make himself so obvious? Nnu Ego asked herself. One would have thought Adaku would be going away after tonight.

'Try to sleep, too, senior wife,' he said to her, and now Nnu Ego was sure he was laughing at her. He could hardly wait for her to settle down before he pulled Adaku into their only bed.

It was a good thing she had prepared herself, because Adaku turned out to be one of those shameless modern women whom

138

Nnu Ego did not like. What did she think she was doing? Did she think Nnaife was her lover and not her husband, to show her enjoyment so? She tried to block her ears, yet could still hear Adaku's exaggerated carrying on. Nnu Ego tossed in agony and anger all night, going through in her imagination what was taking place behind the curtained bed. Not that she had to do much imagining, because even when she tried to ignore what was going on, Adaku would not let her. She giggled, she squeaked, she cried and she laughed in turn, until Nnu Ego was quite convinced that it was all for her benefit. At one point Nnu Ego sat bolt upright looking at the shadows of Nnaife and Adaku. No, she did not have to imagine what was going on; Adaku made sure she knew.

When Nnu Ego could stand it no longer, she shouted at Oshia who surprisingly was sleeping through it all: 'Oshia, stop snoring!'

There was silence from the bed, and then a burst of laughter. Nnu Ego could have bitten her tongue off; what hurt her most was hearing Nnaife remark:

'My senior wife cannot go to sleep. You must learn to accept your pleasures quietly, my new wife Adaku. Your senior wife is like a white lady: she does not want noise.'

Nnu Ego bit her teeth into her baby's night clothes to prevent herself from screaming.

By about the year 1941, it was clear to most people in the country that there was a war going on somewhere. Many did not know why it had started in the first place. But the more enlightened knew it had something to do with the then rulers of Nigeria, the British.

Women who went to the markets realised that they could not get salt as cheaply as before. So scarce were such commodities that in the interior villages salt in cake form was used as money.

At school, children like Oshia could not help seeing images of the war. The school walls were decorated with pictures of aeroplanes of different shapes, some looking like birds, others like fish in the sea.

For the common man in the street, things were not so grim apart from the fact that they could not find cheap fish like stockfish to buy, and the majority of imported foodstuffs became something of the past. But many people were caught in the middle: people like Nnaife and his family, families who had left their farming communities to make a life from the cities. It was comparatively easy when there was no war; one could always be a domestic servant. Now with the war, the masters were at the front fighting. Money was short and so were jobs. And in Nnaife's family there were many more mouths being added to those to be fed.

Nnu Ego and the new wife Adaku became pregnant almost at the same time. Nnu Ego came into labour first and had a set of twins, both girls.

'Your first set of girls, senior wife,' Adaku said by way of congratulation.

'Hm, I know, but I doubt if our husband will like them very much. One can hardly afford to have one girl in a town like this, to say nothing of two.'

'Oh, senior wife, I think you are sometimes more traditional than people at home in Ibuza. You worry too much to please our husband.'

Nnu Ego laughed weakly, as she watched the younger woman tidying the new-born infants. 'I think it's due to my father's influence. I can see him in my mind's eye weighing it up and down, then chuckling over it, and asking his friend Idayi whether it's right for my *chi* to send me two girls instead of just one.'

They both laughed. 'It's a man's world this. Still, senior wife, these girls when they grow up will be great helpers to you in looking after the boys. Their bride prices will be used in paying their school fees as well.'

Nnu Ego looked at Adaku with speculative eyes. 'This woman knows a thing or two,' she thought. So independent in her way of thinking. Was it because Adaku came from a low family where people were not tied to pleasing the rest of their members, as she Nnu Ego had to please her titled father Agbadi all the time? She sighed and remarked aloud, 'You are right. The trouble with me is that I find it difficult to change.'

When Nnaife returned in the evening and was told that his wife Nnu Ego had had two girls at the same time, he laughed loudly as he was wont to do when faced with an impossible situation. 'Nnu Ego, what are these? Could you not have done better? Where will we all sleep, eh? What will they eat?'

'In twelve years' time, when their bride prices start rolling in, you'll begin to sing another tune,' Adaku put in, smiling broadly as if she did not mean to hurt anyone.

Nnaife did not appreciate this woman's boldness, but said nothing. He washed himself and went out to drink with his friends.

'He did not even suggest their names?' Nnu Ego moaned.

'Twins don't deserve special names. This one came first so she is Taiwo and this one is Kehinde – "she who came second".'

When Adaku had her own baby weeks later, Nnaife was

happier because the new wife gave him a son. Unfortunately for everybody, the baby boy did not live for more than a few weeks. He died of convulsions. The death of the baby sent Adaku into deep depression. She became almost impossible to live with. She blamed everybody and everything for her loss.

Nnu Ego tried to reason with her: 'You are still young and conceive very easily: don't give in to this little setback.'

'You can say that now. Do you remember how sad you were, senior wife, when you had the two girls? You would have been happier if they had turned out to be boys instead. Now I had a boy, my only son, and he did not live. O God, why did you not take one of the girls and leave me with my male child? My only man child.'

'But you still have Dumbi,' Oshia said uninvited.

'You are worth more than ten Dumbis,' Adaku snapped at the boy.

'Go out and play, Oshia, and stop listening to female gossip.'

Oshia had heard enough to make him realise that he and his brother Adim were rare commodities, and that he being the oldest was rarer still. And had not his mother told him some time ago that he was a very handsome boy? This was a point, however, that he was beginning to doubt, now that there were other children in the family. He missed the undivided attention he had once enjoyed as an only child; all of a sudden, within a period of a few years, he felt he had been relegated to the background, and if he wanted anything was usually told not to be so childish. His mother was constantly telling him to be his age: 'Don't you know that you are the eldest? You should behave yourself and set a good example.'

Adaku reluctantly pulled herself out of her mourning one evening as it was her turn to do the cooking. 'Oshia! Dumbi! You two go and fetch some water from the tap for the evening meal.'

Dumbi came obediently to take her bucket, but Oshia ignored Adaku.

'Oshia, did you not hear me call you? Go and fetch some

water,' Adaku repeated. 'Dumbi is already on her way.'

'I'm not going! I am a boy. Why should I help in the cooking? That's a woman's job,' Oshia yelled back, and went on playing with his friends.

All the people sitting around in the compound laughed. 'Just like a boy,' they murmured amusedly.

But that childish remark set Adaku off. She started to cry afresh for her dead baby, certain that people were mocking her because she had no son.

'Oshia, come in at once!' Nnu Ego called. 'Why are you so rude to your father's wife? Don't you know that she is like a mother to you?' She hit her eight-year-old son, who shouted back in anger:

'I don't like her! She gives me frightful headaches. I saw her in my dream last night. She was trying to push me into a ditch. I don't like her!'

'What dream are you talking about?' Nnu Ego asked, fear creeping into her voice. She had long sensed that Adaku's grievances were not just that she had lost her own son but that Nnu Ego had two sons already; stories of younger wives harming the sons of senior wives were common.

'Why did you not tell me then? Why mention it now, just when you're being told off?' Nnu Ego persisted in a low voice so that Adaku would not hear.

'You wouldn't have believed me,' Oshia complained. 'You always support her and you ignore me, all the time worrying about Adim and the twins. You wouldn't have believed me.'

Nnu Ego rushed Oshia to the native medicine man, who listened to the boy's story. He did not say that the boy was imagining the whole thing or tell him that he was lying; after all, he had his livelihood to earn. Instead the *dibia* danced and jabbered and spat and convulsed in turn, and then announced in a strange voice:

'The child is right. You must protect your sons against the

143

jealousy of the younger wife. If you bring me two hens and a yard of white cloth, I shall prepare a charm for your sons to wear. No jealousy will be able to reach them after that.'

Oshia was fascinated. He enjoyed the trip to the medicine man, and the feeling of importance it gave him, especially as his mother bought him a big roasted plantain on their way back. Later, root mixtures were prepared for him and Adim to drink, and some black ashes were rubbed on to their veins.

'Will this protect us from Adaku?' Oshia asked in whispers.

His mother nodded and, laying a finger on his lips, said urgently. 'But don't tell anybody.'

The boy nodded, satisfied that his importance was re-established.

Adaku, however, did not stop her moaning and complaining about everything. One evening she was watching Nnu Ego on the veranda counting her pennies and planning her sales for the next day; it was something Nnu Ego always did last thing at night, taking advantage of the cool evening air before retiring indoors to their stuffy sleeping places. Their room was choked with sleeping mats and utensils, and though they had acquired another bed for Nnu Ego, a wooden one which afforded her a little privacy, there was minimal space between the beds.

'I don't know why our husband should stay out all evening with that forsaken guitar, drinking all over the neighbourhood,' Adaku commented.

'Men, they will always have their fun,' Nnu Ego replied absentmindedly, and quickly went on with her counting. As far as she was concerned, the longer Nnaife stayed out, the better. Where would he stay? Here on the veranda as well?

'Do you know that if you play music in the middle of the night you attract bad spirits to yourself and your household?'

'What did you say?' Nnu Ego looked up at Adaku for the first time since she had started her unnecessary conversation.

144

Adaku repeated herself, and Nnu Ego sighed, wondering whether Adaku was going to claim that Nnaife's tuneless music had contributed to the death of her son. *O God, please give this woman another boy so that we can all have some peace.*

'I know that in Ibuza they say that if one sings in the middle of the night one is asking for trouble: I understand snakes love music. I always think that strange, though, because music is a beautiful thing. I don't know why such dangerous creatures as snakes should be attracted to it. Still, that's in Ibuza. There are few snakes here in Lagos, and Ibuza snakes have never seen a guitar-playing musician.' Nnu Ego chuckled in an attempt to throw lightness into the conversation. 'The music our husband plays, that music – it would frighten off anything living, not attract it.'

But Adaku did not laugh. Instead she went on picking her teeth agitatedly and twitching her toes. 'I don't think it's right. Look at us, trying to make ends meet, and he squanders his money on drink and on top of that plays the guitar right into the early hours of the morning, waking up the living and the dead. This town is a mysterious place, not as small as our Ibuza. One day he will invite a bad spirit into this house,' she predicted with a malicious voice.

'No, not to his house, he wouldn't. What is bad in a man having a little fun with his friends? I shall talk to him about the danger of his coming late, but God would not let any evil spirit come into our home,' Nnu Ego said with that type of finality one usually associates with closed doors. She stacked the coins she had been counting and slid them neatly into her money belt.

She duly warned her husband about the danger, and Nnaife grumbled that theirs had not been much of a home to him. There was always moaning from Adaku, there were the babies climbing over him, and there was she Nnu Ego complaining about the cost of food. He stayed out to forget.

'Well, we have a saying that if you cannot bite, then cover

145

your teeth. You accepted her – ' She stopped. She knew that Nnaife still felt it his responsibility to inherit his brother's widows.

'Do you think the other women would not all be here staying with us if I had enough room? So, woman, don't keep reminding me of my duty. I know it very well. I shall come in whenever I like.'

The next day was a Saturday, and their friend Nwakusor was naming his child. Nnu Ego and Adaku and their children had been there all day, cooking, eating and dancing. The children enjoyed themselves tremendously, watching their mothers dance an intricate type of Western Ibo dance called 'Agbalani'. They ran in and out of the circles, making as much noise as they could. None of them was well dressed. Oshia wore his khaki school pants, with one of his mother's butterfly-patterned lappa cloths wound round him and tied in a neat knot at the back of his neck; most of the other boys were similarly clothed. But they had the time of their life. Nnu Ego was given bowls of rice to take home, and Adaku collected some *chin-chin*. They decided to leave as soon as they noticed that the children were overtired, and they left the merriment to the men.

It was not long before all the children were fast asleep. Nnu Ego crawled into the haven of her curtained wooden bed with gratitude. She saw her husband's guitar, and laughed to herself. Nnaife would be staying out late tonight and was determined to enjoy himself, so he had not taken his guitar with him. And he said that he was not superstitious! With a smile on her lips, she checked that the children were all right on their mats, then settled down to sleep herself. She knew that Adaku would be doing the same. She wished her good night.

She had no idea for how long they had slept when the noise of the guitar woke her up. Grumbling, she went blearily towards the door to open it for Nnaife. But Nnaife was not at the door! Then she remembered: he had not taken the guitar with him. So who was playing the guitar? She woke Adaku, and they both listened in fear.

146

They dared not touch the thing. Some time after, a drunken Nnaife walked in. They told him what had happened and, with little ado, he carried the offensive thing from the wall and ran as fast as he could to smash it outside their yard, saying that he would listen to his wives' advice and never play such a ghostly instrument again.

The following morning the story of the guitar that played itself gained so much credence among their friends that people were convinced ghosts had followed Nnaife home on previous occasions and resented his not taking them to the naming ceremony of Nwakusor's son.

When the medicine man was consulted, he said the ghosts Nnaife had disturbed must be pacified with sacrifices. So Nnaife killed a goat, and the whole back of the animal was sent to the medicine man to offer to the ghosts. Friends came and they danced and prayed that all would be well with Nnaife's family.

Oshia did not know what to make of everything. It was one of those happenings which impressed on him early the psychology of his people. Maybe some medicine men could really see into the future, but that man from Abeokuta they had then in Yaba was not so truthful. Oshia knew the real truth of the whole matter: he had caught some mice the day before the incident, and while he was still thinking of the best place to put his new pets his mother had rushed into the room. Knowing that if she saw them she would order him to throw them away immediately, he had quickly put them into the hole in the centre of the guitar hanging on the wall.

'We are going to a naming ceremony,' she had told him, 'so go to the pump and get some water to bathe yourself with. Hurry. We must help them prepare the food, otherwise they will think that we are only ready to eat and not work.'

Oshia had done as he was told, and the rest of the day was taken up by their going to Nwakusor's and returning so very late and tired. Though he suspected that the music players were the mice he had stuffed into the box, he none the less enjoyed the goat

147

and the celebration that had resulted. He dared not tell his parents what actually had happened, especially as the story was repeated so many times that people started regarding Nnaife as a hero. They assured him it was because his music was so good that it inspired the spirits to come home with him. Nnaife even claimed that the last time he had carried the guitar he had felt that he was not alone, that somebody was following him. Later he went on to say that on that very day he had passed the burial ground at Igbobi. And people respected him the more. Many a time Oshia would look at his father and wonder whether those things were part of the art of becoming a man. He soon stopped thinking about the incident and later when people talked about it he was not quite sure that he was not in the wrong. But Nnaife gained the reputation of a master musician whose musk could move even the spirits.

If Nnu Ego had any suspicions, they were not towards her son. She suspected that Adaku had enlisted the help of the medicine man she frequented for her backache, and that he had conjured up the spirits from the graves to come and frighten Nnaife into giving up his guitar and staying more at home. This buttressed the more her resolve to be careful with the way she treated this woman. Adaku had nothing to lose except her girl child, but she, Nnu Ego, had everything to lose.

Her father kept sending messages to her to come and see him because his time was drawing to an end, and though people told her that he was ill Nnu Ego could not bring herself to just go, leaving her boys in Lagos to continue their schooling. She had worked herself up in her imagination to believe that Adaku would harm them once her back was turned. The best she could promise her people in Ibuza was that she would be home when the boys were on holiday, so that her father could see them too. Meanwhile she sent various European medicines and advised him to try them.

She had undertaken to talk to Nnaife about all Adaku's grievances, the guitar apart, but Adaku insisted that the only way to

148

bring home to him the fact that they needed more housekeeping money was to stop cooking for their husband. The evening she suggested this, Nnu Ego stared at her for a while, then asked,

'What plan do you have in mind? I quite agree that we are not given enough housekeeping money. I am sure he spends more than we get on his drink.'

So one day soon after the guitar episode, Adaku and Nnu Ego fed their children secretly, and when Nnaife arrived from work, tired and hungry, he was shocked to find that, instead of food in the carefully covered bowl, his wives had left three pound notes – the month's food money intact as he had given it to them the day before.

'Now what is this?' he asked in bitter anger. His voice was tremulous and he directed his displeasure at Nnu Ego, who seemed to shrink under his stare. If only she could explain that she was doing this for the sake of her children. She looked away, her hands shakily stringing the beads she was going to tie as decorations round the twins' legs.

'The food money you give us is too small. Nwakusor and the other men give their wives double the amount you give us. When we go to the market, we have to keep wandering from stall to stall in search of bargains, because we can never afford anything,' Adaku said breathlessly.

'Is this the only way you could tell me about it? Nwakusor, Nwakusor! How much does he earn? Don't you know that his income is three times mine? Don't you know he is a worker at a recognised trade, while I am only a grass-cutter? You are a bad influence in this house, Adaku. You have become worse since your child died – you're spreading your bitterness all over. Don't I sleep with you? What else do you want?'

He turned to face Nnu Ego. 'And you, my so-called senior wife, you let this woman lead you?'

'Whenever it comes to sacrifice then everyone reminds me

about being the senior wife, but if there is something to gain, I am told to be quiet because wanting a good thing does not befit my situation. I can understand the value of being a senior wife in Ibuza; not here, Nnaife. It doesn't mean a thing. Everything is so expensive now. Are you the only one who hasn't heard that there's a war going on, and that it's difficult to get things in the market? Adaku did not lead me into this – we need more money!'

'Where do you want me to get it from, eh?'

'What about the drinks you buy? What you spend on a keg of palm wine would buy us all a meal.'

'If you were not the mother of my sons, I would have taught you a lesson this evening. But don't push me too far, or I may still do it. Who pays for this room? Who brought you here? You think you can be defiant just because you sell a few wretched cigarettes. I didn't start the war, and what has it got to do with me?'

'I will not reply to your insult, Nnaife. You are hungry, and it is said that a hungry man is an angry one. I will say nothing more, except to remind you that the money we are asking for is to feed your children, not to buy ourselves lappas.'

This annoyed Nnaife so much that he flung his napkin at Nnu Ego, but she dodged it and ran out. On the veranda, Oshia came to her with accusation in his eyes.

'Why don't you cook for Father? Why didn't you use the money for food? It's only paper. If there isn't enough of it, you can tear it up to make more.'

'You don't understand, son, and people don't tear paper money just like that. We need more money to buy more food.'

'But we had a lot to eat today. There are still lots of beans left for Father; why can't you give him that?'

'Oh, keep quiet! You are a spoilt child asking too many questions.'

Suddenly Adaku screamed from inside the room. 'Help! Help! He's going to kill me – you madman!'

'Serves her right,' Oshia said with a wicked grin and ran away.

'I hope you don't become like your father, Oshia,' Nnu Ego shouted after him. She could hear the blows Nnaife was administering to her co-wife. What was she going to do? Nnaife had slammed the door shut but Nnu Ego kept on banging at it for him to open.

'Leave the poor woman alone. Do you want to kill the new child that she is expecting? Open the door!'

When Nnaife did open the door, Nnu Ego grabbed the *odo* handle which she used for pounding food and waved it menacingly over her husband's head, though in the event there was more shouting than physical violence done.

'Don't you know Adaku is pregnant?' she demanded. 'Don't you know?'

Nnaife managed to wrangle himself free from the two shrieking women. By now other tenants living in the compound had gathered round to witness these rebellious women chasing and berating their husband.

'I am not adding a penny to that money,' he said adamantly. 'You can starve, for all I care.' With that he strode out, making his way to the stalls of the palm-wine sellers near Suru Lere.

When all was quiet, and the women were in bed, each nursing her own hurt and falling asleep intermittently, no one knew when Oshia got up. He went quietly to the bowl where the money was kept and sat there in the dark carefully tearing it into pieces. He was still busy doing this when Nnaife staggered drunkenly in.

'Where is the *bloo ... blooo* candle?' he belched. 'Oshia, what are you doing?' While he groped for candles his wives pretended to be asleep. When he had lit one, they heard him burst into uncontrollable laughter.

'Your mothers are really going to like this, Oshia. Ha, ha, ha!'

'What is it, Nnaife? What has Oshia done?' Nnu Ego

demanded, jumping out of bed with so much force that it was obvious she had been awake all the time.

'Look at your son, Nnu Ego.'

'Oh, my God, Oshia, what have you done? You've torn the money into tiny pieces! Now we won't have anything to eat with at all. Oh, Oshia, what shall we do?'

'I only wanted to make more money. Now there's lots of it so you don't have to fight any more,' Oshia concluded. The only money he had ever handled before was in coin, and he knew that somehow you could make a penny go further by changing it into four farthings.

Nnaife chortled loudly. 'Now you must carry your strike to the bitter end. I'm not giving you a penny, because I haven't a penny to give. I am going to bed. Good night.'

Adaku and Nnu Ego thought Nnaife would relent, but after a few days it was clear to Nnu Ego that he was not going to give in.

'Just give us whatever you can; we will manage,' Nnu Ego begged.

'How can you manage with less, when three whole pounds sent you on strike? You'd better carry on the way you started. It's your responsibility to feed your children as best you can. Don't worry about me. I shall take care of myself.'

'I have nothing more to feed them with, Nnaife. Would you like to see us starve?'

'Sell your lappas. You are the chief wife: use your head. After all, you told me you knew what you were doing when you decided not to cook for me. My *chi* has taught you a lesson, not to tamper with a man's stomach. I did not tear up the money, your son did.'

Nnu Ego went on pleading till morning, and when Nnaife was setting out for work she ran after him and begged him again. She had four children and was expecting another, so she had to resolve things; Adaku had only herself and Dumbi to worry about.

'Please help, Nnaife, please!'

152

'All right, I shall see what I can manage to give you when I come back tonight. You have learned your lesson, senior wife.'

On her way back to their room, it occurred to Nnu Ego that she was a prisoner, imprisoned by her love for her children, imprisoned in her role as the senior wife. She was not even expected to demand more money for her family; that was considered below the standard expected of a woman in her position. It was not fair, she felt, the way men cleverly used a woman's sense of responsibility to actually enslave her. They knew that a traditional wife like herself would never dream of leaving her children. Nnu Ego tried to imagine her father's face if she were to return to his house and claim ill-treatment by Nnaife; she would be chased in disgrace back to her responsibility. At home in Ibuza she would have had her own hut and would at least have been treated as befitting her position, but here in Lagos, where she was faced with the harsh reality of making ends meet on a pittance, was it right for her husband to refer to her responsibility? It seemed that all she had inherited from her agrarian background was the responsibility and none of the booty. Well, even though she had now given in and admitted defeat, she was going to point this out to Nnaife that very evening when he came home from work. With that final decision, confidence sprang inside her like water from below the ground and seemed to wash away her gloomy thoughts with its clear, sparkling gush.

It was in this mood of expectancy that she spent the last few shillings she had in preparing Nnaife's favourite dish, a thick and spicy corned-beef stew with peppers and tomatoes. She fed her children as if it was Christmas Day. She could not afford to go on with the strike, not after what Oshia had done; she was ready for reconciliation.

Adaku wondered what was happening when she saw the lay of the food. Had Nnu Ego gone out of her head, spending the profits of her trade so lavishly? What was the matter with her?

153

Even if she was pregnant again, that was no cause for celebration; all it meant was another mouth to feed. Perhaps Nnu Ego had accepted money from Nnaife behind her back. The sly woman! That was probably what had been happening when she went out so early in the morning.

'Senior wife, did our husband give you money to cook with?'

'No, he did not. He promised to bring us some this evening, so I made him this special soup to put him in a good humour.'

'I'm not sorry for what we did,' Adaku said.

'I'm not saying that I'm sorry. All I'm saying is that we can't carry on this way and let the children starve.'

'He wouldn't let us starve. He would have given in in the end.'

'Well, I don't know about that, but I'm not going to play strike with my children's stomachs.'

'Anyway, it's not right for you two to make it up somewhere in secret and leave me in the dark. When a man starts showing preference to one wife then he's asking for trouble. I'm going to wait for him here and have it out with him this evening.'

She sat on the veranda singing scraps of songs, waiting for Nnaife to come home, because she wanted some explanation from him. She had often thought that he showed favouritism to Nnu Ego but had been reluctant before to make an open issue of it. The food money he gave his wives was divided between them, and they would each use it to cook for the same number of days. A husband was meant to share the bed of the wife whose turn it was to cook, unless she was indisposed, pregnant or nursing a child, though like many a husband Nnaife would break this rule as it pleased him. Adaku resented it whenever she heard Nnaife moving in Nnu Ego's bed when by right he should have come to her, but only now did it occur to her that perhaps behind her back Nnu Ego had been bribing him with delicious food, augmenting his money with her own earnings. 'The shameless fool,' Adaku said under her breath.

No wonder she was pregnant again so soon after the twins, because she knew how to sneak behind people's backs and make up to Nnaife. 'Wait until that man returns,' she vowed to herself, 'I shall give him a piece of my tongue.'

But Nnaife did not come home at his usual time. They waited, and while they waited Adaku sang all the songs she knew, then in the failing light she decided to comb out her hair and make tiny plaits in it. By the time she had completed the task, with a small hand-mirror wedged between her knees and still singing angrily, it was twilight and there was still no sign of Nnaife.

Nnu Ego went in and out of the room, doing a mad dance of impatience. Where was Nnaife? What had delayed him, today of all days – when there was no housekeeping money, when she the senior wife had allowed herself to spend more than commonsense recommended, when she knew she was expecting another child, and when she planned to tell her husband that she would not accept responsibility without its reward? Her exuberance of the day was gradually draining away. She had reheated the food so many times by six o'clock that she did not wish to do so again for fear of its losing its taste.

Adaku said nothing but watched her with malicious delight. It served the good wife Nnu Ego right; Nnaife had probably gone on a drinking spree with his friends and just hadn't bothered to come back for his meal. Tired of sitting, Adaku got up and asked in tones of mock politeness.

'Would you like me to take his food indoors? He can hardly eat out here on the veranda now, in this darkness.'

'Yes, please take it in.' Nnu Ego paced up and down, for once allowing herself to show anxiety and agitation. 'Our husband is late tonight,' she muttered. 'I wonder where he is? Grass-cutters don't work overtime.'

'Maybe he has gone straight to the palm wine stalls to drink, instead of coming back to face us.'

'In the ten years since I have lived with him, I have never known him to do such a thing,' Nnu Ego dismissed the suggestion.

'Really? But you can't deny that he is a selfish man.'

'All men are selfish. That's why they are men.'

Adaku began singing again and took the cold stew and rice indoors. But as it neared seven o'clock she too became anxious.

'I think we'd better send Oshia to the Nwakusors to find out if our husband is with them.'

Oshia reported back that Nnaife was not there, nor had he been seen at the palm wine stalls. Within half an hour not only Nwakusor but several other friends and neighbours were there worrying with them and wondering where Nnaife could be.

'He told me he would bring us some money this evening,' Nnu Ego kept repeating to everyone who came to help look for Nnaife.

Eventually Ubani and Nwakusor advised the women to go to bed. 'Look, wives, it is almost midnight and both of you are in a delicate condition. We will stay up to wait for your husband. A man should not be this angry with his family. Go to sleep.'

The men were left sitting outside on the veranda, smoking endless cigarettes.

Inside their room, Adaku forgot her petty jealousy with Nnu Ego and said in a low, near-tearful voice: 'If Nnaife dies, I will run and run and run, and will never be seen again. At my age, to lose two husbands ... it must be a curse!'

'Shh ...' Nnu Ego whispered from her bed which creaked as she twisted and turned in inner despair herself. 'Don't talk that way. He is not dead. You mustn't say things like that.' But her voice was far from convincing; she too was close to tears. She was frightened as well but her culture did not permit her to give in to her fears. She was supposed to be strong, being the senior wife, to behave more like a man than a woman. As men were not permitted open grief, she had to learn to hide hers as well.

She heard Adaku crying, and she envied her her freedom.

It was difficult for men with no qualifications to find work in the early 1940s. In growing numbers they were leaving their village homes to look for jobs in Lagos, and this phenomenon was robbing many areas of their most able-bodied men. Those who left reckoned that it was better to go and work for a master or a company rather than stay on their own farms where income depended upon the whims of the weather and upon their own physical strength. In such circumstances when men grew old their sons naturally took over the farming of the family lands, and their daughters, from wherever they were married, from time to time gave little contributions of tobacco and soap or chunks of wood for warming the fireplaces (for inland in the villages, especially during the Harmattan season, the temperature drops very sharply sometimes to twelve degrees Centigrade or below, which to old people used to the weather being over twenty degrees can seem very cold indeed). But the younger generation like Nnu Ego and her friends preferred to leave this type of life behind. The Yorubas had been in Lagos a long time, since the fall of the great Benin Empire, but the Ibos were one of the last groups to follow this drift. Though they missed the sense of belonging which existed in their village communities, the advantage of working in the towns was that wages were more regular; the payment might be meagre, but they soon learned to tailor their needs to their means.

People seldom took their jobs lightly. They could not afford to. Nnaife was among the lucky few who found work with the government; thus employed, one could hardly be sacked and could rest assured the morning would never come when one was told that was that and there was no more work to be done. On top of that, if one stayed in government service long enough, one was sure of a small pension, something still quite new to most Ibos. Not many people enjoyed such luxuries; those who did were from the few privileged families who came into contact with the Europeans early, and who instinctively recognised the coming trends and were willing to change. In places like Asaba and Ibuza, Ibo towns in Western Nigeria, the inhabitants were very hostile to the arrival of Europeans, so that the few white people who came fled for their lives. The graves of many missionaries and explorers tucked inside the forest bushes tell this tale.

However, Nnaife had been willing to try out this new venture. He did not mind being a grass-cutter, because he knew that one day he would be lucky: he would give the proper handshake to the right clerk who would push his papers in the office for him to be transferred from grass-cutting to employment in the workshops. This was one of the reasons why he still some-times attended church, for most of the preachers and lay-readers were clerks from the railway, and one of them called Okafor had even promised to see to his papers, after Nnaife had given him the appropriate 'dash' of five pounds. Occasionally Nnaife would see this Okafor and shout, 'Good morning, sah!' and the other would grunt his reply; no one expected a 'big man' to be too familiar with such subordinates as labourers and grass-cutters.

There were about twelve of them in his group, and they had devised a way of working harmoniously with one another. One person in turn would be the look-out, watching to see when the head man approached. The others would cut the grass at a leisurely pace, for they had a saying, 'Na government work, ino dey finish': it is government work, it can never come to an end. They justified their slowness by saying, 'If we finish all the work, what will our children do? So we had better take our time.' In the railway compound at Yaba, Lagos, the grass-cutters did not need to worry themselves about what they would do the following day because before a week was out the grass would spring again ready to be cut.

They therefore seemed to be going round in circles, ending up where they began. After a while, one got used to this type of job. Not only did Nnaife get used to the routine, he would have preferred to go on working this way, but for the occasional lack of money. He had become so accustomed to being outside that he feared going to work in the foundry in such a hot temperature that he would have to work almost naked, as he had seen some of his friends do.

On the morning after the problems with his wives, he sat down with his colleagues under the cashew tree, none of them much in a hurry to start their daily work. Nnaife had not brought any food for his breakfast and the others knew why.

'Are your women still on strike?' asked one skinny man by the name of Ibekwe.

The others laughed and so did Nnaife, helping himself to Ibekwe's garri and some dried fish from another person. They all shared their food, so they did not mind him taking part of their provisions.

'No,' said Nnaife in between mouthfuls. 'The shop steward came to me just by the road there, to say that she is repentant and that she admits she was in the wrong.'

The others laughed again. 'You mean they have given up so soon?'

Nnaife shook his head. 'I don't think the other one has. The senior one is a trader, and she knew that if she didn't do something the family – with the exception of myself, of course – would end up eating all her profits.'

'That's why it's good to encourage women to trade, so that they know the value of money. What did you say to her?'

'I didn't say much. You see, I suspect she is expecting another child, judging from the way she is behaving. She is usually a very good woman. She comes from a big household.'

'Pity she could not bring her household here to help you cut

159

the grass,' put in another worker as he got up to look out for the head man. He gave the sign that the boss was on his way, so the others set about swinging their cutlasses in the air, leaving their half-eaten food under the tree, and started to sing as they worked. One man would clear his throat and start a song and the others would answer in the call-and-response pattern typical of African music. Their cutlasses would swing in the air during the call and would land with a swish on the grass towards the end of the refrain. Watching them work, and the rise and fall of cutlasses, was an entertainment in itself. One enthusiastic worker would sometimes stop cutting for a moment or two to do a solo dance before going back to his work. Of course when the head man went away they soon stopped to get their breath back.

During that afternoon, they noticed that there were army trucks coming into the yard. They wondered what was going on though they could not stop work to stare very long. They saw European officers with formidable moustaches, looking strong and wicked, and there were the tall Hausa soldiers with their truncheons who were known locally as Korofos, army policemen. This latter group was very feared. Their methods of searching for deserters were well known. Many young Nigerian men thought it would be fun to join up, especially after going to the Labour Office day in, day out, and having their efforts at finding jobs thwarted, and some found out too late that the rigours of army life were not for them and would run home to their mothers. These army policemen left no stone unturned to locate such a deserter. Perhaps part of the reason they were feared was that few people in the south of Nigeria understood their language; some said they spoke Hausa, some that they spoke a kind of language called 'Munshi'. But whatever they spoke, there was no doubt that they were much taller than the average southerner: most of them were at least six feet three inches tall and many were much more than that. On this day in the railway yard the Korofos were parading up and down as if in search of something. They watched the grass-cutters singing but showed no reaction. The European officers looked beyond them as if they did not exist, just as adults might look indulgently at children, shrug their shoulders and say, 'Let them have their fun.'

There was the usual stampede when the whistle blew and it was time to wash and go home. Some of those who moved fast were already on the bridge over the railway line. Nnaife wished his friends good night and was on the verge of joining the crowd that had just reached the bridge when from all corners came the Korofos swinging their truncheons in the air. A European officer stood behind them saying something to the Korofos. It was not clear what was happening, but by the look of things it was not anything pleasant. Many of the workers ran back into their workshops, others ran out into the open street.

Up went the truncheons and the Korofos were giving orders: 'From 'ere to 'ere! Gwo, gwo into the lorry – gwo, gwo!'

Men screamed like women as some of them were caught. Nnaife was one of them. He found himself being pushed and bundled into the tarpaulin-covered army lorry.

'Why? Why?' workers asked each other. Nobody had an answer.

Nnaife saw a few of the men try to make an escape, but they only felt heavy truncheon blows landing on their shoulders, and their squeals of pain warned the others to stay put and be good 'boys'.

'We don't have slavery any more, so why should grown men be captured in broad daylight?' Nnaife wondered. He was too stunned to think of his family; all that went through his mind was the unfairness of it. He was so preoccupied with this that he could not make out if they were going to Ikoyi barracks on the island or the ones in Apapa or even the ones he had seen so often at Igbobi in Yaba. He was hungry, he was shocked and he was angry. How could one resist against men armed with heavy sticks and guns?

They were ushered into an open field and their names were taken. They were all told to have something to eat and that an officer was coming to talk to them. Nnaife was reluctant at first but seeing others eating he too ate, telling himself that at least the problem of hunger was solved, so that when they let them go he would have enough strength to walk home. He became really alarmed when, after the food, a medical doctor came to examine them one by one. Nnaife knew then that he was done for. It was at that moment that he looked round and saw that his fellow worker Ibekwe was there, looking as stunned as he was. They communicated with each other through looks; there was little they could do but wait and see. The doctor, an Indian, knocked at Nnaife's chest, peered into his throat and ears, before pronouncing him 'all right', that much Nnaife heard. All right for what? He was about to turn round and ask, but a Korofo pushed him along to make room for another man who came in stripped to the waist like himself.

In the corridor where they were asked to wait, most of them had subsided into silence, their minds busy as clocks and their eyes watchful. Soon the medical was over. Some people were called, and Nnaife never saw them again. He and Ibekwe and about thirty others remained, whereas sixty or so of them had been packed into the lorry.

In another room they were eventually told why they had been so enlisted. They were to join the army.

'Army!'

A few men had the courage to shout abuse; others joined in, and an officer with a moustache allowed them to go as mad as they could. After a while, during which time some men wept with tears pouring shamelessly from their eyes, he demanded silence. Later they were told that their wives and relatives would be well cared for. When asked about his next of kin, Nnaife gave the name of his wife Nnu Ego. He was told that the large sum of twenty pounds would be paid to her, and that she would be sent similar amounts from time to time. After recovering from the initial shock of his wife and family getting rich through his going to fight for the white man, Nnaife wanted to know how often this payment would be made. He was informed that it would be about two to four times in the year. They were assured that they would not be serving any longer than one year, since the enemy was on the point of being annihilated. More importantly, they were told, when they returned they would all be promoted in their places of work. Nnaife, for example, would move into the workshop and be apprenticed to a trade, on a higher income.

After all these promises, the men started to think very carefully. This was a chance to pull their families out of the kind of life they had been living; it had never occurred to them before that this was poverty. Why, did not most people live the same way? Anyway, going into the army was bound to raise the standard of living of all of them. Nnaife reckoned that through his taking the plunge his sons Oshia and Adim would be well educated. So also would his brother's three sons at home in Ibuza benefit. Nnaife made up his mind that he must risk it. They were given pen and paper to write to their dependents telling them the best way to spend the money, and since many of the men could not write this was done for them by black officers who had been employed for the purpose.

Nnaife later saw Ibekwe with his head shaved, and wearing a new uniform. He told Nnaife that he had asked his wife (he only had one) to go home to their village and wait for him there. His parents would take charge of his income. His children were very young and would not be starting school until their father returned. After all, they were going to be away for only a year. Nnaife agreed that Ibekwe had made the right decision.

Nnaife himself would rather Nnu Ego stayed in Lagos and continued with her trade and looking after the household as best she could. He said she must send two pounds to Ibuza to pay the year's school fees for the senior Owulum's sons at the Catholic school there; the fees were four shillings a term so that would be sufficient. She should follow the same procedure when she received the next payment, but he cautioned her to regard each payment as the last she would ever get; he did not know where they were going, and he did not know whether he would come back alive. Nnu Ego should give five pounds to her co-wife Adaku for her to use to start a trade. The balance of the money they should use to feed their children and pay the rent. Nnu Ego should see to it that Oshia's and Adim's school fees were paid on time.

He convinced himself that he was doing the right thing. He had no choice, anyway. As a grass-cutter, his income had only been five pounds a month. He had given his wives three pounds of it for food, sent ten shillings to his relatives back home, and paid ten shillings towards his *esusu*, a kind of savings among friends whereby each member of the group collected contributions in turn. Whatever was left Nnaife spent on himself. Things were cheap in those days; several men could get drunk on a keg of palm wine costing just sixpence. Oshia and his brother accounted for eight shillings every three months at school. So on the whole they had been quite satisfied with his small income, until this upheaval. He was quite sure that his wife Nnu Ego would be able to manage.

The following morning Nnu Ego and Adaku were woken by Ubani. He looked sad and Nnu Ego was certain that something terrible had happened.

'Is Nnaife dead?' she asked, steeling herself for the worst.

'No, he is not dead. He is alive, only they have forced him to join the army.'

'The army!' the two women echoed, not believing what they heard.

'How can they force a person to join the army?' was Nnu Ego's incredulous question. 'He is a grass-cutter. Oh, my God, what can we do, Ubani? For me to be married to a soldier, a plunderer and killer of children ... Ah, Ubani, can't we do anything?'

Adaku, shocked, began wailing and shouting. 'I don't know if death isn't better than this! Poor Nnaife, why him, why him?'

'There is nothing we can do. The British own us, just like God does, and just like God they are free to take any of us when they wish.' In those days things were such that Nigerians had no voice. No paper would report what had taken place; even if it were reported, how many of those affected could read, and how many could afford to buy a newspaper?

Nnu Ego then gave in to all the suppressed emotion that was inside her. 'How are we going to manage?' she asked Ubani, who though from the east, had become a close friend. 'What are we going to do with all these children? I can't afford to feed us all as well as paying the rent.'

'Your Ibuza people will be meeting this evening and will discuss the matter. You'll have to learn to forget these superstitions about soldiers. Being in the army is like any other job these days. In fact if all goes well with my friend, he will be better off when he returns. He won't be a grass-cutter any more; that was what my boss told me this morning. Please don't give up hope. You will hear from him soon. Well, I must go now. I've brought a bag of scones for the children – they are a sweet European food. I hope they like them.' With that, Ubani left them.

Their room and veranda were soon filled with sympathisers. Even the Yoruba landlord, who was not popular with Nnaife, lamented, 'What type of life do we live when a man with a large family can be abducted in broad daylight?'

'It is unbelievable,' said Mama Abby. 'I have heard of it happening to other people, but never thought it could happen to someone I know. Why can't they fight their own wars? Why drag us innocent Africans into it?'

165

'We have no choice,' the landlord concluded.

In the evening, they were even more dismayed to learn from Nwakusor that newly-recruited soldiers were usually taken out of the country within twenty-four hours. He tried to reassure the women by saying, 'You know, some young farmers nowadays leave Ibuza for the army because life there is more secure, and they learn a trade which will be useful to them in later life. Nnaife will be sending you some money. So it is up to you what you decide to do. Can you two cope with living in this town?'

'Well, I can go back to trading when we get the money. I have only one child at the moment, so it will not be too bad. After the birth of this baby, I can carry on again. But I don't know about my senior wife.'

'Nnu Ego, you'll be better off in Ibuza,' was the unanimous opinion.

'Yes, I think that would be the best thing. People have been telling me about my father's illness. He is very old now and would like to see the boys.'

The news of Nnaife's abduction soon reached Ibuza. Agbadi sent urgent messages to his daughter to come home. He did not want her to stay there and suffer, and moreover he was dying.

'But how can I go without any money, Adaku? You know what worries me too? We don't even know where our husband is, and whether he is alive or dead. I don't know how I would feel if I was asked to kill people who had never offended me. Poor Nnaife, have you ever known anybody so unlucky?' Adaku shook her head.

The letter from Nnaife eventually arrived and Nnu Ego gave it to Mama Abby to read for her. Then she hurried back to their room to tell Adaku the good news.

'Nnaife is alive and well! He's on his way to a place called India, though he does not know where that is. He has sent us some money and I have to go to the post office to collect it. Your share will be five pounds, so after the birth of your baby you can rent a stall in Zabo market and start trading. I won't be able to do anything like that yet. Too many children and my father's poor health. Mama Abby has advised me to put some of my share away in the post office for the time being.'

'Who will look after it there?' Adaku wanted to know.

'The government. Mama Abby says it will even bring in some interest which should pay for the boys' education. He has sent twenty pounds; two pounds is for Adankwo, our senior wife in Ibuza, so apart from your share the rest is mine.'

'Oh, senior wife, you are a rich woman. If he sends any more like that you will be very rich indeed.'

'Have you forgotten that I have all these children to look after? And he says in the letter that we should not count on anything more. Although he will send more whenever possible, he advises us to make the most of what we have, since life is so uncertain.'

Mama Abby left her own domestic tasks and went with Nnu Ego to the post office. There were so many pieces of paper the clerks there required signed, but after a three-hour-long wait the money was finally actually in Nnu Ego's hand and Mama Abby had helped her open a savings account.

By the time Adaku had used her share of Nnaife's money to establish herself at the Zabo market, Nnu Ego knew she could delay her journey home no longer.

'Please, my young wife, if our husband sends any more money, send it to us by anyone coming to Ibuza. We will get it. My father is very ill and I must hurry. I don't want him to go without seeing me and his grandchildren.'

13 A GOOD DAUGHTER

The journey to Ibuza was long and tortuous. Oshia, resourceful though only nine, took it upon himself to look after his family on the way. Because of Nnu Ego's condition and because her husband was a railway employee, they went by train to Oshogbo, and she was accorded the additional comfort of travelling second-class, since Nnaife was serving the king of England somewhere in India. Though why Nnaife should be fighting in India, when people said that England was defending herself against invasion by some people called 'the Germanis', was quite beyond her. She would have to see to it that proper offerings were made for her unfortunate husband, when she reached home, Nnu Ego thought. The trouble with Nnaife was that he no longer believed in anything. She would certainly make sure that a proper shrine was made for him now that he was the head of the Owulum family.

Luckily for Nnu Ego, they arrived at Abu ano market in Ogwashi Ukwu early in the afternoon. Young Ibuza girls came there to sell roasted groundnuts, and one of these girls was the fifteen-year-old daughter of the senior Owulum widow. When she saw and recognised them, she came tearing into the motor park, hugged each of the children and said she was going home straight away to fetch the young men to help them. Noting Nnu Ego's pregnancy, she instructed her not to move an inch until the men arrived. She left her bowls of groundnuts for the children, then dashed into the market to bring them some salted *ukwa* bean cake, which the youngsters ate with great enjoyment. It was moist and soft, unlike the version they knew that, having been sent all the way from Ibuza, was usually quite dry.

'It's tastier than the Lagos kind,' was Oshia's judgement. 'Look, even the twins love this. They don't eat *ukwa* in Lagos.'

'I shall be back soon,' the young girl Ozili promised.

'Is it far to Ibuza?' Oshia wanted to know.

'No, not far. Only five miles,' Ozili replied, dancing into the footpath that formed a hole-like aperture in the thick forest green before Oshia had time to ask if he could go with her. She soon disappeared, as if swallowed up by the vegetation.

Everyone in the market was shouting greetings to them, and before long Nnu Ego had made a wad of some clothes and was sitting down comfortably on it under a shady tree, talking and laughing with some women Oshia had never seen before. Then, with the help of the other women, his mother washed the twins and Adim. Oshia was taken to a nearby stream to bathe and he enjoyed the plunge. The twins soon went to sleep.

Nnaife's people were the first to come. The babies were slung on to the adults' backs and even Oshia, with all his nine years, had a carrier to take him the rest of the way. Their baggage was packed in manageable sizes so that each young man could balance a bundle on his head or shoulder.

When they had trekked for about two miles and were nearing a settlement called Aboh, the young men from Agbadi's household came to join them. It was a large, joyous and noisy group. But Nnu Ego was told that for the past five days her father had been unable to speak, waiting for her before he gave in to death.

When they reached Ibuza, they went first to Owulum's household. The senior wife Adankwo was beside herself with happiness.

'Welcome, my daughter, welcome. Oh, Oshia, you are a man now. And the twins – they are beautiful. We will soon have young men knocking at our doors. Don't they remind you of Ona?' she enthused to everyone.

'I must go and see my dying father –' Nnu Ego began.

'That is so, good daughter. He is not a dying man, though; he died five days ago, but he will not let go completely until he has seen you. So he suffers in silence. I am glad you are here,' Adankwo went on. 'But first you must eat, then we will go with you. You must take the big children with you. Your father will want to touch them. He is just lying there, on the same hearth where they say you were conceived, and staring into space.'

Yet as soon as Nnu Ego entered Nwokocha Agbadi's court-yard, and the glow of the moon fell on her and on the two rather frightened boys with her, her father spoke:

'Ona, Ona, Ona, stop wringing your hands; our daughter is here.'

Nnu Ego let go of her sons, forgot her tiredness. She rushed to her father, who had become so noble yet so unearthly and frail. His hair was completely white and his body emaciated. But his eyes, those lively, keen eyes, still glowed and the bones of his face stood out strongly in defiance of any illness.

'Oh, Father, I did not imagine ... Why did I not come earlier? Look, look at my children, Father. I have sons, and daughters ... the children – oh, Father, Father.'

Agbadi rolled to one side of the goatskin and gave again that low, wicked chuckle his friends knew so well, though now it sounded ghostly. 'Daughter, I would not go before I saw you. I know of your condition. Stand up and let me look at you. Yes ... magnificent. A full woman, full of children. It is well. Ona, I told you it would be well ...'

People looked round about them in fear, knowing that he was hallucinating. Ona, Nnu Ego's mother, perhaps the only woman Agbadi ever loved, had died a long time before and yet he talked to her as if she were there in the courtyard.

His senior wife, now equally old, and weary as a result of the long vigil they had all been keeping, led the two boys away and prepared a place for them to sleep on a mud couch near their mother. After the excitement of the day they very soon dropped off to sleep.

Twice in the night Agbadi woke, telling Nnu Ego scraps of stories about her childhood and then falling asleep again. Nnu Ego lay beside him, her baby kicking furiously inside her so that she had little doubt that she would have the child before its time. When the kicking became too much, she got up; she knew by the glow of early light that dawn was near. She turned and looked at her father. His eyes were closed but he seemed aware that she had moved and said with a smile.

'I shall come again into your house, but this time I shall bring your mother.' He lifted his hand and touched his daughter's bulging stomach. She dared not ask him what he was saying.

Then he said, 'I must hurry. Most of my age-group are over there waiting for me. Even you, Idayi. I only wished to say goodbye to Ona's daughter ...'

As she held his hand it gradually stiffened. And she knew that her father had gone.

'Goodbye, Father, the last of the great hunters. Come again, come to me again and console me for your loss. Goodbye, Father.' Then she let out a loud cry to tell the world that her father, one of the bravest hunters the world had ever seen, the greatest lover, the noblest and kindest of all parents, had gone.

People woke and rushed in, men who had been keeping vigil in the small huts surrounding the compound. Agbadi's sons and their wives, Agbadi's widows all took up the cry. Cannons, prepared weeks before, were fired into the air. Soon the whole of Ibuza and the neighbouring towns as well knew that an important person had left this earth to go to his ancestors.

The mourning and dancing and the wake went on for days. Nnu Ego could not remember how many goats were killed; until an Obi was buried a goat had to be killed every day, and none of Agbadi's sons would have dreamed of burying him before the fifth day. His other daughters came and helped Nnu Ego shave the heads of the widows and dress them in mourning outfits. She felt an exhilaration, and the strange thing was that since her father had died the expected baby had stopped worrying her, and something told her that she was going to have a boy.

With a great deal of dancing and festivities, Obi Nwokocha Agbadi was set up on his Obi stool and sat right there in the grave dug inside his courtyard. The coffin, a sitting coffin, was very long, for the inmate was a tall man. He was dressed in his chief's regalia, his cap and his elephant tusks were placed across his knee, and so were his hunting weapons, his shield, his iron spear and his cutlasses. He sat there as if he were about to get up and speak. Nnu Ego was well satisfied. Her father was buried thus seated, keeping watch on his household.

After the first burial, the physical one, Nnu Ego had to go to her husband's people's house. Being the first and the best loved daughter, she decided to stay in Ibuza for the second burial, which would send her father finally to his ancestors. After this, his widows would be free to be inherited by any members of Agbadi's family that fancied them. Some of the very old wives would not have to cope with new husbands, because their sons and daughters would provide for them.

Weeks later Nnu Ego came into labour. The baby boy she had came into the world at exactly the same time of the dawn as when her father had died. She wanted to call the child after him, but she did not know how to tell Nnaife's people, for fear of being regarded as an overcivilised woman who chose the names of her children by herself, just because her husband was fighting in the war. She need not have worried. One look at the long-bodied, dry-skinned child on the banana leaf and Adankwo the senior Owulum wife, who had been helping at the birth, screamed:

'It's Agbadi! He is back!'

The noise woke all the sleepers, just as Agbadi's death had woken them all in Ogboli only a short while before. People rushed in to say, 'Welcome, Father.'

Then the oldest of Nnu Ego's half-brothers came in and exclaimed: 'Nnamdio!' meaning: 'This is my father.'

'And that will be his name,' said Adankwo. 'Nnamdio.'

There was dancing and jollity until the early morning when it was time for people to go to their farms.

On the day of Agbadi's second burial, Nnu Ego was surrounded by relatives from both families, the Owulums and the Agbadis. A medicine man who had been following them through the whole ceremony said:

'I can see your father now in the land of the dead, busy boasting to his friends what a good daughter you are.'

There are few women who could feel as honoured and fulfilled as Nnu Ego did then. So happy did she look that people remarked to her jokingly, 'You don't seem to miss your husband very much, do you?'

But she did. She constantly wondered what was happening to him, and to her co-wife Adaku who seldom sent news, but who she heard had given birth to another daughter. Nnu Ego knew that people would soon start saying:

'You have already proved you are a good daughter, but a good daughter must also be a good wife.'

173

After seven months had passed since the death of Nwokocha
Agbadi, people were beginning to wonder when Nnu Ego would
go back to Lagos. Surrounded by in-laws, her own family and a
close community, she knew that when the time came for her to
leave Ibuza she was going to be very sorry; yet she knew too that
she should not remain much longer. It was not that she did not
wish to be there waiting for her husband when he returned from
taking part in the war; it was simply that she was reluctant to go
back to a town where conditions were so demanding. Life here
might be unsophisticated and money short but she had few cares.

One clear night, Nnu Ego sat contentedly in front of the hut
she had to herself, enjoying the cool of the evening. Her children
and the other children of the household had been fed, and the
noises they made in their moonlight games reached her now and
again. Baby Nnamdio was in the willing hands of Adankwo, a
strong woman in her early forties – one of those wiry, dependable
women whom people assumed would always be there. On being
close to her one had the impression of a certain toughness; dry as
twigs in talk as in appearance, she said little though by contrast she
laughed a great deal, displaying a set of magnificent teeth with a
tantalising gap in the middle.

Nnu Ego could hear Adankwo coming up to her, with little
Nnamdio balanced astride one of her hips and holding a stool on
the other side. Handing the boy over to his mother, Adankwo said.

'He has been chewing at my breasts all evening; I think he is
just about ready for some real milk now.'

'Oh, Mother,' Nnu Ego addressed her, in the way appropriate to the oldest woman of the Owulum family, 'you are not so
old and dry. Let him suck more strongly and I'm sure you too will
start producing milk for him. I just want to lie here on this sand

and gaze at the moon.'

'My breast-feeding days are over, daughter. Get up and feed your son; he's very hungry. Also we must talk. Get up.' There was an urgency in her voice, mingled with authority.

'I hope all is well in the household,' Nnu Ego said with concern, rocking Nnamdio gently before putting him to her breast.

Adankwo waited until Nnamdio was fully settled at his mother's breast before she spoke, turning her head a little to one side as if afraid of an enemy listening to their words. She began rather abruptly, and from an angle that seemed at first to be unrelated to the topic Nnu Ego had thought she was going to broach.

'Who told you that the dead are not with us? Who told you that they do not see? A good person does not die and go forever; he goes to another world, and may even decide to come back and live his life again. But must one not be good in this world to have that choice?'

Nnamdio gurgled noisily, lifting a plump foot in the air and clutching at his mother's other breast proprietorially. Though the evening was quite bright, Nnu Ego was glad it was not light enough to reveal the alarm on her face. Her heart beat rapidly. Did the woman think that Nnaife might be dead? Had she received news of it from somebody? She told herself not to be foolish. Catastrophic news would not be imparted to her in this way; it would be done in a more theatrical way. She felt guilty at her own suspicions; one would think she wished her husband dead whereas, on the contrary, she dreaded that harm might come to him.

If Adankwo had been glib of speech she might quickly have dissipated Nnu Ego's anxiety but, apart from the fact that she was a woman of few words, she had an unfortunate way of allowing long silences between her utterances.

'You haven't answered my questions,' she pointed out after a minute or so.

175

'I would give you an answer if I could, but I don't understand what you mean,' Nnu Ego said.

'I mean your father.' Adankwo paused. Then she rapidly went on, like someone who had rehearsed what she was going to say, being even exuberant in her exposition:

'You remember the night your father was dying, when he said he saw your mother? Remember he was telling Ona, who died long ago, that you had arrived from Lagos? Well, your father was a good man. He saw your mother, and he was going to the woman he loved, the woman he had missed all those years in death. But we all knew that your father died in the actual sense of the word about five days before you arrived.'

'I have heard this said many times, but how can it be possible?'

'People die or should die gradually, familiarising themselves with their loved ones on the other side step by step. Your father, however, kept coming back, waiting for you. He kept asking people, "What will I tell my Ona if she asks me how our only daughter is? How could I tell her that I have not seen our child for the past ten years? No, I must see her. I must hang on." And he lay there suffering in silence. Would it then be right for you to offend such a father?'

'Offend him? But how am I offending him?'

'Well, I'll tell you one thing: you're not doing him justice by backing away from the responsibility he entrusted you with. He knew your roots are deep here, that was why he promised to come back to you – yes, I was there in the shadows of the courtyard. We all heard every word.'

'But what responsibility did he leave me that I have neglected?'

'Don't you see, Nnu Ego, daughter of Agbadi? Can't you see that you are running away from the position your *chi* has given you and leaving it for a woman your husband inherited from his

176

brother, a woman whom we here all know to be very ambitious, a woman who has not even borne a son for this family? And you, you have deep roots ... What do you think you are doing? You want to walk with land. You cannot. You have rooted in this Owulum family. You are the senior wife of your husband; you are like a male friend to him. Your place is at his side, to supervise his younger wife. Have you ever heard of a complete woman without a husband? You have done your duty to your father, a man with such nobility of spirit it defied explanation. Now it is to your husband that you should go.'

'But,' Nnu Ego began to protest, 'he is still fighting in the war. I have not neglected him as such.'

'Suppose he has hurried home to see you, to see the new man-child you have borne him, only to be met by Adaku and her whines and ambitions? Do you think that clever thing would put in a good word for you? Nnaife would jump to the conclusion that as soon as he left you preferred to go to your people.'

'I haven't stayed with my people, everybody knows that. I stayed here with his family.'

'That is true, my daughter, but are you there to tell him so? Suppose Adaku took all the gifts he brought from overseas, including money? Don't forget that she is desperate for a son and you have three already. You should be there to see that whatever he brings back is not wasted. You are the mother of the men-children that made him into a man. If Adaku dies today, her people, not her husband's, will come for her body. It is not so with you.'

'What do you think I should do with Oshia? He has settled down so well to being a farmer as well as a schoolboy. He loves the life here.'

'That is true,' replied Adankwo, thoughtfully. 'But there is something new coming to our land. Have you noticed it? We as a family don't all have to live and be brought up in the same place. Let him be trained in Lagos where he was born. He will be able to bring that culture back here to enrich our own. In a few years, he will be able to start looking after you materially. Oshia is now ten. My sons were bringing in their own yams at the age of fifteen. So you don't have long to wait.' She paused as if to gather her thoughts. 'But I would have failed as a mother if I hadn't been here to see that their lands were secure, otherwise where would my sons have built their huts? You buried your father seven months ago. That is a long enough time. You must go back and save your children's inheritance.'

'We haven't got much in Lagos that we can call our own, though. I had to scrape and make do all the time. Even the room we live in is rented.'

'How do you know what you might acquire in the future? How do you know what Nnaife will be bringing back from the war? Things will go well with him, because I have made many sacrifices for his protection. I don't want all to go to that ambitious young woman Adaku. I know her: she was my husband's last wife ... So you must start getting ready tomorrow. And if you are ever in a bad patch with the boys' education, don't forget that girls grow very quickly; the twins' bride prices will help out. But Nnaife would be back by then. Go, and save your sons' inheritance.'

When she arrived back in Lagos, Nnu Ego could not believe her eyes. It was as if she had been away nine years, not months. Things had become doubly expensive and this annoyed her a great deal. Their rent had gone up to seven shillings a month, a measure of garri cost twice what it used to, some common foodstuffs were quite unavailable. And to her dismay she found that Adankwo was right about Adaku. Nnaife had been back on a short visit only three weeks before.

'But why didn't you send a message home?' Nnu Ego asked aggrievedly. 'We would have rushed back to see him. I would have liked to show him his new son.'

'He didn't stay long, senior wife. He was happy that you were in Ibuza, as that was saving him money. He left you five pounds. I was going to send it to you as soon as I knew of anyone going home, but as you can see I've been very busy.'

'Yes, I can see you have been busy making money. Look at all your wares, look at your stalls. I'm sure Nnaife's money went into building your trade.'

'That is not true, senior wife. I didn't ask you to go home in the first place. You insisted on it, so don't blame me if you've lost your foothold in Lagos. Here is your five pounds. I didn't use it for my business, as you seem to think.'

'I see that you are laughing at me. Yes, Adaku, you can afford to make fun of me. You may think you're right, but I'm telling you that you are wrong. Whereas you chose money and nice clothes, I have chosen my children; but you must remember that wealth has always been in my family. I am poor only in Lagos. Go to Ibuza and see how rich I am in people – friends, relatives, in-laws.'

'I don't know what you want me to do, senior wife. There's nothing to stop you going back to your stalls in front of the house, your cigarette stalls ...' Adaku added with a suppressed giggle, knowing perfectly well that neighbours had taken advantage of Nnu Ego's absence and ruined that business for her.

There were four other wooden kiosks where previously hers had been alone. One of the landlord's wives had even started selling things in front of the house. Knowing she could not compete, Nnu Ego was at her wits' end. To get a market stall was out of the question; it had become so costly that if she paid for one with the little money left there would be nothing to spend on stocking the stall. So she took up selling firewood. This did not require much capital, simply a great deal of energy. One had to carry the wood from the waterside, break it into pieces with an axe, then tie the pieces together into bundles for sale. Many other women found it too tiring.

Though Nnu Ego tried to go back to all of them eating together, herself and her children with Adaku and her two girls, as before, she saw that it would no longer work. Adaku was now very rich. She had only two daughters to feed; she talked of sending them to private lessons to learn their alphabet though she had not actually done so yet, nor were they attending any school. Adaku's stall in Zabo market was stacked high with beans, pepper, dried fish, egusi and spicy foodstuffs. She would stay away all day at market, coming in late at night, so there was no point in Nnu Ego waiting for her; nor did Adaku herself ask for food when she came back, so presumably she and her children ate in the market.

This was a life Nnu Ego did not know how to cope with. She felt adrift, as it were on an open sea. No physical help came from friends, for they were all too busy making their own money, and she was always tied down at home with Nnamdio and the twins. She paid few visits to people, not wanting them to think she came to their houses for food. She stopped going to most of the family meetings; one needed to be in fashion to keep in touch. Adaku would attend the gatherings and come and report back to her what had been discussed. Nnu Ego accepted her lot, taking comfort in the fact that one day her boys would be men. But to be so reduced in status as to be almost a maid to a junior wife, and an inherited junior wife at that, dampened her spirit.

When Nnaife had gone to Fernando Po at least she had been by herself. It was one thing to be poor, it was another to be seen to be poor. If only, if only Adaku had taken herself somewhere else! Nor could Nnu Ego go back to Ibuza, not after the talk Adankwo had given her. Apart from the fact that she would look ridiculous, she would be regarded as an ungrateful person, disregarding the heart-to-heart talk from Adankwo who was known for her taciturnity. No, she decided, she would have to grit her teeth and carry on as bravely as possible; everything would be just fine when the children grew up.

Nnu Ego was like those not-so-well-informed Christians who, promised the Kingdom of Heaven, believed that it was literally just round the corner and that Jesus Christ was coming on the very morrow. Many of them would hardly contribute anything to this world, reasoning, 'What is the use? Christ will come soon.' They became so insulated in their beliefs that not only would they have little to do with ordinary sinners, people going about their daily work, they even pitied them and in many cases looked down on them because the Kingdom of God was not for the likes of them. Maybe this was a protective mechanism devised to save them from realities too painful to accept.

As the months passed, Nnu Ego began to act in this way. She did everything she could to make Adaku jealous of her sons. She looked for every opportunity to call the names of her children in full, telling herself she was having her own back. Minor quarrels started between the two women, and Ubani, Nwakusor and their other friends were usually called in to settle the disputes.

It was June and very wet. The amount of rain that fell at that time of year took some getting used to. It came so unexpectedly that day that Nnu Ego was annoyed. True, there had been the thick clouds heralding the rains' arrival, but they had appeared so suddenly that before she was able to adjust her plans for later that afternoon it started to pour with torrents of water being released. She had been up early and had enough firewood for the rest of the week; she calculated that she would have enough for her own cooking and still be able to make a little profit selling the rest, enough to buy the children beans for breakfast. She and the babies would sit outside beside the bread and other groceries she sold at her kiosk in front of the house; Oshia would go and hawk soap, cigarettes, matches and candles, while his brother Adim would sell the roasted groundnuts she was preparing. She was just emerging from the kitchen with the steaming groundnuts when the rain started. Now what was she going to do? If they were kept a day the

181

groundnuts would lose their freshness, and she would not dream of sending Oshia out in this weather. People who knew she sold firewood might come in to ask for some, but still she was going to lose a great deal of profit on account of this rain. With her desperate financial situation she could not afford to lose even half a day's custom. She paced up and down the narrow gap between the beds in their room. She could hear the shrieks of delight from the children as they ran in and out of the rain, enjoying its coolness after the oppressive heat that invariably preceded such downpours. 'What am I going to do?' she murmured, near tears. 'All I have is the five pounds Mama Abby advised me to save two years ago. If I use that now, how will Oshia continue his schooling, and what will happen to Adim? Little Nnamdio is growing, too. Oh, this war, this war ... nobody tells you anything. No one knows where Nnaife is. Maybe in India, maybe in Heaven or even in the north of Nigeria, how do I know?'

'Mother, Mother!' shouted Taiwo, one of her twin girls. 'There is a visitor. Come, Mother. She wants to come in.'

A visitor in this weather? The child must have got it wrong. Who in their right senses would be calling on her now? All the same, she might as well go and see for herself.

Outside the door stood a woman from Ibuza, Igbonoba's wife. She was related to Adaku and like Adaku was doing very well in her business. This woman had the added good fortune to marry an older man who had not qualified to be sent to war, and her husband was one of Ibuza's fairly prosperous people. What was more, this woman, unlike Adaku, had many children, boys as well as girls – in short she had everything any woman could want.

And look at her, Nnu Ego thought angrily, *look at the expensive shoes she is wearing, look at that headtie, and even a gold chain – all this just to come and see her relative Adaku, and in this rain! God, the cost of that headtie! Whatever she paid for it would feed me and the children for a whole month. And she is the daughter of a nobody! Yet look at me, the daughter of a well-known chief, reduced to this...*

'The rain is very heavy – won't you ask me to come in? Your veranda is blocked up with firewood and your kiosk,' Igbonoba's wife said, half in joke and half in anger. Her eyes were following Nnu Ego's and she was able partially to guess her thoughts. Adaku had said she would be home early that day; maybe the rain had detained her. Igbonoba's wife intended to wait for her.

Nnu Ego was still staring at her with glazed eyes. So people still lived ostentatiously like this. Yes, she had seen things in the market like this colourful umbrella, though she had never thought they could be within the means of Ibuza women. Oh, what had she done to deserve being punished like this? She could not stand it, no, she could not! She felt like screaming, but she covered her mouth tightly with her hand.

'Well, if you're going to stand there and stare at me, I'll just step into your veranda and wait for my cousin Adaku.' The woman mounted the two cement steps and looked round for a chair. There was none. So she started to shake the water from her expensive outfit.

Nnu Ego watched her, her mouth still covered, her body shaking.

The woman looked up and asked, 'Are you all right, Nnaife's wife? Why do you look at me like that? I am not your enemy, eh? Why are you looking at me like that, as if you don't want to see me? I have come all the way from Obalende, the other side of Lagos island, and there was no word of welcome from you – '

'Shut up! Shut up and go away! You can't stand here. My baby is crying – go away!' Nnu Ego's voice was so loud that it was more thunderous than the rain. 'Come in, children, it's raining.' The little ones came in and Nnu Ego banged the door shut.

Igbonoba's wife opened and shut her mouth in wonder. She had never in all her life seen such anti-social behaviour. She had never been so insulted. What was the matter with the woman? She

183

acted as if her nerves were taut and almost at breaking point. To shout back at Nnu Ego would be pointless; the rain was howling its protest anyway, and her voice would only be drowned like everything else. If her husband Igbonoba was told this, he would raise hell. As she was struggling to recover from her shock, she heard Nnu Ego and the children singing with forced happiness, and thought: 'Thank goodness I have my own children, otherwise I would jump to the conclusion she was putting on this show of motherhood to make me jealous.' She stood there, waiting both for the rain to lessen and for Adaku, whom she knew would be worried about her.

Meanwhile Adaku grew tired of waiting for the rain to stop, for it seemed determined to go on all afternoon. She and her two little girls chose to brave it and, with an old army tarpaulin they had picked up in the market serving as protection, they ran home.

Igbonoba's wife's eyes were still fixed on the slammed door when she heard the footsteps of Adaku and her two laughing daughters. They were soaked to the skin, because the tarpaulin was only large enough to partly cover their heads.

'I knew you'd be here waiting for me,' panted Adaku as they jumped on to the veranda, 'that's why we had to brave it. It's so heavy, this rain, that it gives one a headache.'

'I know,' replied her cousin. 'Some of the drops hit you like small pebbles; and the suddenness of it! I thought it had to stop soon, since it started almost unannounced.'

'Well, we are all here safe and sound,' said Adaku. 'Welcome. I can see that you have just arrived too. I would hate myself if you had had to wait long. Anyway, my senior is inside – can you hear her singing? She is so devoted to her children.' This was said with a conspiratorial wink.

Adaku opened the door and they all squeezed into the little space of the room. Nnu Ego welcomed them mildly, and Igbonoba's wife noted that she behaved as though everything was perfectly above board. Should she or should she not let Adaku know what had happened? She decided against it. It would cause nothing but trouble and she would be called to be a witness. She did not relish the thought.

Few things are as bad as a guilty conscience. Nnu Ego scuttled round their amused visitor, pretending she had not met her before, and brought out some kolanut with which to serve her. Adaku wondered a little at her behaviour, for her co-wife normally showed only minimal interest in her visitors. She must like Igbonoba's wife very much, Adaku concluded. Nnu Ego averted her eyes, but Igbonoba's wife knew that her actions were begging her, appealing to her for forgiveness. The visitor was sorry for her. Fancy a senior wife lowering herself to such a level. But she said nothing. Nnu Ego realised that socially she had carried her obsession a bit too far; she could only hope this woman would not repeat the story to anybody.

Adaku, however, heard of it three days later, not from Igbonoba's wife nor from Nnu Ego but from her son little Adim. Adaku was too incensed to say a word to Nnu Ego; she simply dashed out to summon their kinsman Nwakusor, the man who had rescued Nnu Ego from death many years before, and she also invited their good friend Ubani. The case was stated to them, but instead of laying the whole blame on Nnu Ego, they made Adaku feel that since she had no son for the family she had no right to complain about her senior's conduct.

'Don't you know that according to the custom of our people you, Adaku, the daughter of whoever you are, are committing an unforgivable sin?' Nwakusor reminded her. 'Our life starts from immortality and ends in immortality. If Nnaife had been married to only you, you would have ended his life on this round of his visiting earth. I know you have children, but they are girls, who in a few years' time will go and help build another man's immortality. The only woman who is immortalising your husband you make unhappy with your fine clothes and lucrative business. If I were in your shoes, I should go home and consult my *chi* to find out why male offspring have been denied me. But instead, here you are quarrelling about your visitor. Why did she have to dress up so extravagantly, anyway, and during the week for that matter?'

Though Ibuza men admired a hard-working and rich woman, her life was nothing if she left no male children behind when she had gone to inherit the wealth, children who were her own flesh and blood. What was the point of piling up wealth when there was nobody to leave it for?

Nwakusor had a word of caution for Nnu Ego. She must guard her reputation. Children were all very well, but they would only enjoy and glory in their parents if those parents had made sure to leave a good, clean name behind them. She should never let it be repeated that the daughter of Nwokocha Agbadi by his eternal sweetheart Ona did not know the art of courtesy to a visitor.

'Don't you realise that the house belongs to you, so why should you feel reluctant to welcome a caller, and an Ibuza woman for that matter?' Nwakusor asked.

Nnu Ego could not say that it was because the woman looked so well off, and because Adaku had been parading her own wealth ever since Nnu Ego arrived back from Ibuza. So she kept quiet, only murmuring: 'This Lagos, it makes me forget my position sometimes. It will not happen again, I promise.'

'Well, you must pay a fine of a keg of palm wine and a tin of cigarettes.'

Adaku stood looking on and saw that she was completely ignored. They did not ask Nnu Ego to apologise to her, and for a time it looked as if they had even forgotten it had been she who invited them to settle the case in the first place. The message was clear: she was only a lodger, her position in Nnaife Owulum's household had not been ratified. Nor did the fact that she was making a lot of money particularly endear her to them. She got the message.

As soon as the men went, Nnu Ego crawled into her bed, which she had now covered with hand-spun mats as she had no money for bed-sheets. Her feelings were mixed, and she wanted to weep, for what she did not know. She felt sorry for Adaku, and the men's hurtful treatment of her, but would Adaku understand if she should tell her so? She also felt relief, knowing that her own fate could so easily have been like Adaku's. Yet all because she was the mother of three sons, she was supposed to be happy in her poverty, in her nail-biting agony, in her churning stomach, in her rags, in her cramped room ... Oh, it was a confusing world. As pangs of hunger gripped the sides of her stomach she shifted slightly, hoping by so doing to lessen her urge to consume a horse. She had eaten very little since morning. The peace-makers had left her a couple of pennies – a fraction of what it cost her to pay her fine of palm wine and cigarettes – which she was keeping to buy the boys a decent breakfast before they went to school in the morning.

She heard Adaku sniffing. So close were their beds that even though they were separated by a curtain one could hear the person in the other bed breathe. Nnu Ego was overwhelmed with pity for Adaku, but how could she express it? The men had been unfair in their judgement. She, Nnu Ego, had been wrong all the way, but of course they had made it seem that she was innocent just because she was the mother of sons. Men were so clever. By admonishing her and advising her to live up to her status as senior wife, they made it sound such an enviable position, worth any woman's while to fight for. She did not care. She spoke to Adaku.

'I am sorry. Maybe you should not have called the men.'

There was a short silence, then Adaku said, 'I am glad I did. I've got what I asked for, I suppose. They have told me what you have been trying to tell me since you returned from Ibuza. I'm thankful to them for doing it.'

'Then what are you going to do, Adaku?'

'What you have been wanting me to do. Leave this stinking

room. Why should I put up with all this any longer? Nnaife does not want me, nor did his people, so why stay? When he came back on leave, he was angry with me for your going home to bury your father. He was hurt to think that you rated your father higher than him; and as for me, he accused me of not stopping you. So he came to my bed only as a second choice. I didn't mind, because all I wanted from him was a male child. But I didn't get pregnant. And you came back only a few days afterwards with so many children of his. I could hardly bear it. And now these men come this evening to rub it all in, as if I didn't know already.'

She sighed. 'Everybody accuses me of making money all the time. What else is there for me to do? I will spend the money I have in giving my girls a good start in life. They shall stop going to the market with me. I shall see that they get enrolled in a good school. I think that will benefit them in the future. Many rich Yoruba families send their daughters to school these days; I shall do the same with mine. Nnaife is not going to send them away to any husband before they are ready. I will see to that! I'm leaving this stuffy room tomorrow, senior wife.'

'To go and worship your *chi*?'

'My *chi* be damned! I am going to be a prostitute. Damn my *chi*!' she added again fiercely.

Nnu Ego could not believe her ears. 'Do you know what you are saying, Adaku? The *chi*, your personal god, that gave you life – '

'I don't care for the life he or she gave me. I'm leaving here tomorrow with my girls. I am not going to Ibuza. I am going to live with those women in Montgomery Road. Yes, I'm going to join them, to make some of our men who return from the fighting happy.'

'Stop! Stop!' Nnu Ego shouted. 'Don't forget that we have young girls sleeping in this room and don't you dare insult me by saying such things in my hearing. Which women are you talking about? You surely can't mean you are going to be that kind of woman ...? You can't. What of your daughters? No Ibuza man will marry girls brought up by a prostitute.'

'I am sorry if I insulted you, but you asked me, remember? As for my daughters, they will have to take their own chances in this world. I am not prepared to stay here and be turned into a mad woman, just because I have no sons. The way they go on about it one would think I know where sons are made and have been neglectful about taking one for my husband. One would think I'd never had one before. People forget that. Well, if my daughters can't forgive me when they grow up, that will be too bad. I'm going to be thrown away when I'm dead, in any case, whereas people like you, senior wife, have formed roots, as they say: you will be properly buried in Nnaife's compound.'

Nnu Ego was silent. Should she blame herself? Had she driven Adaku to take this step? No, it must always have been in the woman to make this sort of move. Even Adankwo in Ibuza had warned of Adaku's ambitiousness. She could stay until Nnaife returned if she wanted to.

Nnu Ego sighed sadly. 'I think you are making a mistake, Adaku. Besides you could have a son when our husband returns.'

'Maybe you're right again, my senior. Yet the more I think about it the more I realise that we women set impossible standards for ourselves. That we make life intolerable for one another. I cannot live up to your standards, senior wife. So I have to set my own.'

'May your *chi* be your guide, Adaku,' Nnu Ego whispered almost inaudibly as she crawled further into the urine-stained mats on her bug-ridden bed, enjoying the knowledge of her motherhood.

The news that Adaku had abdicated her responsibility and become a public woman spread throughout Lagos like wildfire. Ibuza men gloried in the unfaithfulness of women: 'Leave them for ten minutes, they turn into something else.' Many people put the blame on Lagos itself; they said it was a fast town which could corrupt the most innocent of girls. Women shuddered at such a horrible eventuality. They came to Nnu Ego to hear the last detail of it. Most were surprised when she said that there had been no quarrel, that Adaku had simply decided to leave.

'Do you know,' stated one of these Ibuza women visitors, 'I could understand you leaving Nnaife and leaving all his children to him, but not Adaku. Her god really blessed her in this town. I don't see what else she wants.'

Nnu Ego agreed with them, but in her heart she still wondered whether there was anything she could do. The longer she left it, the more impossible it would become. She made attempts to warn Adaku of what people were saying, but her efforts failed. The last time she had seen her at her market stall, she had once more pleaded with her, though even as she did she knew it was a hopeless venture. On that very day Adaku was living up to the meaning of her name: 'the daughter of wealth'. She told Nnu Ego that she was giving up selling beans and peppers, she was buying a larger stall on which she would have abada material for lappas. She smiled to see the wonder and surprise on Nnu Ego's face. She would have passed on her former stall to Nnu Ego, she said, but she was leasing it to someone who would pay her yearly.

'That will take care of my rent, at least,' she finished, laughing.

'You mean you won't have to depend on men friends to do anything for you?'

'No,' she replied. 'I want to be a dignified single woman. I shall work to educate my daughters, though I shall not do so without male companionship.' She laughed again. 'They do have their uses.'

Nnu Ego noticed that Adaku was better dressed – not that she wore anything new, but she put on her good clothes even on ordinary market days. She laughed a lot now; Nnu Ego had never known her to have such a sense of humour. Adaku said she had a separate room of her own, much bigger than the one they had all shared before. Nnu Ego was curious to see it, and only an exertion of will stopped her from saying, 'I'd like to come and visit your new home.' What would people say?

After that she stopped going to Adaku in the market, but not before she had accepted all the edibles from Adaku's old stall. She bought the dry fish cheaply and they were well fed for a month or so. Why should she deceive herself? The woman was better off as she was; she would only be socially snubbed. Nnu Ego said to herself, 'I may not be snubbed, but can I keep it up? I have no money to buy food, let alone abadas in which to attend meetings and church.'

Nnu Ego had scraped and saved to pay the last two terms' school fees for Oshia and Adim, and she congratulated herself on having managed when people began saying that the war was over, that the enemy, whoever he was, had killed himself. That meant Nnaife would be back soon, she thought delightedly. She went to the post office by herself, not wanting to worry Mama Abby who by then had moved with her son into a bigger and grander apartment, and took out three of the five pounds she had there. They said that interest of a whole pound had been added, not that the money was anyway worth what it had been when she had put it in years previously; nevertheless she felt like someone who had inherited a fortune. She rushed to the market and bought a piece of real meat so that she could cook a proper meal for herself and

191

the children. Oshia was so overjoyed that he piled several spoon-fuls of the rice into the empty tomato purée tins his mother had used making the stew and took them to show magnanimously to his friends. 'It's like Christmas,' he boasted to his schoolmates the next day. 'You see, we've won the war. My father and all the other soldiers have killed the enemy. Hitler is his name.'

It was true that the war was over, and talk was going round that those of the soldiers who were still alive would be coming back. It was not known when, and Nnu Ego had no way of knowing if Nnaife was alive. She only trusted her instinct. She was looking forward to Nnaife's return; the work of looking after his large family alone was beginning to wear her down. Recently she was often ill, whether with minor attacks of malaria or tiredness, which she knew was the result of lack of food. She had felt so certain her husband was alive and about to return that she had spent half her savings, on food, clothing and school fees, and for the following two weeks she walked about with high hopes. Then she started to worry.

Suppose Nnaife did not return before the boys' school fees were due again? She knew the Methodist Mission would be making their next demand in a week or two, and she had been so much in arrears before that because she had been late with the last quarter's payment Oshia and Adim had to stay away for two whole weeks. She wished Nnaife would make an effort to write and tell them what was going on, though it was a futile wish; although he had learned the rudiments of reading and writing from a fellow worker in Fernando Po, he was not what one could call an educated man. No doubt many soldiers in the army were literate, and Nnaife in his unsureness would not think of asking his associate fighters to write for him; he would rather keep quiet and laugh it off, or play the guitar which he could not do without for long. Other families Nnu Ego knew of heard from their menfolk from time to time; but nothing from Nnaife. It never occurred to him that his

192

people might worry about him; he knew they could get along without him. After all, life was a gamble; one had to keep gambling right from the day one was born. He had signed the form for part of his income to go to Nnu Ego, and when he had come back on leave that time he had made sure the money would not go to Adaku in Lagos. Little did he know that the whole thing had become confused from that time. Nnu Ego was now in Lagos with the children but no money. Adaku, who he had been trying to punish, had left the family fold to strike out successfully on her own. Nnu Ego was left with dying hopes and demanding children.

She called Oshia one morning, after watching him dress for school. It was one of those days when she felt like not pretending any more. The boy was ten, almost eleven. In Ibuza he would have been initiated into manhood. Had he not been a reliable helper for his young cousins on the farm in Ibuza, joining them as he did in the afternoons after school? He might not be able to read properly yet, but he could write his name, and that was more than his father could do at the same age. So even if he had to stop school altogether now, he would still be better equipped for life than his father. Look at all Nnaife's achievements without an education: he had all these children, he was the only Owulum son alive, and he was the one in charge of his brother's family and his own, she thought grimly to herself. If anyone had asked what financial help Nnaife had ever given to these people, she would have countered simply, 'But they bear his name and will carry it to immortality. He sired these children, and that is what a man is for. That he could not feed them was not his fault; he went to the war. They have a mother, don't they?'

'Oshiaju,' she called gently.

He looked up, surprised to see the thoughtful look on his mother's face, and asked casually, 'Is there something you want?'

She smiled. 'No, son, I don't want anything. But my money is finished now. You see, your father the soldier is not back yet, and

I don't know when he will be back. So learn as much as you can from school, because when they demand the next school fees, I don't think I shall be able to pay.'

Oshia looked the image of dejection and cried: 'But I love school, Mother. All my friends are there. Why do I have to stop so many times? Folorunsho and the others don't do that.'

'This is Lagos, Oshia, and we are immigrants here. For Folorunsho it is different. This is their part of the country. They own Lagos. But don't worry, son, your father will not stay in the war forever. He will come home one day, and then you will make it up. You remember what I have been telling you, that you are handsome? Now I know that you are clever as well. You proved it in Ibuza. You did well on the farm and, when you came back here, you caught up with your education as if you had not missed a day. I know you will make it.'

'What of Adim, then? Is he going to stay on?' Oshia asked illogically.

'No, he will leave and like you wait for your father. You both will start private lessons. They are cheaper, only a shilling a month.'

'But the girls go to private lessons. They don't learn anything there.'

'The twins will have to leave and help me in running the house and in my trade. If they are lucky, they too will go to school when your father returns. They don't need to stay long in school – only a year or two.'

So at the beginning of the next term Oshia and his brother Adim attended a private class at Adam Street, where the teacher taught them how to write neatly and do some sums. All the other complicated subjects were forgotten. Oshia knew that the arrangement was nothing compared to a 'real school' but there was nothing he could do about it. He went about looking glum.

Nnu Ego still sold firewood, garri and other foodstuffs. Every morning neighbours could hear her calling: 'Oshia, Adim, twins, wake up and let us go to the waterside!' There she would buy the firewood for the day's sale and they would all carry it home. She normally left Nnamdio with Iyawo Itsekiri. As she looked at the children trooping in front of her with their little bundles of firewood, she used to say, 'Thank you, my *chi*, that they are healthy and strong. One day they will become people.'

At home after lunch, she would sit by her stall and the twin girls will hawk the foodstuffs from street to street in search of buyers. Adim and Oshia would attend their private lessons. In the evening she would count her money, put aside her little profits to go towards the food bill for the next day, and then go to sleep. The same pattern would repeat itself each day.

Kehinde, the quieter and deeper of the twins, took the breakfast bowls to wash one morning and announced to her mother that the sun would be hot again.

'What is so important about that?' Oshia said.

'Well, you know Kehinde, she is very quiet and observant. There must be a reason for saying that.'

'Our ugu vegetables will all dry out, Mother,' came the voice of Kehinde from outside.

'I told you,' Nnu Ego said to Oshia.

They all ran out of their room. If their ugu should all dry out, that would be a great calamity, because Nnu Ego did not buy vegetables. She grew her own and ugu with its large green leaves was a good standby.

'We will have to sell some quickly before it goes yellow,' Kehinde suggested.

'That will be a good idea. But you and your sister will have to water it during the day.'

'The boys can help too,' grumbled Taiwo the other twin, known in the family as the moaner.

'They have to go to their lesson, Taiwo; and stop moaning. You are a girl, you know.'

'I know that, Mother. You remind us all the time.'

Kehinde just laughed and went on washing her bowls.

'Yes, some of them will have to be sold,' Nnu Ego said, more to herself than to anyone else.

Iyawo Itsekiri was passing by at the time and laughed. 'You Ibos, is there nothing on this earth that you won't sell to make money? You would even sell your children if it were possible!'

'Well, it is not possible, and I do not intend selling my children. But I wouldn't mind sending the girls somewhere to learn a trade if I would be given some money for their services.'

'Oh, you can't be that desperate, Nnu Ego. They are only babies.'

'But they are good hawkers,' Nnu Ego said laughing. 'The money I'd get from them would help me in looking after others. Children sent away like that usually learn something, you know, good trade as well. So they would be well equipped to look after themselves in later life.'

'Oh, go away, Nnu Ego. They learn enough of survival from you. They couldn't have a better teacher.'

Maybe Iyawo Itsekiri was right, Nnu Ego thought as she went on patting her precious vegetables and talking to them, begging them not to dry up. She was so far gone in her musings that the call of 'Mother, Mother!' from Kehinde had to be repeated several times before she turned her head.

'What is it now, Kehinde? Have you noticed a hotter sun?'

The little girl ran up to her, and waved a yellow envelope under her mother's nose before Nnu Ego registered any reaction. She woke up and saw a postman mounting his rickety bicycle and steering it away from their compound.

'Oh!' she exclaimed. 'That bicycle reminds me of Nwakusor's.' Her mind was on the verge of reliving that day on the bridge, when Nwakusor had saved her life, but her little girl would not let her.

'Mother, letter, Mother!'

'Yes, letter, le – ' It might be from Nnaife. Yes, it could be. She had seen the type of envelope before; it was the same as the one that arrived four years before when he had first sent them money. Nnaife, Nnaife ... money ...

Now who was there to read it for her? Mama Abby had moved. She could not give it to any Ibuza person; they were too close. After close relatives had been used to seeing one poor, only the most mature ones among them would be able to stomach one being out of poverty. She ran impulsively to the front part of the house, to the landlord Mr Barber who worked at the Railmen's Secretariat. His family had been kind to her, in a distant, not too familiar, neighbourly way. Halfway there, she changed her mind; no, if it was a lot of money they would increase her rent, and the wives would be jealous. It was better that she be patient, settle the children to their different tasks for the day, and then go in search of her old and reliable friend, Abby's mother.

Not until almost lunch time could she get away. She instructed Oshia to sit by the stall, and that made Taiwo demand to know why he should be let off going to the waterside while they had to sell their oranges.

'Look, it's just for this afternoon,' she assured her. 'He will go tomorrow. We have enough wood for today anyway. I'll be back before lesson time.'

Taiwo pouted. 'The boys have the evening off for their stupid lessons, and they're let off from going to fetch the wood that we have to sell to feed us.'

Desperate, Nnu Ego shouted at the wide-eyed children, 'But you are girls! They are boys. You have to sell to put them in a good position in life, so that they will be able to look after the family. When your husbands are nasty to you, they will defend you.'

'Husbands! Nasty!' They started to giggle.

When she arrived at Mama Abby's, she almost wailed to her,

'I've got a letter! Oh, Mama Abby, I think it's from the children's father. I think so.'

Mama Abby was getting on in years, though she was still extremely elegant and well-dressed, and had a look of satisfaction about her which had not been there before. Nnu Ego was surprised to see her surroundings. There were mirrors everywhere, and there was a separate bedroom, so she did not have to make do with one room as before. Her son Abby had really put his mother in wealth. Nnu Ego bit her lip. O God, let some of her own children be like that, so that she would not suffer in old age as well as now.

Mama Abby adjusted a pair of reading glasses on her nose, something she had never had to do before, and Nnu Ego's first impulse was to enquire whether her friend was going blind. She controlled the urge. It must be just another sign of affluence.

'Oh, it's a note from the army barracks in Yaba. They want to know if you are still at the above address or in Ibuza. If you are still here, which you are, I think – ' Mama Abby was trying to be humorous, but she quickly went on when she saw that the woman in front of her was in no mood for jokes – 'if you are here, and if you are Nnu Ego Owulum, they want you to come to the barracks to collect a package.'

'Package? What package would Nnaife send us, from – where was he when he wrote that?'

'He didn't write it,' replied Mama Abby. 'The office here did. It doesn't say where he is. They just want to know whether you are in Lagos, and if so they want you to go to the army barracks. You know where it is? It's not far.'

Fear gripped Nnu Ego. Maybe Nnaife was dead long ago, killed by bombs, and his flesh scattered over many seas. Not even a decent burying place. *O Nnaife, what has befallen you?* Aloud she asked:

'Please tell me, Mama Abby, is he alive? Look closely into that letter. Is he dead?'

Realising what was going on in Nnu Ego's mind, Mama Abby wondered what she could do. Would they have sent a letter like this if the husband was dead? She did not know the answer. She was not used to army procedure. If Nnu Ego was to go to the barracks by herself, and it was terrible news ... she was a very emotional person. Should Mama Abby advise her to call her people to go with her? But that would take ages, and few of the men from her town could leave their jobs. Much as she did not wish to pry into Nnu Ego's life, she felt that she was the best person to accompany her. At least if it was bad news, she could prevent her hurting herself. And if it was good news which she wanted to keep to herself, well, had she Mama Abby not known of her friend's first savings?

'Let us go together. Abby will not be back until three this afternoon. If we hurry now, we shall soon be back.'

They were not kept waiting long, even though there were many families there. They were handed an envelope with several peculiar stamps fixed to it.

'Where is the package?' Nnu Ego wondered, as she made her thumb mark on the paper. 'Did they not say package in the letter?'

'Well, that is the package,' barked the officer at the counter.

'Do you want me to open it here?' Mama Abby asked with caution. 'Suppose we take it home to read.'

'No, please, let me know the worst. You know, this morning when I got that letter I was concerned to know what he might have written to me and whether he had sent us something to live on. Now, all I want to know is that he is still alive. I feel he is living, but I want to know for sure,' she begged despairingly.

Again Mama Abby put on her smart-looking spectacles, then peered over them, looking for a quiet corner where she could decipher in peace the childish script of whomever Nnaife had persuaded to write for him. As she read, her face began to glow slowly until by the time she came to the end of the letter she was smiling in such a dazzling way that Nnu Ego knew the future held hope and the realisation of hope. Whatever it was, she was now willing to wait.

Still smiling, Mama Abby gave her a piece of greenish paper and told her to thumb it. Then she asked, 'Do you know what this is?'

Nnu Ego began to giggle. 'I think it's the same as he sent last time – some money. How is he?'

While they waited their turn in another queue, Mama Abby told her the contents of the letter. Nnaife had been ill from water-snake bites which he had got because they had had to go to a place called Burma. He asked of the children and herself. He said there were rumours that the war would be ending soon. He now had hopes that they would meet again. He had despaired at first, especially when he had been ill.

There were three letters in all, and they all said almost the same thing. Nnu Ego asked the officer on the counter why they had not been delivered to her, seeing that the first one had been written nearly a year previously, and the officer stammered at her with rage.

'Are you not happy you are getting a big sum of sixty pounds, a man's pay for three years?' he said. 'And here you are grumbling that it did not arrive in time. Do you know what life blood your husband shed to earn this money? Women! Some of our men are so foolish, giving all that money to an illiterate woman.'

Nnu Ego was shocked at the amount. So Nnaife had been sending the money. She could only guess what had gone wrong: the man must have told them she was in Ibuza. Of course the local office had not bothered to check whether or not she was back; and there was no way of her checking. With tears of relief in her eyes, she promised herself that all her children, girls and boys, would have a good education. If she herself had had one, she would have been able to call at this office to check about the money. She would at least have been able to contact Nnaife, and he could have done the same. She and her husband were ill-prepared for a life like this, where only pen and not mouth could really talk. Her children must learn.

She and Mama Abby, the woman from Brass, walked home in silence. By her door Nnu Ego wanted to beg her friend not to tell anybody, but she guessed that such a plea would be useless. Even if Mama Abby did tell anyone, she intended to deny it. The officer at the army depot had said it was Nnaife's blood money, and she was going to use the money to Nnaife's glory. She thanked Mama Abby and would have invited her in for a piece of kolanut had she not said she was rushing back to prepare food for Abby who would soon be home.

Nnu Ego had learned the hard way. She said nothing to the children. She knew that six pounds or so belonged to the Owulum wife in Ibuza. She would send that; meanwhile she would put forty pounds in the post office, and she was not going to wait till the next day to do it. Nervously, as if someone was coming to snatch the money away from her, she quickly made garri for the children and pushed them out to play, saying that she was tired. She had then counted out the required amount, told Oshia that he had to miss his lesson that day as she needed him to watch the kiosk.

The next morning, the children were aghast when she told them that they were going back to school, after so long an absence.

The headmaster was reluctant to take them back at first, dubious that she would be able to pay as had happened before, but she told him not to worry. The children glowed with happiness, and showed their gratitude by studying very hard at school.

She did not say anything to anybody, but either people noticed for themselves or Mama Abby talked. Nnu Ego, too, got a stall in a bigger market in Oyingbo and took up selling abada cloth. Though it was a long way to where they lived in Yaba she did not mind, as she only had to go once in five days. She still kept her wooden kiosk; she would need that as it gave her time to be with her family. She stopped selling firewood, the most back-breaking task of all. For once she stopped worrying about food. The girls were encouraged to continue with their petty trading even though they were at school. They still hawked oranges after school because as their mother Nnu Ego kept saying, 'A girl needs to master a trade to help her in later life.' The boys, on the other hand, were encouraged to put more time into their school work.

'Mother, they keep telling us at school that the war is over and that the enemy Hitler is dead. But when will Father return?' Taiwo asked one evening when they were all sitting by the stall in front of the house.

'I have heard this said so many times in the market that I have stopped hoping. All I know is this, daughter, that when we see your father, we'll see him. We don't even know where he is fighting his own war,' Nnu Ego replied.

'It is not a story, Mother. Some of us will be going to the wharf to welcome some of the returning soldiers. I hope they choose me to go with them and I hope I see my father among them. I will wave and wave and wave,' Oshia expanded.

'Can't you run and meet him and say, "Welcome, Father, I am your son?" I would.'

'You know the trouble with you, Kehinde. You are too clever for your age and too impulsive. You have not stayed long in school. If you had, then you'd know that you are not allowed to do exactly as you like.'

The children went on arguing about the pros and cons of the war. Other children from the next compound joined them until it almost ended in a fight. They completely forgot who started the topic in the first place.

'All this because of your soldier husband,' Iyawo Itsekiri said laughing. She had a kiosk next to Nnu Ego's.

'I don't even know when the man is coming back. His last

letter was over a year ago and in it he said that he would be coming home soon. As I said, that was a year ago. But we still see army trucks and motor scooters all over the streets, and things are still expensive.'

'Maybe it will take time for things to get back to normal.'

'Well, all I want to know is that he is alive and well. I've never had a normal marriage anyway. He was either in one place or the other.'

'It will soon be over. You'll see,' Iyawo Itsekiri assured her friend.

Though Nnu Ego expected Nnaife any minute, she did not wish to put her mind on his arrival. Her business was going well because of her large capital, but many a time she would have liked to relax and not go anywhere, just stay at home and look after her children.

'I have been chosen to go and welcome the soldiers today, Mother, because my school uniform is always tidy,' Oshia boasted some weeks later.

'Liar! You are lying,' Taiwo said uninhibitedly.

Adim and Kehinde just laughed. They dared not oppose Oshia so openly.

'Why was he chosen then?' Nnu Ego wanted to know.

'Because his class was chosen,' Taiwo said.

On the day of the visit to the wharf most Lagos children in their smart school uniforms went to welcome the war heroes. Oshia never stopped talking about them for days.

'They were smart, Mother. They walked with their legs high, marching and waving at us. There were thousands and thousands of them.'

'Did you see your father?' everybody asked.

'No, there were so many of them. I could not tell my father apart.'

I hope this man is not dead, Nnu Ego prayed inwardly. She was still full of these thoughts of foreboding, as she counted her day's sales, when she heard the landlord's wives who were still outside shouting joys of welcome.

'Welcome to our heroes!' they shouted.

The children ran out to find out who it was. Nnamdio was in between their legs and Nnu Ego said, 'Mind your baby brother. You'll knock him over.'

'It's Father, Mother! It is our father – he is back!'

Nnu Ego left her money and ran out and sure enough there was Nnaife. They both started to laugh sheepishly, not giving in to any kind of affectionate demonstration.

Nnaife asked, laughing at the same time, 'And how is our senior wife?'

'Why did you not tell me you were returning today?' was all Nnu Ego could say amidst the confusion.

They all trooped into their veranda, and of course the palm wine sellers in that area got busy. They had missed their Ibo customer all these years.

The celebrations went on for days. Nnaife spent and spent a lot of money until Nnu Ego had to remind him that there were children to be fed and school fees to be paid.

'Aren't you happy to see me back? I did not know that I would return, you know. Can't you see that I have not been well? Look at my swollen feet. They got rotten in the swamp in Burma. Now you want to start your nagging. Let me be.'

Nnaife was ill. He had acquired a kind of yellowish colour which did not look at all healthy. He seemed to have grown more rotund, nervier than before, and tended to speak in an embarrassing whisper. He would be laughing one minute, then start to whisper like a child the next. There was one thing that did not change with Nnaife and that was his lack of judgement. Now that he had money, it had to be spent.

He was happy with his children and very proud to hear about his family in Ibuza. He dismissed Adaku as an evil woman, and declared, 'After I have rested, I must go and see that nice woman Adankwo in Ibuza. She must be longing for a man. For a woman to be without a man for five years! My brother will never forgive me.'

'I know she is yours by right, but she is happy as the senior wife of the family. Her children have grown into energetic farmers, you know. They won't welcome the idea of their mother having another husband,' Nnu Ego warned.

'I am not another man, I am her husband's brother. You have not changed, Nnu Ego the daughter of Agbadi.'

All the male visitors laughed while this was going on.

Then Ubani shouted in joke, 'My friend, Nnu Ego behaved very well during your absence, you know. She fought the war too here in your family.'

'She would be a disgrace to her people if she had not behaved well.'

They all laughed again. Their apartment of one sleeping room and the veranda became a hive of activity. And the children for once knew the joy of a father.

Even that, however, was short-lived. Nnaife maintained that it was his duty to go and see to his dead brother's wife and family. He had to go and thank Adankwo, he said, for the help she had given Nnu Ego. But Nnu Ego was far from deceived at this explanation. She knew that Nnaife's pride was wounded when he found out that Adaku had left his house; from all the rumours people had been supplying him with, he knew that the young woman was doing very well without him. Nnu Ego suspected that he wanted to go home to make Adankwo his wife in the normal traditional way. This woman belonged to him by right of inheritance, but that right had never been exercised. Now Nnaife wanted to stake his claim. Not even when Nnu Ego told him after some weeks that it looked as if she was expecting another baby was he deterred.

'Are you now frightened of having a baby by yourself, my wife?'

'Not frightened. It's only that the whole thing seems to be becoming more painful and dangerous as I grow older.'

'Don't worry, I shall be back before you have the child. I may be reinstated at the loco workshop soon. Just imagine that, I'll be working inside the workshop, not outside on the grass any more,' he announced proudly.

Like all war heroes of the time, Nnaife went home in style. Adankwo, that very composed woman, was taken in, and before long she too became pregnant, with her last menopausal baby. To Nnaife's dismay she refused to come to Lagos with him.

'I shall look after the family compound here. I don't want to go to that one room of yours,' she declared, and her grown-up sons by her former husband supported her in this.

'But I need someone to help Nnu Ego there. She's finding thing difficult now. She needs help,' Nnaife argued.

'You mean you need a new wife?' Adankwo said.

The 'help' soon arrived in the shape of a sixteen-year-old girl named Okpo. Her parents insisted on having nothing less than thirty pounds for their daughter; had not Nnaife brought home all the white man's money from the war? Not to hurt the feelings of his people, Nnaife paid this money, making the Owulum family feel proud of the fact that their son, who had been to the war, was one of the first people to set the pace for things to come. He paid thirty pounds for his woman instead of the usual twenty pounds stipulated by Ibuza custom. Some of the old people who heard of it simply shook their heads and predicted: 'Things are not going to be the same any more.' They were right.

Nnaife rushed back to Lagos. He had spent most of his army money and he knew that if he did not return fast he would sink to a new low. He would have to borrow money from his age-group farmers. Rather than let this happen, he returned, with his new wife Okpo and his new confidence, to Lagos, and to an angry Nnu Ego.

For once Nnu Ego did not bother to hide her disapproval. She refused to share a room with this new girl and all their children. She had been to her medicine man and to the hospital dispenser who helped her whenever she was pregnant, and they both agreed that it looked as if she was expecting another set of twins.

'Where are we going to put them all?' she screamed at her husband and the girl, whom she suspected would soon start breeding as well. 'Have you gone mad or something?' She went on bitterly: 'We only have one room to share with my five children, and I'm expecting another two; yet you have brought another person. Have you been commissioned by the white people you fought for to replace all those that died during the war? Why don't you let other men do part of the job. Even Adankwo whom we regard as our mother is pregnant for you, just you. You have to do something. I don't want that girl sleeping in my bed. I am not giving it up this time, and I don't care what your friends say.'

Nnaife sent for his friends to pacify his senior wife. But their old friend Nwakusor affirmed that Nnu Ego was right, though she should give her husband time to look for other accommodation.

'You know how things are now,' he said to Nnu Ego in a pleading voice. 'Before, you could find a room in less than a day. Nowadays, with these army people about, and with all the money they have, things have become very difficult. Remember that the girl is here to help you look after your children. Your children, remember, A few years ago – it seems like only yesterday – when I saw you on the Carter Bridge, you had no children to mind, let alone needing help to look after them. So Nnu Ego, daughter of Agbadi, you must thank our god Olisa and your *chi* for having blessed you. Your father would not be happy to see you behave this way.'

Nwakusor knew that this was a soft spot. Even in death, Nwokocha Agbadi ruled his daughter. She belonged to both men, her father and her husband, and lastly to her sons. Yes, she would have to be careful if she did not want her sons' future wives to say, 'But your mother was always jealous whenever her husband brought home a young wife.'

'All right,' Nnaife cut in, 'we will look for larger and cheaper accommodation.'

'Cheaper?' Nnu Ego's voice was still raised. 'Is that because you have spent all your army money, the money you were busy making while the children and I were busy suffering? Oh, Nnaife, you are a fool!'

Of course there was no peace after that. Oshia came up with the idea that he was going to the grammar school called Hussey College, somewhere in Warri.

'Why did you not win a scholarship like other boys?' Nnu Ego demanded.

'Only a few people win scholarships, and they have to be very clever.'

'Then why aren't you clever?' retorted Nnaife.

'Maybe if I had a peaceful childhood, and not had to spend my young days selling paraffin and carrying firewood – '

'Shut up!' shouted Nnu Ego. 'So it's all my fault, is it?'

Nnaife laughed and said, 'You answer your father back, eh, son? Well, maybe if your mother was not so keen on getting money, maybe you would have won a scholarship. I had to go and fight. I did not choose to go. And whenever I could get a job, I always did so. So don't blame me.'

It was all so hopeless that Nnu Ego simply broke down and gave in to self-pity. Oshia, her son, blaming her as well. Of course to him his father was a hero. He was a soldier. He was a fighter. He brought money into the family. All the poor boy had ever seen of her was a nagging and worrying woman. Oh, God, please kill her with these babies she was carrying, rather than let the children she had hoped for so much pour sand into her eyes.

208

She heard Nnaife talking like the noble father: 'Indeed you will go to Hussey. I will put all my money into your college education.' As he said that, he brought out a little pass-book, and, swinging it in the air, said boastfully, 'I have a hundred pounds left here. I didn't spend any of my money until I landed in Nigeria. This should pay for your college education. The other children will have to wait until you finish before their turn comes.'

Of course that clinched it. Oshia was the more proud of his father. And what could Nnu Ego say? If she went round making trouble about better accommodation, she knew what her children would say, she knew what people would say, she knew what the new girl who had heard everything would say: they would all say, 'Is not the bulk of his money being spent on your first son Oshia? How many fathers are willing to make such sacrifices?' Her love and duty for her children were like her chain of slavery.

Still, she reasoned, children became people. They would one day grow and maybe help their mother. Look at Abby, an only son; look at Abby ...

With that thought she drifted into sleep that night, only to be wakened in the early hours by labour pains.

Before morning, Nnu Ego had her second set of twins, which Nnaife delivered, as he sat on the upturned mortar which they had brought from the kitchen. Okpo was there to help with hot water, knives and things. Nnaife was not very pleased with the outcome: all this ballyhoo for two more girls! If one had to have twins, why girls, for Olisa's sake?

The arrival of her new twin daughters had a subduing effect upon Nnu Ego. She felt more inadequate than ever. Men – all they were interested in were male babies to keep their names going. But did not a woman have to bear the woman-child who would later bear the sons? 'God, when will you create a woman who will be fulfilled in herself, a full human being, not anybody's appendage?' she prayed desperately. 'After all, I was born alone, and I shall die

209

alone. What have I gained from all this? Yes, I have many children, but what do I have to feed them on? On my life, I have to work myself to the bone to look after them; I have to give them my all. And if I am lucky enough to die in peace, I even have to give them my soul. They will worship my dead spirit to provide for them; it will be hailed as a good spirit so long as there are plenty of yams and children in the family, but if anything should go wrong, if a young wife does not conceive or there is a famine, my dead spirit will be blamed. When will I be free?'

But even in her confusion she knew the answer: 'Never, not even in death. I am a prisoner of my own flesh and blood. Is it such an enviable position? The men make it look as if we must aspire for children or die. That's why when I lost my first son I wanted to die, because I failed to live up to the standard expected of me by the males in my life, my father and my husband – and now I have to include my sons. But who made the law that we should not hope in our daughters? We women subscribe to that law more than anyone. Until we change all this, it is still a man's world, which women will always help to build.'

The two baby girls were given the names Obiageli, meaning 'She who has come to enjoy wealth', and Malachi, meaning 'You do not know what tomorrow will bring'.

After staying packed in that airless room for an uncomfortable three-month period, Nnaife knew that they had to make a move. Though their landlord had promised them another room whenever one came vacant, none of his tenants wished to go because he charged the old pre-war rents. So Nnaife and his family moved to a mud house in the Onike area, an area where there was no running tap water and no electricity, to which flocked young Ibos who would rather save money than pay the new exorbitant rents some landlords were asking. Rooms were also becoming difficult to find because so many of the discharged army lived in Lagos. They were all given good compensatory posts with fatter pay packets, and of course this made prices rocket.

However, Nnu Ego was glad to have a room of her own with her children. She did not mind the mud much, and the children found the changed and exacting atmosphere very exhilarating. They loved drawing water from the wells and got their drinking water from Zabo market on their way from school. Despite these inconveniences, their rent was higher than before. Nnu Ego was sorry to leave her friends – Iyawo Itsekiri, Mama Abby and others. They all promised to come and see her, and Mama Abby told her not to worry, for her children were growing fast. 'Wasn't it lucky his allowances for you arrived in a lump? What would have happened to you?'

Nnu Ego replied that God was wonderful. If she had not kept her mouth shut about it, Nnaife would have forced her to use the money to pay for Oshia's education, and she would have got nothing to show for her sufferings. All Nnaife gave her by way of presents was five pounds, part of which she used to buy a new piece of the best George material she could find, putting the rest as a down-payment on an old sewing-machine somebody was

211

selling for six pounds. She paid this off gradually and was happy she did this, because she started to teach herself to sew. She had been attending classes at Mama Abby's, twice a week, before they moved. She could not cut complicated blouses yet, but she could stitch up their torn clothes and make the plain blouses known as bubas. For this you did not need to measure, and the shape was always the same. With all these little bits and pieces, she allowed Nnaife to have his way with his new wife Okpo. Even if Nnu Ego had wanted to raise a row, people would remind her that he had spent all his life-blood money in sending her son to school.

The day came for Oshia to leave home for his new college. Adaku and Mama Abby came to wish him good luck.

'You should not have bothered, Adaku; after all, you were not particularly happy with Nnaife when you were living with us. All these yards and yards of abada material. Why, one would have thought the boy was getting crowned and not just going to college.'

'Well, it is like getting crowned in a way. Imagine a son of Nnaife going to an expensive place like that. And don't forget Oshia is still a brother to my girls.'

'How are the girls anyway? I am so bowed down with my own problems that I have not had the time to come and see them.'

'Oh, they are in a convent school. They live there and come home only during holidays.'

'Really?' Mama Abby cried. 'Adaku, you have always surprised me. Those girls of yours may end up going to a college too.'

'She wants them to and they will make it. I am beginning to think that there may be a future for educated women. I saw many young women teaching in schools. It would be really something for a woman to be able to earn some money monthly like a man,' Nnu Ego said looking into the distance.

'But Kehinde and Taiwo are still at school, are they not?' Adaku asked.

'Oh, no, they only attended for a couple of years. We have

212

Adim and Nnamdio to think of and, with Oshia's big school fees, we cannot afford fees for the twins. I think they can read a little. I personally do not regret it. They will be married in a few years. They can earn an added income by trading. The most important thing is for them to get good husbands,' Nnu Ego said finally.

Nnu Ego went with Oshia to his new school in Warri. Her heart sank when they arrived. Here were the sons of very rich men, one could see from the cars that brought them. She called Oshia gently and said: 'You must not go the way of these rich boys. They have so much money in their families. Son, I wish you did not have to come to this school, I wish you had chosen one of those in Lagos where things are cheaper and you meet ordinary people.'

'I won't copy them, Mother. I will work hard. If I had stayed in Lagos, I don't think our home would have been conducive to my studies. There are so many quarrels over money, and me having to help selling this and that.'

'You are not running away from your people, Oshia, are you?'

'No, Mother, I am not. But here I can make the best of my ability.'

Nnu Ego went back to Lagos and to the old routine of scraping, saving, counting every penny. Before, her refrain used to be: 'All will be well when Nnaife returns from the war.' Now it was: 'All will be well when Oshia returns from college.' Did not all the *dibias* consulted before he was born say that he was going to be a great man?

Some years later, Adim too wanted to go to secondary school.

'Your father is at the end of his tether now, and I can't possibly ask him to pay for your fees,' Nnu Ego had to explain to him. 'It would not be fair on him and on the others. He has made so much sacrifice for us, and you know that he does not find it easy to give. He surprised us all with Oshia's school fees. So if you pass into one of the local schools, I will try and meet your fees somehow; if not, you will have to stay till you get to standard six and then go and learn a trade. They take young people as apprentices at the railways.'

'But, Mother, why? Don't I deserve help too? Is it my fault that I am a second son? Everything in this house is Oshia's. He must have the best of everything. You answer to his every whim, Mother. Sometimes I think we the rest of your children don't exist for you at all,' Adim cried in disappointment.

Then as quickly as his temper had risen, it subsided, without Nnu Ego saying a word. He seemed to be talking to himself. 'I shall go to a secondary school. I shall even go further than that: I shall be trained to be something, not a stupid mechanic in the railways. I will, you'll see, Mother. I will.'

Nnu Ego smiled with a touch of hope. 'As long as God is with us, I shall help you whenever I can. Your brother is the direct heir, the first son of your father; he needs to be specially treated. If you can wait, when he finishes his education, then we will all be better off. Oshia will pay for you too.'

Adim was only eleven but he knew many, many things which his parents did not know. He had heard his friends talk of their brothers going overseas to study this and that. Most of the said brothers were people who had been through the type of secondary schools Oshia attended. Adim knew, after talking to his brother during the holidays when he was home, that though he would like to help his parents, that help was going to be a very long time in coming. Only last Christmas, after the feasting and the merry-making, he and Oshia were sitting in front of their mud house, watching the insects make their nightly rounds. He had said to him, 'Just think, Oshia, in two years, you will be out working and earning a lot of money. That will be a real help to Father and Mother.'

Oshia had laughed at him, as if he was talking nonsense. Adim waited for him to explain why he was apparently so amused.

214

Adim had been closer to his parents, and he knew that they would not last much longer under the stress of the family burden. Their father Nnaife seemed to be sinking more and more into himself. Even he, Adim, could remember when he was a different person. He too hoped very much for Oshia to hurry up and help his people.

'It's true, what I'm saying, isn't it?'

Oshia was looking into the darkness as they sat side by side, not touching, but Adim could feel him resenting his questions. 'What help can one give with only twelve pounds a month? That is what they pay now, even with a good Cambridge school-leaving certificate.'

Adim did not know what to say. It sounded a lot of money to him. The school he dreamed of attending was only six pounds a year for day boys; if his brother could earn twelve pounds and ten shillings a month, then they would be rich. That was a great deal of money, he told his brother enthusiastically; 'What will you do with all that money? I'm not sure our father earns up to that.'

Oshia had laughed again. Adim hated the air of remoteness he was putting between himself and the rest of the family. His mother had complained and nagged him about the silences he was displaying, like somebody bored stiff with his people.

'You are too young to understand, Adim. I don't want to live like my parents. Education is a life-long project. If I stop now, I shall only help them half the way. I intended to go further after leaving school. Say four to five years after that ... then I shall be able to do something for them. Not now.'

Adim opened his mouth and closed it again, swallowing the night air.

'What of me, what will become of me?' he had mouthed into the darkness.

He got up with a very heavy heart, remembering all the firewood he had helped his mother carry just to make ends meet, remembering the year in which there were locusts and he had

215

stayed out for days bagging the insects to make delicious fried snacks for sale, all because 'my brother is at college, and when he comes out, we will be rich!' It now looked as if he was never going to finish his own education. He had slept little that night; he was determined not to sacrifice his life for any brother. He had a right to his own. He had heard his father say so: every man had a right to his own life, once it had been given to him. He thought of his younger brother Nnamdio, who at the age of six had not started school, and who would not even sit still for five minutes at a private lesson, and he smiled sadly. He too would find his own path.

'No, Mother,' he finalised now. I don't think I will wait for my brother to finish his education before I go for mine. I'll make the best of what I can have now, while my brain is good.'

Adim worked hard both at school and at home. He asked himself many times if his brother Oshia was right in his attitude of aiming for the highest peak in whatever profession he was going to choose before stopping to look back and help the other children. He could see by his mother's size that she was pregnant again. 'I don't understand these adults. First we do not have enough, yet they keep adding to the family. Maybe Oshia is right.'

When Oshia came home on holidays, Nnu Ego tried to acquaint him with Adim's aims.

'I don't blame Adim for wanting to go to college, Mother. I think the boy is right.' Then he paused for a while, knowing that what he was going to say would sound like a bombshell in Nnu Ego's ears. 'After Hussey, I shall be going to a university.'

'What is a university? Have you not learned enough?'

'No, Mother, not enough. I can't help Adim, not yet anyway. I can't even help myself ... oh, Mother, don't look like that. Things will be all right, only they would take longer staying in Nigeria, and studying here is the greatest part of it. Going abroad to a university is just topping it up. The most difficult part was getting through the course here. It would be such a waste to have had this good foundation and not be able to build anything on it. Soon I should be like my father ...'

'What is wrong with being like your father? He gave you life. I will not allow myself to listen to my son denigrating his father. He is no longer a strong man, not after that horrible war. He is not perfect; far from it. But he had hoped ... oh, God, we all had hoped that the *dibia* and all those medicine men were speaking the truth.'

'What truth? What truth are you referring to, Mother?'

'They told us that you were going to be a great man, that you would help us in our old age, just like sons in Ibuza used to help their parents.'

Oshia started to smile, stifling the urge to laugh out loud. 'Mother, do you mean the type of medicine man you used to take me to? The one that said that the ghosts were in Father's old guitar?'

Nnu Ego nodded. 'Such *dibias* helped us look after you.' There was no point in telling her that most of those *dibias* only told her what she wanted to hear. 'Me a great man indeed!' Oshia said to himself.

Aloud he said, 'I don't think I will be greater than any boy in my class.'

Nnu Ego did not know what to make of a statement like that. Had she been mistaken all along? No, her father could not have been wrong. Of course the boy did not know what he was talking about.

But Nnu Ego became subdued, her enthusiasm began to flag so much so that Nnaife, who was always full of his own woes, noticed it and asked, 'What is the matter with you? You behave and walk as if there is no life in you at all.'

'I don't know, Nnaife. It is this child. I don't think I am carrying it well.'

'Since when has pregnancy been a disease to you? And a

217

seventh pregnancy at that?'

Nnu Ego did not reply. There was no need to. Luckily for her, the new wife Okpo was not an ambitious girl. She coiled up to her warmly as if she were her own daughter, and would do anything Nnu Ego said, because she had been orphaned early in life, she knew suffering too. So Okpo went to the Zabo market for Nnu Ego.

Nnu Ego was now a woman of forty, approaching middle age though she felt like the oldest drone imaginable. She guessed in the morning, when everybody was leaving the house, that she was nearing the end of her term. The baby was due to arrive at any time. How would she, almost an old woman, go round the yard asking for help just because she was having her ninth baby? That would be ridiculous. Soon her eldest twin daughters would be betrothed, and they would remember that their mother was a coward in childbirth. When the girls eventually left with their wares, and Okpo had gone to the market with Nnamdio and the younger children, Nnu Ego knelt in the middle of her room, holding on to the bed post, and, with her teeth dug right into her lower lip to prevent herself from screaming, she gave birth to a baby not bigger than a kitten. She had only lain there for what she thought was a few seconds to get her breath back; but when she woke up, she saw the baby and herself in the pool of blood. The child, a girl, was lifeless. She was dead.

Nnu Ego stared at the picture she made with her dead daughter in horror. She felt like crying, but at the same time did not want to. She felt the loss of this little piece of humanity, this unfortunate little thing she had carried while climbing up to Zabo market, this thing she knew was probably being hurt as she had bent defiantly down to wash clothes for her sons. Oh, poor baby, she thought. *I am sorry you are not staying; I am also glad that God has seen fit to take you back. My own reward, the joy of knowing that at this age I can still have children for my husband. The joy of making the world know that while some of our friends and their wives are at this moment making sacrifices so that they may have children, I can have one without any effort at all.*

Then she started to feel guilty. Had she wanted the child to die, was that the interpretation of the slight relief she had experienced when she crawled to the dead child to check what sex it was? That it was a girl had lessened her sense of loss. Oh, God, she did not wish it. She would have been happy to have the child. God, please don't let her thoughts torment her so. Please God, give her something to hold on to, some faith to assure her that she deliberately had not killed her own child in her heart. But the thought kept recurring, until she felt she was hearing it in the voice of her father: 'Nnu Ego, why did you not call for help when you were in labour? Just because one child was proving a disappointment to you, do you have to refuse all the others? Nnu Ego ...' The voice seemed to be repeating itself. She felt herself slipping, all her senses going with her, like somebody being drugged into an unwanted sleep. She tried to fight the feeling of fluid engulfment spreading around her, but despite the fact that she struggled desperately to explain to her father how it had all happened, she had to give way. The force pulling her was stronger than her will.

She heard a dull thud somewhere, like footsteps, but she knew little else until much later.

When she came to, she tried to open her eyes, but they seemed gummed together by some kind of oil. She could hear people talking, and the room was hot. She moved gently, feeling pain round her joints. She guessed that her mouth was at least free, so she asked hoarsely, 'Could someone tell me what is going on?'

She sensed the relief of those surrounding her. She heard the voice of the *dibia*, intoning his magic more fervently than ever. She heard Adim call, 'Mother, so you are back!' She wanted to ask him where she had been, but the energy with which she had called out at first had now gone. Something cooling was being applied to her gummed-up eyes.

219

They told her days later that she had been very ill, and that in her illness, she had given birth to a beautiful baby girl, who had since died and whom they had buried as she was too ill to see the child. Nnu Ego would have liked to know if they were saying that to save her pain. She still searched in her memory for any sign that she had been looking forward to the arrival of the child.

It took her a long time to recover, and even when she was pronounced completely well by the medicine man, she was very unhappy and absentminded. Could she have so deteriorated into the kind of woman who would not want her own child because she could not afford to feed or clothe her? Why, once she had been about to end her own life because a child she had had died in its sleep. Was that why God let things happen like this? Was that why God had given her two sets of twins to make up for the loss? She could not confide in anyone.

She was still in this emotional muddle when, one afternoon, as she sat in front of their house doing some sewing, Adim burst in, happy and glowing with a sense of achievement.

'Mother,' he cried, 'I have gained admission to St Gregory's College.'

Nnu Ego's heart missed a beat. She quickly rallied round, and arranged her face to smile at this boy who had been such a help to her. 'Oh, yes!' she replied with faked enthusiasm. 'Oh, yes, that's very good, son. Really good. And you shall go, of course you will go.'

Adim was not deceived. He was too close to be unaware of the hardship. 'I am glad, Mother, but believe me, I shall work somehow to help make things easier. If it comes to the worst, I can always stop in the fourth year, when I will have gained my class four certificate, what they used to call Junior Cambridge.'

'Oh, my dear husband!' Okpo shouted with joy. 'This is good news. All the children in this family are so clever. And that makes us very proud women. Even the new child I'm carrying will not

220

lack anything. Now they have two big brothers who have been to high school. Oh, I am so glad, aren't you, Mother?'

Nnu Ego nodded numbly, thinking, 'Another child? Into all this mess?' Then she heard Okpo saying:

'Mother, you know those pieces of material you were making into clothes for the little one that we lost, may I take them for my baby? I am sure mine will be a boy. I had a girl last time.'

Then Nnu Ego remembered, and the remembering made her love this bubbly girl Nnaife had brought into the house ... What, she wondered, could have made her forget that she had been making clothes for her baby? Oh, yes, she had expected her. She had wanted her. But God had thought otherwise. Her death had been an accident. Not deliberate at all. So this was the answer.

She replied jokingly, 'You young people are so full of optimism. You've only just found out about the existence of your child, and you are planning a big tower for it already. Of course you can take the clothes.'

Okpo nodded, laughing. 'Yes, we shall all work to see my little husband Adim through the nice school; and when he has finished, he will take care of his little brother here, and the one here will be his cook, and my husband, my little husband Adim will pay for his education. And my baby will do the same for his children. Is that not our philosophy, Mother? Is that not what you and my big husband and father Nnaife have been trying to teach me all these years?'

Nnu Ego nodded. For once Nnaife had done the right thing. This girl would see him through old age. She believed in him. Nnu Ego loved the way she never called the male children of the household by their names without the prefix 'My little husband'. Even little Nnamdio was well respected by her. So unlike Adaku, this one.

Adim laughed: 'Eh, so that's why you married my father, so that you can have clever children?'

Okpo nodded in agreement. Her face was full of glad anticipation. Okpo, only seventeen years of age, and Adim, who was approaching thirteen, seemed to possess the same emotion. This youthful emotion appeared on the surface immediately, without any coy excuse; they were not faithless in their future, they were both enthusiastic, vigorous, and open.

Nnu Ego laughed with them, and she knew then that, had they lived in times gone by when families used to stay together, several generations living and dying on the same portion of land, Okpo's children would never suffer. For she saw the look of childish love that went from her son to this young girl his father had married. If it had been that time, if Nnaife should die, Okpo would never need to go back to her people, because on a day like this, she had given the boy Adim the spontaneous reaction which he needed and which said: 'Well done. We know you will do your duty by us when you grow up.'

Nnu Ego was grateful Okpo was there at the time to do this, and at the same time, to clear her own conscience so that she could rest assured she had not killed her dead baby in her heart.

She let herself be carried with youthful optimism, and all of them worked to see Adim through college.

Everybody referred to Nnu Ego, as she proudly carried her back-breaking firewood up from the waterside, as the mother of very clever children.

The Ibos have a saying: 'People come and people go.' By the mid-fifties Nnaife knew that even if it was not time for him to go finally to his Maker, it was high time he moved nearer. For generations the Owulums had been laid to rest in their corner of Ibuza, Idum-ohene, and he had been hoping one day to go back there; he had not consulted the rest of his family, for as far as he was concerned he was the family. He was looking forward to when Oshia left school and took over earning for the family; then he, Nnaife, would no longer have to work and would lead a life of indolence and ease, drinking palm wine with his friends ...

When Oshia gained a grade one in his Cambridge School-leaving Certificate it was a great triumph for him. Though Nnaife did not understand the full significance of such a brilliant performance he rejoiced with his son, and Nnu Ego was too happy for words.

'I've been offered a good job at the Technical Institute,' Oshia said. 'I have to do some science research work. I have always been interested in science. Just think of it, Father.'

Nnaife did not know where to begin his thinking but he laughed politely. He celebrated his son's success with palm wine and *ogogoro*, inviting Ubani and Nwakusor and all his old friends and army colleagues, and even allowing their former Yoruba landlord to come and congratulate him.

'Well, it won't be long before you can retire and let Oshia educate his brothers,' Nwakusor exclaimed, his eyes aglow with wine. 'The girls will marry soon, I gather. Honestly, Nnaife, that unwilling bride of twenty-five years ago has really done you proud.'

'It hasn't been easy living with a daughter of Agbadi, I tell you, my dear friend. Not any man could have coped with her. But she has given me brilliant children. Adim will do well like his brother,' Nnaife boasted.

It was a happy and hopeful occasion for the Owulums and their friends. People agreed that it was worth the trouble one had to go through to train children in a difficult place like Lagos.

'But things are changing fast,' said Ubani, who still lived with white people in the railway yard. He was regarded as better informed than his friends in the workshop. 'They say that in the not-too-distant future we shall be ruling ourselves, making our own laws.'

Overhearing this, Nnu Ego asked the men: 'Do you mean we'll have a black District Officer in a place like Ibuza?'

'Of course, Mother, that is what we are saying.'

'And a Nigerian Reverend Father, and all our doctors Nigerians?'

'Yes, Mother,' Oshia replied with exaggerated patience.

'But, son, these new Nigerians, will they do the job well?' Nwakusor asked.

'They will do it even better, because this is their country. They have never been given the chance before. Now things are changing and Nigerian politicians are springing up and demanding our rights, especially after people like you, Father, have fought in the war.'

'Was that the reason they forced me to go to Burma? I still do not understand who we were fighting. We kept marching up and down and the white officers were shooting in the air ... oh, well. My friends, I think we are overstaying our welcome in this town. I don't know what all this new talk is about. This is what I know!' Nnaife downed another glass of palm wine.

'Yes, palm wine does not change,' Ubani agreed. 'Oshia, we'll be coming back when you tell us officially that you've earned your first salary. This is your father's do. We'll come to yours then.'

Oshia never did call them to a palm wine party. There was a small living apartment attached to his post at the Institute, and he had to use his salary to maintain this. Moreover, as soon as his examination results became known to the authorities, he was recommended for a scholarship award to the United States of America. A few months later he won it. But he could not find a way to tell his parents.

'Oshia, when are you going to buy your father a bottle of white man's whisky to toast your *chi* for making you pass your exams?' Nnu Ego prompted.

'What's wrong with the sixpenny bottles of local *ogogoro* he has been drinking all these years? I can't afford a whisky party. As a matter of fact, I am saving to go to that university I told you about some time ago, Mother. I still want to go. They have given me a scholarship. If I don't take the opportunity offered me now, it may never come again.'

'God, Oshia, please don't tell your father, it will kill him. He is becoming impatient about you not helping in the family.'

Indeed, at the end of the month, Nnaife could bear it no longer. He called angrily to eight-year-old Nnamdio to go and fetch Oshia for him.

'What is it, Father?' Oshia asked.

Sensing that there was trouble coming, Nnu Ego suggested weakly, 'Nnaife, why don't you eat before you start your man-to-man talk?'

'Woman, why don't you go to your cooking place and let me talk to my son? Now, young man, when are you going to take on your family responsibilities? Have you not sense enough to know that a father shouldn't have to ask that of his son, he should do it automatically?'

'What responsibilities, Father?'

Nnaife's bottled-up wrath exploded, and he thundered: 'Adim! Nnamdio! You two come here.' He turned back to Oshia. 'These are your responsibilities, to say nothing of myself and your mother, who still carries firewood like a paid carrier.'

225

'I don't understand, Father. You mean I should feed them and you too? But you are alive and well and still working – '

'Shut up! Shut up before I lay you flat and show you that you haven't grown too big for me to handle. Didn't you hear my friends saying the other day that I should soon rest after the work I have done all these years and that you should take over?'

'I can't take over, Father. I am going to the States. I have won a scholarship, though I shall have to pay for my board. I did even hope that you and Mother might help me out – '

'Help you? Help you!' Nnaife's voice had become a menacing whisper.

Adim, now a tall sixteen-year-old, was standing by and saw that the exchange was getting too heated: 'I shall soon finish my education, anyway, and will help Nnamdio until brother Oshia returns.'

'Wait until you are asked to speak. I am talking to this fool on whose stupid head I spent all the money I sweated for in the army.'

Nnamdio's contribution was: 'I don't want to go to a silly school. I want to be a hunter. A hunter with the title "Killer of elephants".'

Nnaife and Oshia ignored the two younger boys and wallowed in their anger.

'Do you know, sometimes I curse the day you were conceived,' Nnaife hissed.

He sat down on one of his old chairs and covered his eyes. He looked so very old. 'I wish you had died instead of my first son Ngozi.'

'Nnaife, Nnaife, are you well?' Nnu Ego enquired from the doorway. 'What senseless talk is that? What dreadful things are you saying to your sons?'

'Not to me,' Adim protested. 'Nobody thinks at all about me. It's only Oshia, Oshia every time.'

'He is no longer my son. Regard him as one of the lost ones.' Nnaife stood tall and looked Oshia straight in the face. 'I do not wish to see you ever again, since you have openly poured sand into my eyes. Out of my house!'

'I can do without seeing your face, old man!' Oshia retorted with heartfelt self-righteousness. He stamped out.

One could feel the presence of the tangible silence that followed.

Then Nnaife said in a small voice, 'Tomorrow I am going to put in my resignation. I am going home on pension. I don't understand anything any more. O my *chi*, where have I gone wrong?'

Nnaife did not go to see Oshia off on the day he left for the United States. Nnu Ego, Okpo, Adim and several of their friends went to the airport to wave him goodbye. It left an emptiness in Nnu Ego's heart that was hard to communicate. Please, God, teach him to be used to being alone, for a person like Oshia who put ambition first at the expense of his family was always a loner, Nnu Ego thought as she returned home dry-eyed. Friends and well-wishers were surprised to see that she did not cry; and when they predicted that soon her son would be back and driving her about in a big car, she knew that they had all missed the point. She was not destined to be such a mother. She realised that now. Her joy was to know that she had brought up her children when they had started out with nothing, and that those same children might rub shoulders one day with the great men of Nigeria. That was the reward she expected.

But not Nnaife. If there was any gain to come from his sacrifices, he wanted it now, and preferably in cash. Glory was worthwhile, too, but to Nnaife what was the good of a big name without money? He felt very bitter at Oshia, and, though he knew Nnu Ego would have waited hopefully for him until the plane left, he made no effort to be there for his son's departure. He purposely stayed late at work that day, and when he did arrive home, he was in a nasty mood. Nnu Ego however was determined to know why he had not showed up.

Nnaife pointed out to her that the children were her children. 'Will they remember me when I am old? No, they will remember only their mother. And have you not noticed that women stay longer than men on this earth? So why should I give up my day's work for a son who has spat in my face?'

'He has never given me anything. In fact he was expecting us to give him something before he left. He was expectant to the very last minute. I saw the disappointment on his face. Why do you all make life so impossible for me? Where am I going to run to?' Nnu Ego cried bitterly from her heart. But there was no answer for her. It could not be given. 'Sometimes, seeing my colleagues, I wish I didn't have so many children. Now I doubt if it has all been worth it,' she thought to herself. She noticed that Nnaife was beginning to refer to them as her children, whom she had borne to kill him before his time.

His anger grew when he knew that it was going to take a longer time for him to be granted his retirement pension than he had expected. Nnu Ego did not have long to moan about all this. Another child was causing a big problem.

Most Ibos, at the time, did not like their children marrying Yorubas. One tribe always claimed to be superior to the other. Even an Ibuza girl who chose another Ibo person outside Ibuza as a friend was regarded as lost. To go so far as to befriend a Yoruba man was abominable. Yet that was what happened. While Nnu Ego and her husband were busy planning and scraping for their sons, they took it for granted that the girls, the twins now blooming into young women, would automatically take care of themselves.

They were now fifteen. They looked very much like their mother, fair-skinned, and with the narrow face of Agbadi. They were growing tall too, and this was emphasised by the fact that throughout their young lives they had never really had sufficient to eat. They had never been hungry, but they had suffered from all the illnesses that accompanied malnutrition. They had yaws when they were taken to Ibuza as babies, they had protruding stomachs when they were five, and still occasionally the skin of their lips and at the sides of their mouths was cracked and torn, though they had learned to cover this with some of the brown burning juice, the colour of honey, which oozed out of wet wood that was set alight and forced to burn; apart from curing soreness the stuff coloured lips a dark brown. The Owulum twins were very beautiful. They did not go to school, but they had learned to read and write in the few evenings they could be spared to attend lessons. They could sew, and had been taught through their mother's strictness to be very quiet. They were identical in appearance, but not in character; the one called Kehinde, 'the second to arrive', was much deeper than Taiwo, 'she who tasted the world first'.

The parents knew that they played with everybody and were very polite. But it never occurred to them that it could go deeper than that. Young Ibuza men were beginning to come for them, and Taiwo, the eldest by ten minutes or so, had had her day of formal bride-price paying fixed. Her future husband was a young clerk who had come to Lagos only a few years before. He had previously been teaching in Onitsha and although he was well educated, he knew he would be happier with a wife who did not have much education. He told himself that as long as the wife could bear children, keep his room clean and wash his clothes, he was perfectly satisfied. That Taiwo was beautiful and quiet he calculated as an added bonus. Nnaife quickly approved of this man, knowing that his daughter was striking a good bargain, and he was in a hurry to get as much money as possible from his children before retiring. Thank goodness, he had no older brother, so the whole bride price would come to him. One evening Nnaife called Kehinde and asked her what she thought of a certain young man who, though he had not gone to college like Taiwo's prospective husband, had a good job at the railway. He was not prepared for the answer he got.

'I am not marrying that man.'

For the first time, Nnaife really looked at Kehinde. He had never had much time for his daughters. One planned for and had sleepless nights over boys: girls, on the other hand, were to help in running the house and be disposed of as soon as possible, unless one was asking for trouble. He was already counting on the money he would get for Taiwo; who did this one think she was? None the less, he knew it would not pay him to lose his temper.

'But why?' he asked, putting on as gentle a voice as he could manage.

'Because, because ... I don't know, Father. He grew up in Ibuza. I don't like him,' came the hesitant reply.

Nnaife laughed coarsely. He was amused and at the same time relieved. His daughter, he told himself, was still very young. 'You don't have to like your husband,' he assured her. 'You don't even have to know him in advance. You just marry him. You are lucky you already know this one, and that you know what job he is in. Things have changed. Before, you might not have known him at all. Anyway what is bad in his being born in Ibuza? Are you not from there?'

Kehinde could not put her feelings into words. She frowned, and started to chew at her lip.

'My retirement time is coming,' Nnaife continued, 'and I don't see why you should come home with us where you would be forced to marry a farmer. You know what farming is like? You wouldn't like it at all. Take it from me, your father: you would hate it. So I want to see you and your sister well settled before we go back.'

Kehinde shuffled her feet, head bowed, still chewing at her bottom lip. She moved away towards the door, then she turned and spoke:

230

'Father, I want to marry and live with Ladipo, the butcher's son. I don't want an Ibuza man!'

She ran out before Nnaife could say a word. The room seemed to him to have grown darker all of a sudden. Who was Ladipo? A Yoruba man from a Muslim family? Nnaife knew the butchers who lived down the untarred road. The family hawked meat round the houses every weekend, especially if they had any leftovers from their Zabo market stalls. How had his daughter become involved with them? How did she come to know them so intimately as to be able to think of marrying one of them? No, he must be dreaming. The girl must be mad. He went behind the curtain in their room and had a glass of chilled palm wine which he had been saving for after his evening meal. He could not wait. He wanted to blot out his burning worries. But the drink did nothing to alleviate the pain. He must have it out with Nnu Ego. Why, he had thought the woman's children were a blessing to him. Now he was beginning to see that they were a curse. He could not bring himself to cry, but he felt the lump in his throat all the same.

He was draining his second glass of palm wine when Nnu Ego entered, carrying his food. She took in the situation and asked in a painful tone:

'Is my food so bad that you have to get drunk before you have even tasted it? What do you call this behaviour, Nnaife, the son of Owulum?'

He stared at her for a while. It was an intense look, and hatred with anger worked on his face, each trying to gain supremacy over the other. He remembered the day this woman had come to him, now twenty-five years ago, young, slim and beautiful, a reluctant bride. How he had wanted her then! He had been ready to stake everything he had for her, even though she had not liked him. What had sobered her opinion of him were the children she started having in quick succession. Was that not why she had come to him in the first place, to use him as a tool to produce the children she could not have with her first husband? Now the house was full of her children, *her children* – none of them had so far showed any loyalty to him, their father. God, what was he to do now? Send this woman away, tell her never to come near him again?

'Damn you and your food, Nnu Ego,' he repeated aloud. 'I shall curse till I die the day you came to my threshold. I wish I had never met you.'

It was a good thing the food was damned, because it dropped from Nnu Ego's hand.

Okpo, who was bringing in the washing water, opened her mouth aghast. 'What is the matter with you two?' she gasped. 'Mother, has something happened? Have you heard bad news?'

Nnaife was growing old fast and, like an old man, he had become too sensitive even to bother to offer his wives any explanation of his now frequently explosive behaviour. His skin had acquired a kind of ashy dryness due to exposure in the foundry workshop where he now worked as a supervisor. He had also acquired stooping shoulders and a protruding belly. He wore no shirt and one could see that his breasts were forming like those of a young girl. Pointing a shaking finger of blame at Nnu Ego, he threatened:

'I have a mind to tell you and your brats to leave this house immediately. I was not created to suffer for you till I die.'

Understanding was gradually dawning on Nnu Ego. She could guess that his anger was connected with the children. She was becoming fed up of this two-way standard. When the children were good they belonged to the father; when they were bad, they belonged to the mother. Every woman knew this; but for Nnaife to keep hurling it in her face at the slightest provocation was very unfair. She decided to have her own back, not caring that Okpo the young wife was there watching and listening.

'I didn't bring the children from my father's house. You gave them to me. Leave your house? What house have you got? How

232

many people live in mud-covered houses in Lagos? I am only waiting for my share of your pension money. I worked for it as well. After that, if you don't want me, I can go back to my people.'

'Oh, Mother, stop,' pleaded Okpo, 'stop saying wicked things you will be sorry for later. Please come out and stop.' She managed to drag her, still shaking, out of the room.

Both Nnaife and Nnu Ego were too incensed to discuss what the cause of the quarrel was. Nnaife was too full of bitterness to eat. Nnu Ego went to the back yard, had a bath then announced that she was going straight to lie down. No one missed Kehinde, until it was too late.

The children and Okpo had their evening meal in near silence. Adim went away to do his school work and Nnamdio went to play with his friends. Taiwo noticed that her sister was not eating with them, but assumed it was because she was upset over their parents' arguments, which were becoming more frequent these days. First it had been over their brother Oshia; then over their father's pension; two days before it had been over Adim. Taiwo could not wait for the final arrangements for her going away to her husband's home to be finalised. She would go and start her own home somewhere else. She knew she would have her own problems, too, but at least they would be fresh ones.

Later, when she was preparing to go to bed, she missed her sister again. They both slept on the same mat, and Taiwo had bought some soft cotton blankets from the pocket money her fiancé had been giving her. These had been spread over the mat she shared with her sister, and it had been Kehinde's turn that day to wash them. Taiwo called loudly about the compound for her. Okpo asked her whether Kehinde had been seen since mealtime, and it was then that they both realised they had not seen her for most of the evening.

'And it's getting late now. Where could she be?' Okpo asked with concern. 'We'd better wake Mother.'

233

'Let's ask everybody else first, before asking Mother. The mood in which she is at the moment, I don't know ...'

The ghost of a smile passed across Okpo's face at Taiwo's remark, and for a split second Taiwo thought maybe Okpo, that superficially bubbly girl, was enjoying it all. It was possible that she was not what she seemed. Maybe she had even been praying that things would go wrong, for who would benefit from it all if not Okpo? Her father Nnaife would not marry again, of that Taiwo was certain. Okpo was still having babies, and with the lump sum of his pension money she would be better off if Nnu Ego gave up and left the house. Taiwo promised herself to think more of this later. Meanwhile, she was looking for her twin sister.

Adim was soon called but, search where they would, they could not find Kehinde. Eventually Nnu Ego had to be summoned. She was surprised when she was told of it, for she had never had any trouble with the girls before. It had always been the boys who had caused the headaches, because they would always be members of the Owulum family. The part of the daughters was to be of little trouble and allow themselves to be used by their family until they were transferred to their men. So where would a girl, a grown-up girl, go at this time of night, when all had gone to bed? Nnu Ego could foresee what was coming – more blame for her, the mother. If a thing like this should leak out to their people, Kehinde would definitely acquire a bad reputation, and once that started, all the girls in the family would be tabooed. People would say: 'If her mother had done her work well, why should the girl leave home to wander about Lagos at this time of the night?' Ibuza people in particular had very vivid imaginations when it came to their girls. They would gossip and say, 'Do you know where she has been? Do you know what she has been up to?'

Nnu Ego begged everyone to keep it quiet, and they looked everywhere once more. She suggested they should start checking at the houses of their Yoruba neighbours; after all, it did not matter if they knew. They would never marry any of the girls anyway. So she did not mind some kind Yoruba neighbours joining in the search.

It was nearing two o'clock in the morning when Nnu Ego decided it was better to face Nnaife's annoyance now than his blame later for keeping Kehinde's disappearance a secret. When she went into the room and saw him, she was filled with indecision. She wished she did not have to wake a man who was peacefully having his nightly sleep. Nnaife was snoring gently, his mouth half open, his wrapper flung loosely about him. He was only partly covered but it was obvious that he did not care, for who else had the right to come into the privacy of his curtained bed but his wives and his children?

Taking a deep breath, Nnu Ego called softly, 'Nnaife, Nnaife, wake up. We're looking for Kehinde. Nnaife, wake up!'

He opened his heavy eyes slowly, frowned at seeing Nnu Ego. *Even in his sleep he hates me*, she thought, brittle-eyed as she watched the frown that came and went: *we tolerate each other for the children, just for the children*. People blamed her later for telling a sleepy man the whole truth before he was fully awake. But how was she to know he had had an argument with Kehinde? If only she had been told. If only Nnaife had given a hint ...

'Kehinde is missing. We don't know where she is.'

Nnu Ego screamed at his reaction. She thought he was going to kill her, cut her up into bits. He was talking, talking as though he was still asleep, though his eyes were wide open and staring. He hastily and haphazardly tied his wrapper, exposing the part he was supposed to be covering; his behaviour was not without purpose, but one would have thought that his senses had left him.

'Kehinde! My daughter! The butcher – I'll butcher him!' With that, he bent down under his bed – anger made him so agile, so quick – reaching for the big cutlass which he kept there for emergencies, since that part of Lagos was often troubled with

235

armed robbers. He picked up the cutlass, swung it in the air, as if aiming it at Nnu Ego, his eyes still glazed from sleep. Nnu Ego let out another piercing scream, warning the people outside to clear out of Nnaife's way because it looked as if he was going to commit murder. But his wife's scream seemed to reach him, and he dashed out, swearing under his breath.

'That butcher and his son – I will teach them! My daughter!'

His family could not hold him. He was so wild, he was so determined. Adim somehow guessed where he was going, though how he knew was something of a miracle. He ran fast, jumping over a small bush that separated the butcher's house from their own. He went in there and shouted in Yoruba: 'Wake up, all of you, somebody is coming to kill your father. Wake up!'

That was what saved the butcher and his family. Some of the young men of the house were sleeping on the veranda as it was a hot night. They got up, wakened by the noise and the screams of the Owulum women, and one of the men crawled under a broken kiosk for safety when he saw the flash of a cutlass in the night; the other joined Adim in waking the butcher, who was groggy with sleep. Nnaife dashed in brandishing his cutlass.

Adim's young voice could be heard, shouting, 'Please hold him, hold him! Don't just hide there – hold him!'

The appeal in that urgent voice coupled with the screaming voices of women, made everybody run round in confusion.

Nnaife dashed into the butcher's house, bellowing, 'My daughter with a Yoruba husband? She is better dead – and with her the father of her man! Where are they?' His cutlass was still in the air, held high. No one dared come near him face to face.

When he turned his back on the standing kiosk where some Yoruba young men had been crouching, one of them jumped on Nnaife from the back, taking him unawares. But Nnaife's cutlass landed once, on the young man's shoulder and he let out a piercing scream. Before the cutlass slashed at the wriggling man the second time, Adim came from behind and hit his father's arm with a stick, making it go limp. The cutlass fell.

All the other hiding men came out and they held Nnaife. The mother of the youth whose shoulder had received the deep cut started to cry.

'What has my son done? Why do you have to go mad on us? We have never given you any trouble? You are Ibos and we Yorubas, what have we done to you?'

'I shall still kill you. No child of mine is marrying a tribe that calls us cannibals. A tribe that looks down on us, a tribe that hates us,' Nnaife growled, struggling in the hands of his captors.

'So that is it!' shouted the senior man of the Yoruba family, the man Nnaife had wanted to kill originally. 'Your girl is only a girl. You cannot prevent a girl from marrying anybody she likes.'

'We don't do so in my town Ibuza. I will choose husbands for all my girls. They are too young to know their own minds.'

'Look, this is Lagos, not your town or your village.'

'But I came from my village! If my daughter has been touched by your son, know this: that when these men leave, I shall kill you.'

Nnaife in his mind thought he was in the Ibuza of his childhood where arguments of this sort were wont to be settled by sheer force. He was the more surprised when an ambulance arrived, followed quickly by six strong and fierce-looking policemen.

'You see, you see, Nnu Ego, you see what you have done to me! One of your daughters is responsible for their taking me to jail.' He turned once more to the senior man and threatened in front of the policemen: 'I shall be released in a day or two, but I shall come and kill you.'

'Is that so?' asked one of the policemen. 'And what has your neighbour done to you?'

'He abducted my daughter and he is a Yoruba man!' Nnaife replied, in his whining whisper.

'Have you the daughter? Where is she?'

Kehinde came out from the knot of people standing in the shadows watching the whole proceedings. She was crying gently and begging the policemen to please let her father go.

'But we can't let your father go. He almost killed a man, and he is threatening to kill one if he is free. We have to uphold the Law now, young woman. And did the Yoruba family abduct you?'

'No, no,' Kehinde answered slowly. 'I ran to them. And I am going to marry Aremu the butcher's son.'

Women started to cry, the voices were unmistakable. They were those of Okpo and Nnu Ego. Nnaife looked lost. He could not believe that a daughter could betray her family so.

One of the policemen came up with a handcuff and clasped it round Nnaife's wrist. The clasping sound somehow managed to cut through the babbling and crying voices. The sound reached Nnaife's heart and the hearts of his two young sons watching helplessly, unable to lift a finger to help their father.

They bundled Nnaife into the waiting police van but as they were doing so, his night cloth which he had thrown around him loosely was coming off, about to reveal his nakedness.

'Please wait, please wait!' Nnu Ego shouted, shaking with emotion. 'Please, policeman, let me tie his lappa round him more securely. He is the father of all my children, he is my husband.'

Nnaife stood there unmoved, as Nnu Ego tied the lappa tightly, making an extra knot so that, however much he was pushed and tousled, it would not come off.

'We shall always try to hide your nakedness, Nnaife, and may your *chi* guide you in this.'

Nnaife stared into the darkness, unseeing, as the Black Maria was slammed shut, and then was driven away.

The days that followed were filled with seeing this policeman, that lawyer, that doctor – a sea of faces to Nnu Ego. She understood little of what was being said. All she prayed for was Nnaife's release. Everything was costing her money, money she did not have. Adim's schoolwork began to suffer and the boy was losing weight. It was true what they said, she thought, that if you don't have children the longing for them will kill you, and if you do, the worrying over them will kill you. One day she called the boy and talked to him seriously.

'Look, Adim, it seems I am alone with you in this game of living. Your father blames me and you, my children. Ibuza people blame me: they say I did not bring you all up well because I spent most of my time selling things in the market. They are predicting that none of you will come to any good. Are you going to fulfil their hopes by rejecting yourself too? You can blame me if you like, but listen, good son; so far you and your sister Taiwo are my only hope. I hope in you two, not only that you will feed me in my old age but that you will wipe the tears of shame from my eyes. So don't let yourself go. Face your school work; it is your salvation.'

'Do you know, Mother, I wrote to Oshia in the United States, and he said he was sorry for what has happened, and that he would pray for us all, but there was little else he could do.'

An unmistakable gleam of hope shone in Nnu Ego's tired eyes. 'Eh! So, the boy still remembers us? O my *chi*, I wish you had told me. May his *chi* help him. How is he? Do they treat him well over there?'

There was a slight pause during which Nnu Ego stared at her moving toes, and Adim looked closely at her in confusion. He did not understand his mother.

'Well, if you had asked me,' she went on, 'I would have told you not to write him. He must be busy building his own future, worrying about it. It is very painful to be at that age.'

'But, Mother, could he not have helped in any way?'

Nnu Ego smiled. 'How can he help us when he is not in his country? He probably does not have enough to eat. I know the Ibuza people say nasty things behind my back, but look, son, they are sending our only lawyer, Nweze, to plead for your father, and I have to look for money to pay for your last year at school, and with my *chi* helping me, I shall get it for you. So why do you have to worry Oshia when he is not in a position to help? I don't want him to worry or to think that he brought all this on us. When you reply tell him that we all love him and that we all pray for him too.'

For the first time since he was young, Adim – the tough boy, as they used to call him – broke down and cried. 'Mother, you say you'll pray for him? Mother, he started all this. He did, and nobody else. It was anger over him that made our father lose his sense of direction.'

Nnu Ego laughed, and stretched out her work-worn hand to help Adim, who noticed with horror how bony his mother's hand was and how all the veins that ought to have been covered with healthy flesh now stood criss-cross in relief. And her teeth, those teeth that used to be her pride, had been badly neglected and were beginning to have black smudges round some of their edges. He knew his mother was not old in age, but she had never looked this old to Adim. She looked like a woman in her seventies. Oh, poor woman, he thought.

Nnu Ego, unaware of his thinking, said:

'Don't blame anyone for what has happened to your father. Things have changed drastically since the days of his own youth, but he has refused to see the changes. I tried to warn him ... but, no matter. The fact is that parents get only reflected glory from their children nowadays, whereas your father invested in all of you, just as his father invested in him so that he could help on the farm.

Your father forgot that he himself left the family farm to come to this place. He could only help when he was well settled in a good job. For you, the younger generation, it's a different kind of learning. It also takes longer and costs more. I'm not sure that I'm not beginning to like it. My only regret is that I did not have enough money to let the girls stay at school. So don't blame your brother for anything. And don't forget Oshia is my son, just like you. Some fathers, especially those with many children from different wives, can reject a bad son, a master can reject his evil servant, a wife can even leave a bad husband, but a mother can never, never reject her son. If he is damned, she is damned with him ... So go and wash, put on your clean school uniform and hold your chin up. I shall see to it that your fees are paid before we leave. After that I'm afraid, son, your life is in your own hands and those of your *chi*.'

'Thank you, Mother,' Adim said simply, and he determined to do well in his forthcoming examination.

Many Ibuza people turned up at the hearing. Nnaife looked lost. He stood there listening to report after report about himself. The lawyer read a long report about how Nnaife had been in the army, how he had been taught to kill without thinking if an enemy invaded his territory. Nnaife, he said, had been half asleep at the time of the incident and had acted instinctively because he thought the local butcher and his son were stealing his daughter. This was obviously the result of the fact that Nnaife, like a typical Ibo, loved his family. The court was told that with a salary of only ten pounds, thirteen shillings and fourpence, Nnaife had educated one of his sons who was now in the United States of America reading science. When the defending lawyer said this, the court gasped. 'He is the father of a future leader,' people murmured. Sensing this, the attorney warmed up and asked Nnaife:

'And your second son, Adim, what is he doing?'

'He too is at St Gregory's.'

'Who pays his school fees, Nnaife?'

241

'A father pays his son's school fees.'

There were mutters from the prosecuting lawyer but one questioning look from the presiding judge silenced them, though not before somebody had laughed rather nervously.

Nweze, the defending lawyer, knew that something had gone wrong, but he led his client boldly.

'Your sons are doing well. But if your daughter Kehinde had been tainted it would have reflected on them, would it not?'

'Reflect! Reflect! All the members of my family would have suffered. The work I have done all these years would go down the drain. No good person would want to marry the other girls, and my sons would find it difficult to marry a good Ibuza girl because people would point at us and say, "Look, there goes a member of the Owulum family. One of his daughters ran away to a Yoruba man. The family is unstable. The family is this, the family ..."'

'Ahem. Ahem. All right, Nnaife Owulum. The court has seen that it is important for a man to defend the honour of his daughter, not just for her sake but for the sake of the other members of the family.'

The prosecuting attorney did not seem unfriendly. He at first seemed to be in sympathy with Nnaife, and Nnaife not knowing the ways of the court fell for it.

'So because there are so many children, you drink sometimes?'

'Well, a man has to do that to live. With two wives nagging about the shortage of food, asking for endless school fees, and children all over the place, I drink once in a while.'

'Don't you drink every evening? You have a regular palm-wine climber who brings you palm wine every evening. Remember, Mr Owulum, that you have sworn by your *chi*, and your god would not like you to tell lies.'

'Of course I am not telling lies. Yes, I drink palm wine every evening, but as for the real thing, *ogogoro*, I drink that only when I

242

have company or when there is something to celebrate.'

'So on that evening you finished a whole shilling keg of palm wine on an empty stomach before your evening meal? Hm ... your daughter must have annoyed you.'

'Yes, she said she was going to marry the Yoruba people and not the man I have chosen for her.'

'Are the Yoruba people that bad?'

'I don't know anything about them and I don't want to know. They don't give housekeeping money to their wives, they are dirty, they call us Ibos cannibals – oh, they do all sorts of things. My daughter will not marry one of them.'

'If your daughter married the man you chose, you would be given a big bride price because she was brought up in Lagos, is that not so?'

'Why, yes, a good husband is expected to pay well for a good girl. That is the way to prove his manhood. If he cannot afford to pay, then he does not deserve a wife. But the Yorubas, they don't do anything like that. They just give the father a bowl of drink and buy the bride a few lappas ... no, not enough for all the food the child has eaten since she was born. And her mother has trained her to be a good trader.'

'Has she now? Hm ... Also if your daughter was found virtuous, your Ibuza in-law would bring you over twelve big kegs of bubbling palm wine, to show her chastity, is that not so?'

'Yes. Yes, I have lost even that, even that after-bride palm wine, I have lost that too.'

'That is a pity. A great pity. So when you took the cutlass to your neighbours' house, you were not just fighting for the honour of your daughter but for the bride price she would have fetched and the palm wine your in-laws would have given you?'

'Your honour,' intervened Lawyer Nweze timely before Nnaife made a greater fool of himself.

Lawyer Nweze led Nnu Ego through the bewildering

experience. No, she had not known that her husband had had an argument with their daughter Kehinde; she did not know that Kehinde had a Yoruba boyfriend; she had not known that Nnaife had drunk too much. She had not seen him brandish a cutlass before. The cutlass was hers. She used it for breaking firewood. Nnaife kept it under the bed to frighten off any prowling robber. Yes, Nnaife was the best of fathers, the best husband a woman could wish for. Yes, he spent all his army money on his children, he had never stopped working, and even the sons of his dead brother had been trained by him up to standard six. He loved his children dearly. Yes, he must have been sleep-walking when he threatened the butcher, and thank God, the boy whose shoulder had been cut was coming on fine.

There was an obvious sigh of relief from Nnu Ego when Lawyer Nweze sat down to allow the prosecuting lawyer to question her.

'You remember, Mrs Owulum, that you have sworn by the Bible, which is, like your *chi*, very binding.'

Nnu Ego looked again at the innocent black book and wondered whether it had the power to make a liar go mad, as an angry *chi* could. She nodded. She knew all that.

'Well, your second son is at St Gregory's. Who pays his fees?'

'I do, I pay his fees with the profits I make from selling firewood and other things.'

There was a suppressed ripple of laughter in the court.

'But your husband told us he pays the school fees, how is that?'

'Yes, he pays the school fees.'

'Do you mean the two of you pay Adim's school fees?'

'No, I pay.'

The laughter that followed this could no longer be suppressed.

Even the judge smiled unwillingly.

'Mrs Owulum, will you please explain.'

'Nnaife is the head of our family. He owns me, just like God in the sky owns us. So even though I pay the fees, yet he owns me. So in other words he pays.'

'Oh, I see. And you clothe and sometimes feed the family, too?'

Nnu Ego nodded, not knowing that with that one nod, she had nailed the last nail in Nnaife's coffin. It became clear that she was doing nearly all the providing and that when Nnaife was away in the army for four years, she had only received two allowances, even though she then had five children to look after.

And he went on probing Nnu Ego, 'When your husband returned from the army did he not go to Ibuza?'

'Yes, he did.'

'What did he go for?'

'I don't know, to see his family at home. Ibuza is his home.'

'Did he bring anything with him?'

'Yes, he brought a new wife.'

'And did he not do something else in Ibuza, say give someone a child?'

'Yes, he made my senior wife pregnant. Her husband died, you see.'

Three-quarters of the court was filled by Yorubas to whom this kind of custom was strange. They looked at the pathetic figure of Nnaife sitting there, being responsible for all these children. Even the judge looked at him with a kind of masculine admiration.

'Your husband is a very strong man,' the prosecuting lawyer said cynically and the court roared in laughter.

'You say your husband is an ideal man, a very nice man.'

Nnu Ego nodded.

'Has he got a nasty temper?'

'No, he hasn't. He only gets angry when he is drunk.'

'And he drinks often, every day?'

245

'Well, he is a man, isn't he? Men are expected to be like that. My father – '

'Ahem. We are talking about your husband, not your father.'

'My husband is like any other man. I would not have married any man who did not behave like a man.'

'Even to the extent of carrying a cutlass?'

'He was drunk and his daughter's honour was at stake.'

'And the bride price?'

'Yes, and her bride price. It's her father's money.'

'You're right, Mrs Owulum. But the trouble is that we are now in the twentieth century and in Lagos. No one has a right to carry a cutlass, not even your husband.'

'I think you should leave that to the jury to decide,' intervened the judge.

The lawyer did not stop his cross-examination there. He went in detail through the happenings of that evening. Why had Nnu Ego dropped the food? Why was it she did not know her husband had been drinking? Why had she been so frustrated that she had gone to bed early?

By the time Nnu Ego had struggled through the whole answers, the jury, most of whom were Europeans, had the whole picture. Nnaife was sentenced to five years' imprisonment.

Outside the court, Okpo still had the energy to cry. Adaku came up and touched Nnu Ego and said, 'Senior wife, I am sorry.'

'But I don't understand it. Why were they all laughing at me? Was I saying the wrong things? Things surely have changed, but Nnaife still owns us, does he not?'

'I'm afraid even that has changed. Nnaife does not own anybody, not in Nigeria today. But, senior wife, don't worry. You believe in the tradition. You have changed a little, but stood firm by your belief.'

'Try to forgive my condemning your leaving Nnaife when you did. I am beginning to understand now.'

246

'Forget it. Look, all your friends are here. There's Mama Abby ... it's not so bad, senior wife.'

By the time she got home, Aremu's people, who were very fearful of court cases, had brought the family food and drinks. Some of the younger children were being taken care of by Kehinde's new people, and the butcher was very sorry that Nnaife had to stay in jail for the next five years. Nnu Ego was grateful that though she was now penniless she had such friends, and still had her children.

Throughout the whole nightmare period, from the night Nnaife was taken into a cell to the morning of the day on which he was finally convicted, Nnu Ego had allowed herself to wonder where it was she had gone wrong. She had been brought up to believe that children made a woman. She had had children, nine in all, and luckily seven were alive, much more than many women of that period could boast of. Most of her friends and colleagues had buried more children than they had alive; but her god had been merciful to her. Still, how was she to know that by the time her children grew up the values of her country, her people and her tribe would have changed so drastically, to the extent where a woman with many children could face a lonely old age, and maybe a miserable death all alone, just like a barren woman? She was not even certain that worries over her children would not send her to her grave before her *chi* was ready for her.

Nnu Ego told herself that she would have been better off had she had time to cultivate those women who had offered her hands of friendship; but she had never had the time. What with worrying over this child, this pregnancy, and the lack of money, coupled with the fact that she never had adequate outfits to wear to visit her friends, she had shied away from friendship, telling herself she did not need any friends, she had enough in her family. But had she been right? Nnaife had looked at her with so much venom that she knew that when it neared the time of his release, if she was still alive, she would find a way to live with her own people. That man would never stop blaming her for what had happened to him; his people, and many of the Ibuza people in general, blamed her for bringing up her children badly. There was Oshia in America, not caring at all, and though Adim was keen on having a footstool in Nigeria Nnu Ego suspected that he too would prefer to leave his family and go abroad, judging by the way he was going. She still had the three youngest ones on her hands, and no money, and with the first flush of youthful energy gone, the prospect of getting an adequate living was grim. She knew she would be better off in Ibuza, where at least there would be no rent to pay and, if it came to the worst, she could always plant her food at the back of her hut.

She was slightly reassured when that very evening who should visit them but Lawyer Nweze. She was so embarrassed at the honour, she hardly knew what to do; it was like being visited by royalty. She gave him all she had in the way of kolanuts and bunches of spinach from her small plot nearby – not that Lawyer Nweze wanted any of these things, though he knew how offended she would be if he did not accept them. He told her that there was some likelihood of Nnaife being released from prison after serving only three months, because some 'important' people had decided that he had not been responsible for his actions when he had attacked the Yoruba butcher. He would lose a great part of his gratuity, but they would give him a small pension: it would be nothing near what he ought to have got, but in the circumstances it was better than nothing. The family was to keep quiet about it, otherwise people would think that the lawyer defending them had done some underground deal. He had only come to tell them because he thought it would cheer them all up. He left soon afterwards, leaving behind a family almost dizzy with gratitude. He had warned them again that not a word of it was to be breathed to anyone. As soon as Nnaife was released, he would be taken directly to Ibuza, so few people would know his whereabouts. They would think that he was still in prison. This knowledge would pacify the butcher's family more than anything.

Within a few weeks, it was necessary for Nnu Ego to go back to Ibuza. She could not afford their rent and she had no courage to start struggling all over again. And the weepy Okpo would be taken off her hands. She called Taiwo's young man and asked him where he stood.

'Are you willing to take my daughter as your wife, or not?'

The suitor said he wanted to marry Taiwo straight away if Nnu Ego had no objection to a quiet wedding. The bride price was quickly paid; it belonged to Nnaife, so Nnu Ego made sure that she let it be paid to Nnaife's representative, Adim.

'Now you hurry, before the palm-wine drinkers start paying us any visits. Pay the whole year's school fees for yourself,' Nnu Ego advised her son, 'put six pounds into the post office so that you can use it to supplement your food until you find yourself a job. Abby said you can come and live with him, as a servant. It will only be for a short while. Many people have volunteered their homes to you, but I want you to trust tested friends, not relatives. If you are hungry, you have two married sisters; you can go and eat with them. But don't do it too often, otherwise you lose your self-respect. It is better to lose respect among people who do not know who you are; don't do it nearer home or it will rebound on your people. You must work partly for your keep, helping Abby to clean his shoes, wash his new motor cycle ...'

Nnu Ego spent six pounds to get her daughter ready. She gave her enough cooking utensils to last a long time and bought her many pieces of lappa material. Adaku, too, surpassed herself; one would have thought it was her own daughter getting married. Even if it was to be a quiet wedding, it must be done in style. Taiwo was a good girl and had served her family, so deserved the best. She was married at St Paul's in Ebute Metta, in a snowy white dress.

Her husband was young and handsome, a well-educated man. Many mothers bit their nails and wondered why such a nice man should condescend to marry a girl from a family with so dubious a reputation. In the evening, after a long day of dancing and drinking and merrymaking, Taiwo was taken to her husband's house in a car hired by their butcher neighbour from one of his relatives who was a taxi-driver. The Yoruba in-laws made the whole thing more colourful than many people anticipated. They all attended the church in identical *aso-ebi* cloths, and brought their own food and their friends. Taiwo thanked her sister who, already pregnant, seemed to have gained the respect of her new home.

A week later, with a truck packed full with odds and ends, Nnu Ego left Lagos for Ibuza, having said a fulsome goodbye to all her Lagos friends. With her went Nnamdio, who still refused to go to school, her second set of twin daughters, now aged seven, Okpo and her two children. Taiwo's husband, Magnus, insisted that they take Obiageli, one of the little girls, and though Nnu Ego thought seriously about it she did not want the child to grow up feeling she had been sent away.

'But, Mother,' Magnus said to her then, 'your daughter was a virgin. By the look of things, we shall be starting a family quite soon. You are going to be busy settling down at home, and I will be the last person to trouble you about coming here to see your grandchild. So leave Obiageli here with us. She will be able to start school and will help her sister in running the house.'

Nnu Ego still hesitated. It came to the stage when Adim had to step in. He argued with his mother until they nearly reached Iddo motor park, from where they were to set off.

'Look, Mother, Magnus is an enlightened man. He will see to it that Obiageli is well brought up. She'll be better off in Lagos. What's more, you need a little rest, Mother. You have worked too hard all your life. You have to join your age-group at home, dress up on Eke days and go and dance in the markets. It's going to be a good life for you. Don't saddle yourself with so many children.'

'But that's it,' Nnu Ego replied with tears In her eyes. 'I don't know how to be anything else but a mother. How will I talk to a woman with no children? Taking the children from me is like taking away the life I have always known, the life I am used to.'

'Mother, you still have Nnamdio and Malachi; some women only have two anyway. Let Taiwo take Obiageli. You are bound to be spending half your time in Ibuza and half here in Lagos anyway. Kehinde will soon be having her child, and do you think she would go into labour without you being near her? It will soon be Taiwo's turn to start breeding, and she will need you, too. You're not going to be as idle as you feared. And that young wife of Father's and her children ...' Adim started to say.

Nnu Ego looked round the motor park and saw her daughter Taiwo coming to meet her there. Beside her was Magnus, who had taken the day off from where he worked in the Treasury to come and see his mother-in-law off. Taiwo glowed with health and was full of happiness. She was wearing a new cloth, a gift from Magnus, and looked very well-to-do. No one would have dreamed that she could only read and write very simply. They were joking, husband and wife, and she was laughing, pointing at something. He playfully hit her lightly with the folded newspaper he was holding. Then, seeing Nnu Ego, they ran like schoolchildren towards her. Her cup of happiness was full. Yes, this was something. She was happy to see her children happy.

When it was time for them to pack themselves into the mammy-lorry that would take them to Ibuza, Magnus and Adim insisted that Nnu Ego should travel in front, holding the baby Malachi with her, so that she would not have to worry.

'But the front costs three times what the back costs, children. Do you know what you are doing?' Nevertheless she went up to the front, to the envious glances of the other passengers.

'Mothers come first,' said the driver with an exaggerated

show of courtesy. 'She is your mother, is she not? She looks so young to be the mother of all of you.'

Nnu Ego stepped in like a queen to her coronation. Then she looked down and said to Magnus. 'My son, take Obiageli. See that in fifteen years' time she becomes a well-educated Miss.'

'Yes, Mother.'

She waved to her daughters, each of them standing by her husband – Kehinde pregnant, Taiwo radiant – and Obiageli held tightly and with love by Magnus. She waved and waved, and they all laughed, until they started to cry.

'Mother, pray for us, that our life will be as productive and fertile as yours,' Kehinde called after the moving lorry.

The driver grinned at Nnu Ego. 'It's nice to have daughters,' he remarked.

Nnu Ego dried her tears and said primly, 'Oh, I haven't just got daughters, I have a son in "Emelika", a boy in grammar school, and another who is going to be a farmer.'

'Oh, you are a rich madam,' the driver said. 'You must tell me where you stay; I like to know important people. You see, when you talk with them, they give you ideas of how they made it. A son in America? Goodness, you must be full of joy, madam!'

The lorry sped down to Agege on its journey to Ibuza. Nnu Ego closed her eyes; her head was aching a little. She eased Malachi on her lap, for the child's weight was making her stiff. She listened with one ear to the driver's monologue.

'This life is very unfair for us men. We do all the work, you women take all the glory. You even live longer to reap the rewards. A son in America? You must be very rich, and I'm sure your husband is dead long ago ...'

She did not think it worth her while to reply to this driver, who preferred to live in his world of dreams rather than face reality. What a shock he would have if she told him that her husband was in prison, or that the so-called son in America had never written to her directly, to say nothing of sending her money. If she should tell him that, he would look down on her and say. 'But you're above all that, madam.' Nnu Ego chuckled at her thought, just as her father would have done.

At home in Ibuza, Nnaife's people branded her a bad woman, and she had to go and live with her own people in Ogboli. She had expected this, knowing full well that only good children belonged to the father...

Nnaife was soon released and he too came home, living with his young wife Okpo. But he was a broken man; and his wife Nnu Ego, similarly, was going downhill very fast. It was not that she was physically poor; her daughters sent help once in a while. However, what actually broke her was, month after month, expecting to hear from her son in America, and from Adim too who later went to Canada, and failing to do so. It was from rumours that she heard Oshia had married and that his bride was a white woman.

For a while Nnu Ego bore it all without reaction, until her senses started to give way. She became vague, and people pointed out that she had never been strong emotionally.

She used to go to the sandy square called Otinkpu, near where she lived, and tell people there that her son was in 'Emelika', and that she had another one also in the land of the white men – she could never manage the name Canada. After such wandering on one night, Nnu Ego lay down by the roadside, thinking that she had arrived home. She died quietly there, with no child to hold her hand and no friend to talk to her. She had never really made many friends, so busy had she been building up her joys as a mother.

When her children heard of her sudden death they all, even Oshia, came home. They were all sorry she had died before they were in a position to give their mother a good life. She had the noisiest and most costly second burial Ibuza had ever seen, and a shrine was made in her name, so that her grandchildren could appeal to her should they be barren.

Stories afterwards, however, said that Nnu Ego was a wicked woman even in death because, however many people appealed to her to make women fertile, she never did. Poor Nnu Ego, even in death she had no peace! Still, many agreed that she had given all to her children. The joy of being a mother was the joy of giving all to your children, they said.

And her reward? Did she not have the greatest funeral Ibuza had ever seen? It took Oshia three years to pay off the money he had borrowed to show the world what a good son he was. That was why people failed to understand why she did not answer their prayers, for what else could a woman want but to have sons who would give her a decent burial?

Nnu Ego had it all, yet still did not answer prayers for children.

254

AWS CLASSICS

The book you have been reading is part of Heinemann's
African Writers Series Classics (www.africanwriters.com).
The AWS Classics consists of eight titles:

For a catalogue giving information on all the
African Writers Series titles write to:
Heinemann Educational Publishers,
Halley Court, Jordan Hill, Oxford OX2 8EJ.

United States customers should write to:
Greenwood Heinemann, 361 Hanover Street,
Portsmouth, NH 03801-3912, USA.